Eleven Exiles

Accounts of Loyalists of the American Revolution

edited by
Phyllis R Blakeley
and John N Grant

Dundurn Press Limited

Toronto and Charlottetown
1982

97539

Acknowledgements

The preparation of this manuscript and the publication of this book were made possible because of assistance from several sources. The editors are grateful to the **Ontario Arts Council** for a Writer's Grant award. The publisher wishes to acknowledge the ongoing generous financial support of the **Canada Council** and the **Ontario Arts Council**.

J. Kirk Howard, Publisher

Editor: Bernice Lever
Design and Production: Ron and Ron Design Photography
Typesetting: Howarth and Smith Ltd.
Printing and Binding: Editions Marquis Ltée, Montmagny, Quebec

Published by
Dundurn Press Limited
P.O. Box 245, Station F,
Toronto, Canada
M4Y 2L5

Canadian Cataloguing in Publication Data
Main entry under title: ·
Eleven exiles

Includes index.
ISBN 0-919670-62-8 (bound). -- ISBN 0-919670-63-6 (pbk.)

1. United Empire Loyalists - Biography.*
2. American loyalists - Canada - Biography.
I. Blakeley, Phyllis R. (Phyllis Ruth), 1922-
II. Grant, John N.

FC424.A1E54   971.02'4'0922   C83'094124-X
F1058.E54

Eleven Exiles

Accounts of Loyalists
of the American Revolution

Contents

List of Illustrations and Maps

Dedication

Dedicated to all those men and women who came, and are still coming, as pioneers to this land, and to their children, especially Norman, Cheryl, Alison, Marianne, Jennifer, Julia, Heather, Andrew.

Foreword

Eleven Exiles: Accounts of Loyalists of the American Revolution provides accounts of individual Loyalists who were forced to flee their homes and create a new place for themselves in what remained of Britain's empire. These biographies were written specifically for this publication by a number of authors from a variety of fields. The dictates of available source material has determined that these works are of various length, style and composition.

The editors wish to express their thanks to the authors for their co-operation, to Bernice Lever and Kirk Howard of Dundurn Press for their patient assistance and guidance, to Mary Beacock Fryer for her conscientious checking of and comment upon this manuscript, and to the Ontario Arts Council for their financial support.

Phyllis R. Blakeley
John N. Grant

Migration Routes from the Thirteen Colonies

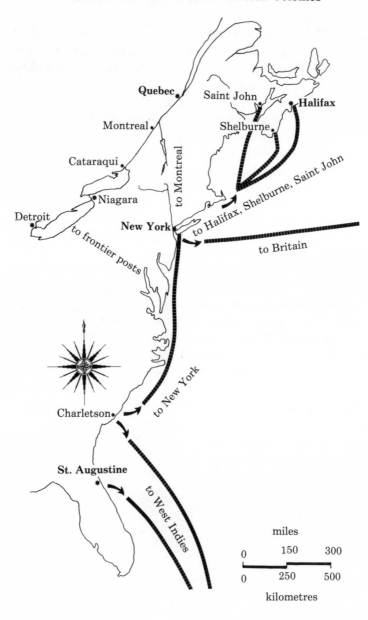

Chapter 1

' ... those in General called Loyalists'[1]

by John N. Grant

When the American Revolution erupted in Great Britain's North American colonies, individual citizens were faced with personal decisions of enormous importance and difficulty. Some flocked to the banner of the Continental Congress and joined the battle against Parliament and King. Other citizens, equally convinced of the rightness of their cause, declared themselves for their King, speedily sought shelter wherever the British army could protect them; many sought to join the King's troops and fight for the re-establishment of his authority. Other Loyalists might have 'spent their nights in prayer for the success of the King' but, being fearful of the hostility of their rebel neighbours, spent their days in silence. Between these two poles were thousands of other Loyalists whose sentiments, whether declared or not, were known to rest with the King but who tried to remain peacefully in their homes. During the years of the War of the American Revolution (1776-1783), and after the peace settlement, many of these Loyalists or Tories as they were termed by the Rebels were driven from their homes and forced to flee.

Contemporary definitions of Loyalists were often not very complimentary. One proclaimed that 'a Tory is a thing whose head is in England, . . . its body in America, and its neck ought to be stretched'[2] and another insisted that while 'Every fool is not a Tory, yet every Tory

11

is a fool'.[3] While such descriptions might be expected from their rebel countrymen, in England Edmund Burke also denounced the Loyalists proclaiming in the House of Commons that 'It was our friends in America that had done all the mischief. Every calamity of the war had arisen from our friends; and if such were to be our friends, I wish to God that we might hear of them no more'.[4] Ignoring partisan descriptions, the Tories, unorganized and less united, were 'simply those who remained actively or passively loyal to George III and opposed the Declaration of Independence even if they had taken a Whig position earlier . . .'.[5]

Prior to 1763, indeed prior to 1773, it would likely have been impossible to distinguish future Rebel from future Loyalist. Most would have no doubt denied that such an eventuality as independence was desirable let alone possible. Yet by 1783 independence was a reality. Many excellent accounts have treated those eventful years and no effort will be made to duplicate them here. (A Chronology of the important events of these years is supplied in Appendix A). However, it should be emphasized that up to 4 July 1776 and the Declaration of Independence the Loyalists

were every bit as American as their Whig brethren. They feared social change and any increase in the power of the democratic element in society, but one looks in vain for Loyalists who were opposed to Liberty or the rights of Englishmen. The great majority did not even favour the 'new' English legislation after the Seven Years War. The quarrel was over the *mode* of opposition; the Loyalists would not admit violence and believed the future of their country would be ruined by revolution and independence. It was not a case of colonial rights or 'passive obedience', but rather whether the colonies' future well-being could be best assured within the empire or without. The Loyalists had a fundamental trust in Britain, the Whigs a fundamental distrust.[6]

John Adams, rebel spokesman and future President of the United States, asserted that likely one-third of the people were Loyalists, one-third patriots and one-third were neutral. This, however, 'appears an overdecisive judgement on the ways of men. The great majority in each colony were trimmers who went with the Tide; and certainly far less than one-third of the colonists were ready to declare themselves Loyalist until it was clearly wise to do so.'[7] In support, Wallace Brown points out 'that the majority of Loyalists never left America in the first place'[8] but became reassimilated into American life after the hostilities were over. However, by that time, some one hundred thousand Loyalists had become political exiles from their native land. Authorities estimate that there were twenty-four émigrés per thousand of population in the American Revolution and only five per thousand of population in the French Revolution.[9] Only by such comparisons can the true upheaval of the American Revolutionary War be demonstrated. However, it was often safer to leave than to stay. 'Loyalist homes were attacked, their jobs made forfeit, and all legal action was denied them. From 1777 the states began the practice of banishing prominent Loyalists, and everywhere they ran the risk of tar and feathers'.[10] Beaten, robbed, and sometimes murdered, the greatest trials of many Loyalists came not with their struggles to start over in a new land, but prior to their exile from the old.

The Loyalists came from every avenue of colonial life. A majority were farmers or landowners and therefore rural residents. A sizeable minority however 'were in commerce or a profession, or held an official position, and accordingly they usually lived in the towns, most of which were on the coast'.[11] Artisans, merchants, servants, shopkeepers, innkeepers, labourers, seamen, lawyers, teachers, doctors, clergymen and office holders were also represented in the Loyalist ranks. There were more who were poor than rich and colonial minorities appear to have been over represented.[12] These minorities included religious groups like the Quakers and Mennonites, native people such as Mohawk nation who moved into Canada and racial groups like the approximately 3,000 Black Loyalists[13] who came to Nova Scotia.

The Loyalists left an area that was geographically immense, with a relatively small population. While nine-tenths of the people lived in the countryside, there were five major cities, the largest of which, Philadelphia

The Battle of Rhode Island in 1776 showing the landing at Newport

at 40,000, was probably bigger than any other city in the British Empire except London. The most easterly parts of the colonies had, with a history prior to 1776 almost as long as their history since 1776, enjoyed the pleasures of civilized life. Although distrusted by the frontier, eastern colonial centres were culturally sophisticated containing libraries, newspapers and learned societies. They boasted nine universities at a time when England only had two and, in general, their education laws were more liberal.

When the Loyalists left their old homes, they carried much more than their loyalty with them. They also brought their cultural, educational, legal, political and religious values. Their numbers created new communities like Shelburne, Nova Scotia, which was for a time the fourth largest English-speaking city in North America. Loyalist religious demands caused the creation of the first colonial Bishoprics and the growth of various Christian denominations. The Loyalists' educational concerns led to the establishment of universities throughout the colonies, while their political objections forced the British Government to review the system of land holding in Quebec and eventually led to a revised political system in that Province. The creation of newspapers, magazines, and a new élite also marked the Loyalist presence in their new homes. Their active participation in political affairs, often in opposition, underlines the fact that while they were undoubtedly loyal, they were not lackeys of government. In their response to their circumstances, they soon mirrored much of that which they had left behind.

The journeys of the Loyalists began from all corners of the colonies. In real numbers the greatest Loyalist colony was New York followed by South Carolina, Massachusetts, New Jersey, Pennsylvania, North Carolina, Connecticut, Virginia, Georgia, Maryland, Rhode Island, and Delaware. Their destinations were equally diverse. Some fled to England, others to Florida, Bermuda and the West Indies. The majority, however, moved northward into what remained of Great Britain's American Empire where they formed the backbone of the second British Empire. By ship they travelled to the Maritimes and Quebec while others on foot or by ox cart or handcart entered British territory to settle in what is now Ontario and Quebec.

While the greater percentage of the Loyalists remained in the new United States, the territory that is now the Dominion of Canada received approximately 50,000 exiles. The majority, perhaps as many as 35,000 came to Nova Scotia while up to 10,000 more settled in the old province of Quebec.[14] Their immediate impact was to overwhelm the old population and cause the creation of two new Atlantic colonies, New Brunswick and Cape Breton Island, and eventually the Province of Upper Canada (Ontario). While the long-term influence of the Loyalists may be more difficult to measure, it is, for many historians, no less certain. W.S. MacNutt has written that

> the Communities formed in 1783-84 gave assurance of the maintenance of a British Empire in North America. Sir Guy Carleton was emphatic in his assertion that continued British control of the remaining colonies depended entirely upon the Loyalists. What is of greater contemporary significance is that the essential ingredients for the Canada of 1867 came into being.[15]

In their struggle to survive the first years, the Loyalists likely suffered no more hardships than did the earlier and later pioneers who helped develop this country. The Loyalists have been described as 'a worthy people not very different from the Americans who had preceded them, and the Americans who followed them, except perhaps they had an exceptional reputation for loyalty, which may have led some of them to claim a monopoly of this virtue'.[16] While this estimation may well be accurate, there remains no doubt that the Loyalists can lay a legitimate claim on history for a place of their own.

The Loyalists included here came from throughout the rebellious colonies and ended their journeys both in British North America and elsewhere. They include government officials, merchants, mechanics, labourers, farmers, and professionals. The biographies include the rich and the poor, Whites, Blacks, Native peoples, and women.

These narratives are, with some exceptions, of persons who either were or became members of the 'upper class'. Because historical writing depends upon the availability of sources, this limitation is not unexpected. These narratives, however, appear to support the myth that loyalism was the creed of the élite in American society. This is far from the truth. If loyalism embraced leaders such as Oliver Delancey, Sir John Johnson and Edward Winslow, aristocrats like George Washington of Virginia and Philip Schuyler of New York were high-profile Rebels. The 'lower orders' were equally divided on the issue of independence, and American society was split down the middle by this fratricidal conflict.

As a group, Loyalists did not leave much literature expressive of their aspirations, and the effect of the revolution on their lives. The few who did tended to be the wealthy, educated class. Some of the rank and file, especially if they were from the frontiers where educational opportunities were limited, were illiterate and required assistance in preparing their memorials and petitions for compensation. Most of these memorials are brief and devoid of emotion, and at best would make narratives of a few paragraphs. This problem is graphically illustrated by the story of Private Truelove Butler, whose given name hints at Puritan ancestors, but who had a farm somewhere in northern New York. In his memorial he stated that in October 1780 a band of Rebels arrived outside his house. Butler, his wife and children, escaped into the woods, and the Rebels burned the house and barn and destroyed most of the grain and provisions he had stored against the coming winter. After the Rebels had gone, the Butlers gleaned what they could from the charred ruins, and set out for Canada. Truelove did not say which way they went, but an educated guess would be Pointe au Fer, the most southerly British blockhouse on Lake Champlain, where many other Loyalists sought protection.

Truelove became a recruiting agent for a below-strength provincial corps, the King's Loyal Americans, and made journeys into New York in search of Loyalists willing to leave their homes and enlist with the British army. In 1781 the King's Loyal Americans were amalgamated with another below-strength corps to form a new regiment, the Loyal Rangers. Truelove then served under Captain Peter Drummond. He retired towards the end of 1782, for his name is not on the last muster roll of the Loyal Rangers that was compiled on 1 January 1783.

The regiment was disbanded on 24 December 1783, and the Butler family joined the bateau brigades up the St. Lawrence in the summer of 1784. Truelove and his family made their home in the Township of Elizabethtown. The land board records do not show on which lot the Butlers settled, but Truelove's name is on a 'Return of Disbanded Troops and Loyalists, Settled in Township No. 8 (Elizabethtown) Mustered 12 October, 1784'. No more is recorded of Truelove Butler, but his son, Truelove Jr., was a Reformer and a founding member of the Leeds County Agricultural Society in 1830.

The evidence on Private Mathias Snetsinger is even skimpier. He served in the first battalion, King's Royal Regiment of New York — Sir John Johnson's corps — in Captain Samuel Anderson's light company. Mathias probably came from Schenectady area in the Mohawk Valley where other Snetsingers lived, and the family, like many others in that neighbourhood, was of German origin. The muster roll of Captain Anderson's company shows that Mathias — whose name is given as Mathew — was twenty-three years old and an American. Records preserved by his descendants state that he enlisted at age seventeen.

Mathias was awarded a farm lot near Moulinette, Ontario, but he may never have resided on it. He married the widow of Private Jacob Austen, who had served in the grenadier company of his battalion. What became known as the Snetsinger homestead, where his descendants lived until 1913, was the original Austen land grant, the east half of Lot 9, Concession 3, on Toll Gate Road in Cornwall Township, also near Moulinette.[17]

In the past, Loyalist history was rarely well presented. More recently however increased scholarly interest has been concentrated on the Loyalists. Their place in the history of English Canada has always been assured as they represent the first major immigration of English-speaking persons into largely unsettled territory. Much more important than their numbers would warrant the Loyalists placed their imprint on the societies they augmented or established and created an ideal to which later arrivals could only aspire. Increased interest in, and awareness of, the Loyalists has appeared in the United States as a result of the bicentennial celebrations of the Revolutionary War and its aftermath. Much of the new work has presented them in a more sympathetic light, in many cases, portraying them as the victims rather than simply the villains of their unsettled times. This has not always been the case. W.S. MacNutt has pointed out that

> Early American scholars regarded the Loyalists as a shameful and reactionary minority resistant to inevitable destiny and to the myth of liberty with which the Revolution has been enshrouded. British historians have tended to ignore them, the first of many loyal minorities sacrificed in the liquidation of empire. Yet there is nothing peripheral or forgettable in their contribution to Canadian history. For over thirty years they composed the principal English-speaking ingredient among the elements that were to transform British North American into the Canadian nation, a link between colonialism and nationality second to none.[18]

An American historian has pointed out that 'a revolutionist who is unsuccessful is likely to be condemned as a criminal, whereas he who succeeds is sure to be dubbed a patriot, a statesman, a hero, or a saint. It is always too much for human nature to glorify the losing side.'[19] However, this has been the lot of the Loyalists. A loser as far as the War was concerned, a 'Tory', a traitor, a villain as far as the victors were concerned the Loyalists became the patriots, heroes and saints of Canada's early history. While no doubt that as individuals they possessed a combination of both the good and bad qualities ascribed to them, it is equally certain that 'they had all lost much for their Tory principles', and likewise believed that they 'were a chosen people' a feeling that 'did not die with the first generation of Loyalists'.[20] It may be best to see the Loyalists as individuals, not as heroes or as villains, but simply as individuals facing the public and private affairs of their lives as best they could. As individuals

St. George's Anglican Church, Sydney, N.S., built in 1789

their hardships, suffering, and heartaches take on a new form and a new reality. As neighbours parted and families split, there were heartaches that did not mend, even when public attitudes softened between the former foes.[21]

The sentiment expressed by a Loyalist woman in Halifax, corresponding with a relative in Massachusetts in 1815, no doubt expressed the feelings of many when she wrote:

> You have, I am certain, joined me in blessings to a merciful God for once more granting us the blessing of peace . . . I glory in the pious and learned race from whence I sprang, and cannot help regretting that I lived at a time when it pleased an infinitely wise God to scatter us over the face of the earth.[22]

Some years later, in 1828, Stephen Jones, a Loyalist resident of Weymouth, Nova Scotia, wrote to his 90-year-old brother in Adams, Massachusetts, reporting the death of a relative and commented on the dispersal of their family to 'different provinces, countries and towns'.

> Our Father was interred in a vault under Trinity Church, Boston, our mother at Keene, N.H., Elias at Adams, Mass., Josiah and Simeon at Sissiboo, N.S., Ephriam in Canada, Jonas in England, Charles in Virginia, and you will probably lay alongside of Elias, and I beside my two brothers here. There will then be three together here and two at Adams and Mrs. Minot at Concord.[23]

The division of an empire obviously was felt, and continued to be felt, by individuals and families as clearly and deeply as the new political order was felt in international affairs.

The American Revolution is the story of the destruction of an Empire and the birth of a new nation. It is also the story of thousands of people, individuals whose stories should be remembered and should be told. The stories that have been included here cannot be said to be typical if only because of the fact that so few individuals left enough records to allow historians to even partially recreate their lives and stories. They may, however, be representative in that each individual, and the Loyalists

were above all individuals, had to face personal conscience and public demands and decide if the two coin-
cided or could co-exist. For many they could not and the
exiles of the Revolutionary War were created.

1. W.S. MacNutt, 'The Narrative of Lieutenant James Moody', *Acadiensis*, I, 2
   (Spring, 1972), 72-90.
   Mary Beacock Fryer points out that some confusion exists over the designation U.E. with Loyalists and writes:
   On 7 November 1789, at the request of Lord Dorchester, the former Sir
   Guy Carleton, who was then governor-in-chief of Canada, the Legislative
   Council passed an Order-in-Council. It was in accordance with Dorchester's wish to put a 'Mark of Honour' upon the families who had adhered to
   the 'Unity of the Empire' and joined the Royal Standard in America before the Treaty of Separation in 1783. The land boards in Canada were ordered to prepare a list of these families, to distinguish them from other
   settlers. Although the resulting Privy Council list was not entirely accurate, it does provide a means of identifying who, in what are now the
   provinces of Ontario and Quebec, had the right to call themselves U.E.
   Loyalists. The designation has not been commonly used in the Maritimes
   as no similar list was compiled for the Loyalists who settled there.
2. D.C. Harvey, 'Commemorating the Loyalists', Public Archives of Nova Scotia, M. G. I., vol. 1891, TF,82 14, p.2.
3. Wallace Brown, *The King's Friends: The Composition and Motives of the
   American Loyalist Claimants*, Providence, Rhode Island: Brown University Press, 1965, p. 252.
4. E.R. Barkan, ed., *Edmund Burke on the American Revolution: Selected
   Speeches and Letters*, New York: Harper Torchbooks, 1966, pp. 213-214, n.
   4.
5. Brown, *King's Friends*, p. 252.
6. Brown, *King's Friends*, p. 270.
7. Esmond Wright, *Fabric of Freedom, 1763-1800*; New York: Hill and Wang,
   1961, p. 126.
8. Wallace Brown, *The Good Americans: The Loyalists in the American
   Revolution*, New York: Morrow, 1969, p. 251.
9. R.R. Palmer, *The Age of Democratic Revolution*, (New York, 1959) as quoted
   in Wright, *Fabric*, p. 154.
10. Wright, *Fabric*, p. 154.
11. Brown, *Good Americans*, p. 241.
12. Brown, *King's Friends*, p. 282.
13. James W. St. G. Walker, *The Black Loyalists: The Search for a Promised
    Land in Nova Scotia and Sierra Leone 1783-1870*, New York: Africana
    Publishing, 1976, p. 12.
14. Brown, *Good Americans*, p. 192. Brown's work is also the source of the in-
    formation concerning the colonial homes of the Loyalists.
15. MacNutt, 'Sympathetic', p. 11.
16. Harvey, 'Commemorating', p. 7.
17. For these examples and the proceeding paragraph, the editors are indebted
    to Mary Beacock Fryer's critique of the draft manuscript. Beyond her own
    familiarity with the period, Mrs. Fryer's sources include:
Public Record Office, A O/ 13. Memorials of New York Loyalists, in alphabeti-
    cal order. Memorial of Truelove Butler.
Public Archives of Canada. MG. 13. WO 28, Vol. 10, part 4, pp 457-73.
PAC. Haldimand Papers, transcripts, B 168, p. 84. Copied by Dr. H.C. Bur-
    leigh.
T.W.H. Leavitt. *History of Leeds and Grenville*, (Brockville, 1879), pp. 44 and

200.

Ontario Archives. Muster Roll of the first battalion, King's Royal Rangers of New York, 1783, Montreal.

J.F. Pringle, *Lunenburgh or the Old Eastern District*, (Cornwall, 1890), p. 372.

J.G. Harkness, *Stormont, Dundas and Glengarry; a History 1784-1945*, (Oshawa, 1946), pp. 243-244.

18. W.S. MacNutt, 'The Loyalists: A Sympathetic View', *Acadiensis*, v. 6, n. 1 (Autumn, 1976), p. 19.

19. Charles M. Andrews, *The Colonial Background of the American Revolution: Four Essays in American Colonial History*, rev. ed., New Haven and London: Yale University Press, 1931, p. 182.

20. Margaret Ells, 'Loyalist Attitudes', *Dalhousie Review*, v. XV, n. 3, 1935, pp. 326-327.

21. Neil MacKinnon, 'The Changing Attitudes of the Nova Scotian Loyalists to the United States', *Acadiensis*, v. 11, n. 2, (Spring, 1973), pp. 43-54.

22. Thomas H. Raddall, *Halifax: Warden of the North*, rev. ed., Toronto: McClelland and Stewart, 1971, p. 154.

23. C. St. C. Stayner, 'Weymouth and the Joneses', Public Archives of Nova Scotia, M. G. I., vol. 1644, No. 85, p. 15.

"The father was taller and stouter than his son, [Joseph] strongly built, with a remarkably benevolent expression of countenance, and a fine head." Joseph A. Chisholm, Vol. I Speeches, *p. 88.*

Chapter 2

John Howe, Senior

Printer, Publisher
Postmaster, Spy

by John N. Grant

John Howe was a young newspaper apprentice when the disturbances began in New England and he took an exciting, active part in the American Revolution. Although his family had lived in Massachusetts for 140 years, Howe's convictions led him to leave Boston and all the other members of his family. As a Loyalist, he sailed alone to Halifax in 1776 where he enjoyed many careers including newspaper publisher, Postmaster, and even spy.

The grip of the winter had been broken, but the wind still blew cold from the north. The chilling gusts seemed to carry an ominous message as the ships tacked off shore and set sail for that part of His Majesty's colonies that many would later refer to as Nova Scarcity. As they moved away, the eleven hundred refugees must have wondered if they would ever return. The many anxious passengers must have worried about what was to be their lot, what it would mean to be driven from their city, and on whose charity they would be forced to rely in the weeks to come.

On board one of the crowded transports young John Howe watched his native Boston recede from view. The movements his sharp eyes picked out were likely the rebel forces occupying the city from their fortifications on Dorchester Heights. And no doubt looters, under the guise of liberty, were already at work. It was 17 March 1776. John Howe was twenty-two years of age, and he was alone. It was not that he did not know anyone on board the transports. His employer and business partner was there,[1] and as a newspaperman and fellow Loyalist he knew, and was known by, many of the eleven hundred refugees, and even by some of the three thousand British regulars. Even so, he was alone. His father, his brothers, his uncles — all of his family remained in rebel New England. Of his whole family, he alone had chosen to follow the King's colours into exile. He alone had elected to leave Boston, a centre of New England life for one hundred and forty-five years, and had opted for the primitive conditions of Halifax, Nova Scotia's twenty-seven-year-old Capital. His eyes must have betrayed his concern and his thoughts must have centred around what had brought about the 'disgraceful spectacle' of the power of Britain in full flight.

John Howe's roots lay deep in the rocky soil of Massachusetts Bay Colony. The first of the colonial line of his family had emigrated to America in 1636 from Broad Oak, Essex, England.[2] The succeeding generations had been farmers and artisans. His father, Joseph, 'a reputable tradesman in Marshall's Lane'[3] was a tin plate worker in Boston, where John Howe was born on 14 October 1754. After the good general training that the liberal education laws of Massachusetts allowed, John Howe's father apprenticed his son to learn the newspaper business. It is almost certain that young Howe was placed with the Drapers, as the families were reported to have been related.[4]

The Draper family owned the famous *Massachusetts Gazette and Boston Weekly News Letter,* the oldest newspaper in America. Established in 1704 by Bartholomew Green, the paper had passed to John Draper in 1733. Thirty years later, in 1762, the business was continued by his son Richard Draper. The 'dispute between Great Britain and the colonies induced the government particularly to patronize *The Massachusetts Gazette . . .* '[5] and it remained staunchly loyalist throughout the hostilities and siege of Boston. A government organ, in fact if not always officially, 'the Thursday paper' with a circulation of 1,500 copies weekly,[6] was the only one published in Boston during the siege.

In 1774, Richard Draper had taken John Boyle as a partner in publishing the *News Letter*. One month later Draper died. 'His widow, Margaret Draper, succeeded him as proprieter of the paper, and Boyle was for a short time her partner; but they separated before the commencement of the revolutionary war'.[7] Apparently Boyle's sympathies and those of Mrs. Draper lay in opposing political spheres. These political differences, however, presented John Howe with an important opportunity. Despite the fact that he had just completed his apprenticeship, Howe became her partner and remained in business with her until the evacuation 'when the publication of the *News Letter* ceased, and was never revived'.[8] Mrs. Draper was included in the 'Confiscation and Banishment Act' and her young partner, named in the same Act, followed her into exile.[9]

These were exciting times for a young man in Boston. As the centre of New England's opposition to the British Government's post-1763 policies, the city had seen the defeat of the Stamp Act, the rise of the Sons of Liberty, and the successful use of trade embargoes and non-importation and non-consumption agreements. Here the constitutional argument of 'no taxation without representation' had been debated and here the seamier methods of opposition, of mob action, tar and feathering, and rail riding, had been used to effect. Here a Committee of Correspondence had been established and here the halls of the colonial assembly and town meetings rang with the eloquence of John Adams, James Otis, Samuel Adams and John Hancock. Here too, men had ranged themselves with one party or another, for or against the government. It became the worst kind of dispute as even relatives turned against each other. As a contemporary put it:

Nabour was against Nabour,
Father against the Son and

the Son against the Father,
and he that would not thrust
his one blaid through his
brothers heart was cald an
Infimous fillon![10]

Either as printer's devil, reporter or interested spectator, John Howe had direct contact with such events as the infamous Boston Massacre and the equally well-known Boston Tea Party. He 'was present when the soldiers were tried for firing upon the mob in Boston, knew Otis, Adams and Hancock and had heard them often in Faneuil Hall.'[11] In 1774, the British government passed the Coercive, or Intolerable acts to punish Boston and the colony of Massachusetts Bay for the 'Tea Party', and for years of insubordination to the Crown. Political emotions were highly aroused. As staunch an adherent to his principles as any of his better known contemporaries, John Howe stood against common public opinion — on the side of the King.

The military situation in Boston was grave. The city was surrounded by a hostile countryside. The Minutemen and other colonial militia were openly training and stockpiling arms and ammunition in various locations. General Thomas Gage, Governor of Massachusetts Bay and Commander of His Majesty's forces, realized that the time for action had come. 'So much trouble was brewing he could no longer mark time in Boston. Great stores of supplies and ammunition were daily being assembled . . .'[12]

General Gage decided that the threat to Boston had to be eliminated and sent seven hundred soldiers to destroy the stores at Concord. Warned of their coming by Paul Revere and William Dawes, colonial militia assembled at Lexington where the first skirmish was fought. Continuing to Concord, the British forces destroyed whatever supplies that had not been carried off and ran a gauntlet of deadly sniper fire as they retreated the 25 kilometres to Boston. The losses of 19 April 1775 'were heavy on both sides, the British 273, the Americans 95'.[13]

John Howe likely covered the story of Lexington

and Concord and the 'shot heard around the world'. But whether he did it or not, there is no doubt of his presence during the 'Battle of Bunker Hill'. The British forces had intended to place garrisons on both Bunker and Breed's Hill but their plans quickly became public knowledge and the colonial forces occupied them first. Gage, now joined by Generals Howe, Clinton, and Burgoyne, mounted an attack upon the rebel positions on Breed's Hill. Led by General Sir William Howe the British forces advanced, were repulsed and advanced again. Finally, a bayonet charge cleared the Hill and drove the rebels from the peninsula. The victory, however, left the British command little cause for rejoicing:

> The patriots sustained casualties above four hundred; but Gage was forced to report more than a thousand for his army. Over 40 percent of Howe's men were slain or wounded. Britain could not afford to buy many hills at such a price.[14]

During the assault, John Howe saw the battle of Bunker Hill from one of the old houses and in later years described to his youngest son the picture of ' . . . Sir William Howe charging up the slope with the bullets flying through the tails of his coat'. Not content to be merely a spectator or reporter, John Howe assisted in the care of the wounded. 'That night he sat up with a young officer whose leg had been amputated and who he cured of a raging fever by letting him drink a bucket of cold water'.[15] These were exciting times for young Howe for more than one reason as reports suggest that following the day and night of the Battle, he proposed to Martha Minns, the sixteen-year-old daughter of William and Sarah Minns of Boston.[16] She was later to become his wife and to bear him six children.[17]

The military stalemate in Boston was finally broken when captured artillery from far away Fort Ticonderoga was installed on the heights overlooking the city. The military command quickly realized their position was untenable. 'The result was a decision to evacuate Boston and to remove to Halifax.'[18] The British regulars and the eleven hundred Loyalists of the city who did not wish, or dare to remain, set sail on 17 March, St. Patrick's day, thereby giving the later day Irish of that city two reasons to celebrate.

There was likely little celebration among the refugees who arrived in Halifax on 30 March and 1 April, 1776. The arrival of the fleet had more than doubled the population of the town and had brought all the attendant difficulties:

> The influx of army officers and 'loyalists' . . . created a tremendous demand for necessities in the town. Rents soared to the heights. So did the price of provisions. The merchants, the landlords, the brewers, the madames of the bawdyhouses reaped a harvest, but the ordinary townsfolk . . . found themselves in open competition with a horde of strangers for a roof above their heads and the very food upon their plates.[19]

Even the youthful spirits of a John Howe must have been dampened by such a prospect.

Many of the Loyalists were forced to take shelter under canvas on the Commons while others had to remain huddled on unsanitary hulks floating in the harbour. Where John Howe or his partner, Mrs. Margaret Draper, spent their months in Halifax is unclear. Mrs. Draper actually remained in Halifax for only a short time before sailing to England to seek, and to receive, a pension from the Crown.[20] John Howe's duty lay in the opposite direction. Later in 1776, he returned to New England, accompanying the British forces to New York. He was also with them when they occupied Newport, Rhode Island. On 16 January 1777, the first issue of the pro-British newspaper, the *Newport Gazette,* appeared — John Howe, publisher. Howe and his newspaper remained in Newport until October, 1779, when he, together with his young wife, again retreated to New York. A year earlier, on 7 June 1778, he had married Martha Minns, and she was with him when the troops withdrew. On Christmas Day, 1779, their first child, Martha, was born in New York City.[21]

In 1780, although the disastrous news of Yorktown was still a year away, the situation in America was grim. The colonial dispute had grown into a world war, with France, Spain and Holland supporting the colonies.

At twenty-six years of age, and with a family to support, John Howe reached a decision. The time had come for the Howes to establish themselves in one of His Majesty's loyal colonies. In 1780, the Howes were again on the move, leaving New York and journeying to Halifax. His son later explained that John Howe had 'left all his household goods and gods behind him, carrying away nothing but his principles and the pretty girl.'[22]

When John Howe left New England, he may well have 'abandoned his prospects and property'[23] but he brought much more than 'his young wife and a few poor possessions'.[24] He also brought his religious convictions as a Sandemanian. His religious beliefs were essential to his being and may not only help explain his loyalty but also the course of his later life. Sandemanians were the followers of Robert Sandeman, a Scottish convert to the Glasite Movement. The Movement was founded by John Glas, a popular minister of the Church of Scotland who had become dissatisfied with the teachings of his Church. Finally, suspended by the established Church he continued to preach, urging his followers to return to the 'simple faith and practices of the early Christians' calling for the separation of Church and State. One of the most famous converts of John Glas was Robert Sandeman, who married Glas's daughter and who was ordained to the ministry. After serving various congregations in Scotland, Sandeman 'journeyed to London and founded several English churches, where his followers were called Sandemanians'. Thereafter, he was invited to New England where, following his arrival in 1764, he commanded considerable attention as a preacher, but it was a year before a congregation of followers was formed. This is not difficult to understand when one considers the leader's emphasis on good works, charity, support of the poor, and in such troubled times, the commands 'Fear God and honour the King' and 'if it be possible . . . live peacefully with all men'. Many of the Sandemanian converts were leading members of their communities and considered by their fellow New Englanders to be 'Tories'. Indeed, although pacifists, many of the Sandemanians became Loyalists, left their native New England, and followed the King's colours to Hali-

31

fax. There the emigrants re-established their Church and its members enjoyed its fellowship for the one hundred and thirty years of its existence. While not one of the original members, John Howe had early become an adherent and throughout the years remained a staunch supporter of the Church.[25]

When John Howe returned to Halifax, he was no longer alone. Not only did Martha and their daughter accompany him, but members of his wife's family had immigrated and were there to greet them on their arrival, and some time later his sister Abigail joined them.[26] The town had grown in the years of his absence. By the end of the war there were fourteen forts, blockhouses and barracks in and about the town proper. The streets were thronged with soldiers, sailors, French and American prisoners, Indians, Loyalists, German market gardeners, and Black immigrants, both freemen and slave. For those who had been in a position to take advantage of the war, it was a time of prosperity, a prosperity which was demonstrated by the appearance of splendid new residences, country estates, and flourishing business houses. The Inns and Coffee Houses like the 'Golden Ball', the 'Great Pontac' and the 'Split Crow' were filled with customers. The inner city, however, was filthy, riddled with disease and offered every known vice to those who could afford them. Henry Alline, the Nova Scotia evangelist of the New Light Movement, wrote of his visit to Halifax in 1783: 'I preached in different parts of the town and have reason to believe that there were two or three souls that received the Lord Jesus Christ. But the people in general are almost as dark and vile as Sodom.'[27] John Howe likely kept his family in 'downtown' Halifax for as short a time as possible. He soon moved them outside of the city, to a 'long, low cottage of one story and a pitch, which stood on the eastern slope of the Northwest Arm',[28] where his family grew and where he resided for the rest of his life.

Immediately upon returning to Halifax, he established himself as a printer. It is reported that he had brought with him a printing press that 'had once belonged to Benjamin Franklin, and the first that the philosopher had ever possessed'.[29] But no matter if he used the Franklin press, a Draper press, one he brought from Newport, or one he acquired elsewhere, John Howe was a good printer. On 28 December 1780 the first number of *The Halifax Journal* appeared, printed by John Howe 'at his Printing Office in Barrington Street, nearly opposite the PARADE'.[30] In the best tradition of the *Boston News Letter* the *Journal* was a 'Thursday' paper. The weekly paper remained in the Howe family until 1819 and continued to be published until about 1870.[31]

> The *Halifax Journal* had about half of its space occupied with foreign news or essays reprinted from European publications, a short section headed Halifax, and date of issue, containing shipping and other local news. It included less official matter (proclamations, laws, notices of the provincial government) than the *Nova Scotia Gazette,* and more advertisements. These were remarkably well composed, illustrated with small cuts, and unlike the practice of most early Canadian papers, changed frequently in layout and location on the page. Howe . . . set a new standard of newspaper printing in Eastern Canada.[32]

The *Journal* also reported the debates of the Assembly but remained largely 'free from party ties, prepared to advocate the best interests of Nova Scotia regardless of section, class, or party'.[33]

Although the *Halifax Journal* was the frontpiece of his business, Howe also did general printing. He produced pamphlets and sermons for the Methodists, New Lights, Freemasons, Temperance Societies and other groups. As early as 1781 he presented to the public an *Astronomical diary or Almanack,* a practice he continued, either in partnership or alone, for many years.

The most important 'Colonial News' that Howe reported during his first year of publication concerned the disastrous defeat of Lord Cornwallis at Yorktown in October 1781. Two years later, the final evacuation of New York brought new thousands of Loyalists to Nova Scotia, again flooding the streets of Halifax with displaced persons. Although challenged and for a time outstripped by Shelburne, the city grew in size and in importance as a military and political centre. The arrival of the Loyalists settled the eastern part of the province and caused the further partition of the old province of Nova Scotia by the creation of the new provinces of New Brunswick and Cape Breton Island.

As the years passed, and his family both increased and grew, Howe gradually became a recognized figure in Halifax. His social position developed also, as by 1785 he was considered to be a friend of both Lieutenant-governor Edmund Fanning and Governor John Parr.[34]

Both a professional and personal interest of Howe's was demonstrated in 1789 when he participated in the development of the first literary movement in British North America. In that year *The Nova Scotia Magazine and Comprehensive Review of Literature, Politics and News* was established. The eighty page monthly was at first edited by the Rev. William Cochran, President of Kings College, Windsor and printed by John Howe. In July, 1790, however, Howe took over the editorship himself. He announced that there would be no alteration to the original editorial plans 'except in the department of POLITICS; which, unless articles very important offer themselves, will occasionally give way to more amusing and instructive miscellanies'. The *Magazine* contained a potpourri of material. As its sub-titles suggested it was indeed 'A Collection of the Most Valuable articles which appear in the periodical publications of Great Britain, Ireland, and America with various pieces in verse and prose never before published.'[35] The content matter ranged from 'Observations of the Natural History of the Cuckoo', to 'A Plan of Liberal Education For the Youth of Nova Scotia, . . . ' to 'The Advantages of Raising Cabbages'. It contained the proceedings of the British and Irish parliaments, book reviews, poetry, and letters to the Editor. Items of local interest included articles on the Acadians, the Agricultural Society and the Knight Baronets of Nova Scotia. World affairs and matters of technical interest were not omitted either. The September 1789 issue contained news of the 'Progress of the Revolution in France'; and a discourse on the 'Method of Curing Smokey Chimneys' which included the caution that:

A smokey house and a scolding wife Are (said to be) two of the greatest ills in life.[36]

Unfortunately, the subscription list of the *Nova Scotia Magazine* was not as extensive as its range of content and in March 1792 it failed.

The year of 1790 was one during which John Howe especially needed the strength offered by his religious faith. On 25 November of that year, after having borne him six children, his childhood sweetheart and wife of twelve years, died.[37] He took many years to fill the void left by his wife's death.

During the years of the 1790s Howe built his newspaper into a strong business, and became recognized as a printer-publisher of great skill. As a result, when the position became available following the death of Anthony Henry (Anton Heinrich), John Howe received the appointment as printer to the Government of Nova Scotia.[38] As King's Printer he produced the *Nova Scotia Royal Gazette* beginning 1 January 1801. The *Gazette* was the only newspaper in which government proclamations and official information had to be published and, although it also carried general news, it was at least 'always semi-official in character'. As the provincial printer, Howe was also responsible for publishing the *Debates of the House of Assembly* and any other official proclamations or papers. The *Halifax Journal* also continued to be published by 'John Howe or John Howe and Sons',[39] so even at this early date the Howe family played an important role in molding the opinions and views of their countrymen. These must have been busy times for John Howe, although by 1801 John Howe junior, now seventeen years of age and trained in his father's shop must have been of considerable assistance. The official nature of the position and of the paper was one that another son of John Howe's would chafe under. In a letter to his sister he complained that, 'being the servants of government, . . . we cannot extend our concern in any way so as to make more employment and more profit, because we can never take the popular side in anything that may be going forward . . . ' Party politics, however, seemed to be of no real interest to John Howe, just as 'profits' never seemed his motivation for anything. Again his son would complain, 'Our father's fortunes would almost teach us to renounce his principles.'[40]

Following his appointment as King's Printer, Howe appeared to have developed a strong connection with 'official' Halifax. In 1801 he wrote a report entitled, 'Statements of fact relating to the Isle of Sable'. It was concerned with the necessity of establishing a lifesaving station on Sable Island and was used by Lieutenant-governor, Sir John Wentworth to support his efforts to create a 'Humane Establishment' on that Island. The Report was compiled just after the wreck of the Duke of Kent's transport the *Francis* and contained accounts of the actions of wreckers, the sad tale of Mrs. Copeland and her ring, and a reckoning of the large number of ships lost at Sable Island. Howe's arguments for the establishment of a lifesaving station, for the purpose of humanity, of security to trade, and the preservation of cargo, were sound. Using Howe's work as a base, Wentworth built his case and by 1802 was able to convince the Legislative Assembly of Nova Scotia to vote financial support for the venture.[41]

The year 1801 also saw John Howe receive the commission to be 'Post Master' in Halifax.[42] On 6 August 1803 he furthered his position in the Post Office by accepting the appointment as 'agent manager and director of His Majesty's Packet boats in Halifax',[43] and by 1808 was termed the 'Deputy Post Master General of Nova Scotia'.[44] Although the position was not financially rewarding, he held this office until his retirement in 1818. Years later his son wrote of the private arrangement which had brought his father to the Post Office:

He had a hard bargain at the Post Office. A Mr. Brittain, who held it, it was supposed was going to die. My father was pursuaded to give him 200 pounds a year for the good will of the office. The arrangement was made. Brittain lived seven years and a half during which my father paid him 1,500 pounds. As the office took up much of his time, and greatly increased his expenses, this heavy payment laid the foundation of debts and sources of perplexity which ran over half his life. He held it about seven and a half years after Brittain died, the salary being 290 pounds out of which he had to pay 100 pounds a year to a clerk. He got 1,425 pounds out of it in that time or 75 pounds less than he had paid to Brittain. The upshot of it was he did the duty of Post Master General for 15 years and lost 75 pounds.[45]

John Howe had been more than a caretaker in the office. Although before 1818, very little progress had been made in improving the postal service because of the lack of roads he did open new routes and establish new way-offices and postal facilities. The position was a challenge. 'The existing roads were almost impassable and the government had to provide a grant of £100 in 1816 to carry the mails and passengers twice weekly between Halifax and Windsor'. Howe assured his supervisors in London that 'Had I consulted my own comfort, I should never have encouraged the new Arrangements'. He also explained that while he had 'greatly increased the trouble and anxiety of the office, and added much to the expediture of Stationary' (sic) it had been done to 'afford general accommodation to every section of the Country.'[46] Authorities must have been satisfied with his efforts for on his resignation the position passed to John Junior who held it until his death in 1843.

John Howe's expanding position in the community was marked by his acceptance of additional public responsibilities. By 1803 he was already serving as a "Fireward for the Town of Halifax"[47] and in 1804 he was commissioned to be a 'Justice to Keep the Peace'.[48] At the same time that his public duties were increasing so were his private responsibilities. In 1798, John Howe married the widow Mary Ede Austin. Now father of six, and stepfather of five, John Howe's second wife bore him two more children. In 1804, in his cottage overlooking the Northwest Arm, John Howe's last child was born. It was a boy, named Joseph in honour of his grandfather.

John Howe never lost his love of his 'native sod' and at least as early as 1789[49] he had returned to visit family and old friends in Boston. During the years that followed, he returned whenever he could to walk on the 'Commons' and revisit the scenes of his youth.[50] Speaking in Boston, son Joseph pointed out to his hosts that,

My father, though a true Briton to the day of his death, loved New England and old Boston especially, with filial regard. He never lost an opportunity of serving a Boston man . . . and so it was, all his life. He loved his Sovereign, but he loved Boston too, and whenever he got sick in his later days, we used to send him up here to recruit. A sight of the old scenes and a walk upon Boston Commons were sure to do him good, and he generally came back uncommonly well.[51]

However, whenever loyalty to the King and love for 'New England and Old Boston' came into conflict, loyalty always carried the day, and as Britain struggled for her existence against Napolean's Europe, conflict with the United States seemed to be inevitable.

A combination of old disputes left over from the Revolutionary War, and problems arising from the conflict between France and England caused acute tension between Great Britain and the United States.[52] With the renewal of the Napoleonic Wars in 1803, the British insistence on the right to search neutral shipping for contraband, and their provocative habit of impressing American sailors, became increasingly annoying to the United States. In June, 1807, the fight between the *H.M.S. Leopard* and the *U.S.S. Chesapeake* during an impressment attempt, brought the two nations close to war. A speedy British disavowal of the action, and a pacifist president, averted the danger, but, to many it was merely a temporary postponement of military conflict. Both France and Britain had imposed sanctions on neutral commerce. Napoleon's 'Continental System', which closed European ports to British goods, instructed French authorities to confiscate neutral vessels that complied with British rules. The British responded 'with Orders in Council stipulating that all French controlled ports were blockaded; only those vessels which cleared through a British installation and paid British tariffs would be exempt'.[53] President Jefferson's response to these provocations from the European belligerents was to threaten economic sanctions against whoever persisted in interfering in American neutrality. The resulting embargo against British trade was undoubtedly more than an inconvenience to that country, but it was disastrous to parts of the United States and 'sacrificed what New Englanders had won after generations of enterprise on the sea'.[54]

The strong feelings that emerged in 1807 precipitated preparations for war on both sides. In the Maritimes, military governors replaced civilian administrators and increased attention was given to fortifications, militia forces, and military stores. Attention was also paid to the internal affairs of the United States:

It could hardly be unknown to all high officials in British North America that Jefferson's embargo policy was decidedly unpopular to New England. The murmurings of the disaffected and the comparative looseness of the federal bond were other patent facts of the time. As a result we find British officials both in England and in America endeavouring to obtain a more exact knowledge of the political situation in the United States with a view of profiting thereby should war ensue.

Because of the important commercial relationship between Nova Scotia and her New England neighbours, as well as for defensive considerations, Sir John Wentworth had, in 1807, dispatched a secret agent, 'a person well qualified, to observe whatever may be agitating', to the United States. This action was apparently approved by his London superiors for when Sir George Prevost became Lieutenant-governor of Nova Scotia in 1808, he was instructed to

. . . use your utmost endeavours to gain Intelligence with regard to the projects of the American Government . . . and particularly those of the States bordering upon His Majesty's Territories . . .

Accordingly, Prevost sent a 'respectable and intelligent Inhabitant of Halifax, first to Boston, then Washington, Norfolk, and New York', to obtain whatever information he could about military preparations and about the feelings of the populace concerning war. As a spy, John Howe quickly fell into the spirit of the game and proved to be most competent. He arrived in Boston, on 22 April 1808, claiming to local authorities that he had come 'on a visit to my friends' and informed Sir George that he had generally received the utmost cooperation from the Americans, and although 'attacked in a

violent democratic Paper, . . . it excited no other sensa-
tion here than general contempt . . . . Although astonished at 'the great number of new and elegant building
which have been erected in this Town, within the last
ten years . . . ', Howe pointed out that because of Jefferson's Non-intercourse Act . . . 'there are at least 500
Stores and Houses to let, as the late occupiers of them
have been either obliged to go into the Country, or to
turn their attention to other pursuits. . . . ' Howe suspected Jefferson of being in league with France against
Great Britain and wrote that, 'But as Philosophers in
general make wretched Politicians, so has he totally mis-
calculated his measure and the effects it would produce.
In his endeavour to injure Great Britain, he has reduced
his Country to the utmost state of suffering'. This 'suffering', especially in New England, kept that part of the
United States in a ferment reminiscent of the 'Essex
Juno' of 1804, when New England Federalists, under
Aaron Burr, conspired to leave the Union.

Beyond the political situation (and the prophecy
that Madison would succeed as the new president), Howe
reported on other matters. He pointed out that 'The Em-
issaries of Bonaparte are numerous in this country' with
'frequent opportunities to do mischief'. Included among
their nefarious efforts . . . 'to corrupt these people, is to
introduce French Schoolmasters in the Country Villages
. . . under a pretence of teaching the French Language'.
The presence of other foreigners in the United States
was noted as well. Howe wrote that there were seven
thousand Irishmen in New York and commented on
their 'great and fatal effect on elections in this city' and
suggested that,

> Every day's experience shews, (sic) that men who will
> be restless and intriguing under one Government, will
> be so under every other. A great part of the Intrigues
> which agitate this country, originate with men whom
> the Nations of Europe have been compelled to spue out
> from among them, and wherever they get a footing,
> they will be a perpetual source of disease to the body
> politic.

Howe also commented on the state of military prep-

John Howe, Senior

arations in the United States, generally suggesting that the Navy was unprepared, the shipyards inactive, and the army under-manned. The militia, he suggested, 'have a wonderful disposition to imitate everything French, and if they have not the military talents of that nation they certainly shew (sic) they are not behind hand with them in vain or tinsel quality', and concluded that 'the best of them appear to me to be inferior to the Militia Light Infantry Company of Halifax.'

After travelling throughout New England, Howe moved south to New York, Philadelphia, Baltimore, and Washington, visited a cannon foundry at Georgetown, and worked his way homeward through New York and Boston. Before closing his report, he cautioned his superiors to tread softly. He left the United States not doubting that the Administration was anti-British, but believing that it could not, 'without some new subject of irritation excite generally a War Spirit in this Country at present, I am perfectly satisfied.'[55]

Howe's Report was well received in Halifax and London, but during his absence peculiar events had unfolded in Nova Scotia. At Government House, Sir George Prevost received a secret traveller himself. Aaron Burr, the former Vice-President of the United States, who had killed Alexander Hamilton in a duel, arrived in Halifax under the alias of 'Mr. Edwards'. A man of many schemes, Burr unfolded a plan before Prevost and Admiral Warren concerning the Spanish possessions in America and the 'establishment of an Anglo-Saxon, a British-American, hegemony in that part of the world'.[56] Prevost sent Burr off to London where his scheme eventually came to nothing. Meanwhile, it was deemed desirable to seek additional intelligence about American affairs and Howe was prevailed upon to make a second trip. On this trip from 10 November 1808 to 5 January 1809, Howe had thirty-six specific questions to answer.

Howe's second spy mission was carried out under the guise of being the 'bearer of Dispatches to the British Minister'. Again, he started at Boston and moved through New England southward to Washington and beyond. His observations, carefully made and recorded, were primarily concerned with internal political affairs, military preparations and plans, and the public disposition toward war.

Again, Howe pointed out the economic problems caused by the policy of the American Government. He wrote:

> The Embargo has completely federalized all the New England States, and may eventually lead to a division of the Southern and Northern States, and such is the difference of sentiments and habits between them, and the acrimony with which they speak of each other, that such an event is by no means improbable, and indeed many openly express their wish that it may take place.

This proved to be an observation of some insight when it is considered in the light of the 1814 Hartford Convention, and later civil conflict.

Politically, Howe suggested that the Federalists 'generally wish a reconciliation with Great Britain', but that the Democrats were 'with few . . . exceptions, . . . in favour of France', and that the 'President for the ensuing four Years will undoubtedly be Mr. Madison'. This, however, did not disappoint John Howe as he felt that the government 'do not at present think it will be for their Interest to be at War with Great Britain'. Howe attributed the same attitude to the population as a whole, writing, 'Mad as Parties are in America, I do not think, that a Majority of the Population wish a War with Great Britain'. At the same time, he cautioned his superiors that the Orders-in-Council should be repealed. If they were, he felt, ' . . . reconciliation will ensue. If they do not, we shall probably go to War'. If War did follow, Howe expected an attack on British North America.

> The Conquest of Canada, they contemplate as a matter perfectly easy; and whenever they speak of it they build much on the disposition of the Canadians as friendly to them. They reckon also, on a ready welcome from a number of Americans who have of late years become Settlers in Upper Canada. And this last circumstance at least may well lead His Majesty's Government to consider, whether it is politic to admit as settlers near the Frontiers, men of this description.

The capture of Nova Scotia, because it 'is so much surrounded by Water', was more of a puzzle to the Americans, but they did not seem '. . . to imagine there would be any difficulty in effecting the Object'. Howe's opinion, while he advocated 'Precautionary Measures of every kind . . .', was that '. . . Should the trial be made, they will, at least, not find the conquest an easy one'.[57]

John Howe was no ordinary spy, as his interviews with President Jefferson and president-elect Madison suggest. Likewise, his clear observations, lucid descriptions and perceptive opinions, mark him as a man of ability and insight. Time was to prove Howe correct for the Orders-in-Council were not repealed quickly. While it does not matter if the War was really caused by maritime rights, expansionist sentiment, or nationalism, the offending 'Orders' provided the basis for Madison's declaration of War in June, 1812.

The period of the Napoleonic Wars and the War of 1812, were years of great prosperity for Halifax, as the harbour was filled with ships and the taverns were filled with sailors. Nova Scotian privateers brought dozens of French and American prizes to Enos Collins' new warehouse. The city of ten thousand cheered the victory of the *H.M.S. Shannon* over the *U.S.S. Chesapeake;* it watched the regiments come and go; and a whole generation of Haligonians grew up knowing nothing but war. Halifax was the site of a military prison, and throngs of French and American prisoners-of-war were held at Melville Island and in the near-by countryside. John Howe was a frequent visitor to the island prison and many a Boston man had reason to be grateful to him. Many years later, Joseph Howe, on a visit to Boston, was approached by

> . . . one gentleman (who) told me that my father had during the last war, taken his father from the military prison at Melville Island, and sent him back to Boston. Another on the same evening, showed me a gold watch sent by an uncle who had died in the West Indies, to his family. It was pawned by a sailor in Halifax, but redeemed by my father, and sent to the dead man's relatives.[58]

Collectively, Howe might term 'The Republican Virtue' as 'the Virtue of a Strumpet',[59] but as individuals, these Republicans remained his brothers.

The news of Waterloo precipitated joyous celebrations in Halifax. After one hundred and one 'loyal' toasts, the party broke up, only to be reconvened some time later when a final peace was concluded among the belligerents, including the United States. Peace brought a return to quieter times in Halifax. It also brought approximately two thousand Black refugees, largely from the Chesapeake and Delaware Bay areas. First quartered in the barracks of the now empty military prison, the new arrivals were settled in communities around the Capital. John Howe concerned himself with their welfare and often served as a lay preacher in Black communities.

Following his adventures as a spy, John Howe returned to the routine of a busy daily schedule. The Post Office, which he had been forced to neglect during his trips to the United States,[60] continued to take up a large portion of his day, as did his newspaper business. He also remained active in the public affairs of the city. In 1810, he was again commissioned as a Justice of the Peace as well as a Justice of the Inferior Court of Common Pleas. In 1815, he was given an additional responsibility when he was commissioned as Justice 'for the better and more effective administration of the office of Justice of the Peace and for the establishment of an active, vigorous and effectual Police'.[61] The creation of a police force had long been a matter of concern to the merchants and other property owners in Halifax. Although soon after the city was founded in 1749, the settlers were called upon to elect one constable from each of the 13 ships' companies to provide a basis for law enforcement, many years passed before a regular agency was established.[62] After long years of war, the port was filled with the outcasts of a dozen societies, and the need for a regular force was great. However, the fights between press-gangs and townsmen, soldiers, sailors and civilians, underlined the reason for the lack of a police force and jail. This type of service in a community of any size required incorporation if it were to be handled with any efficiency. However, the incorporation of Halifax was constantly refused because it ran contrary to the wishes of the military authorities. The nightwatch, even when armed with a one metre long staff to assure attention, and an iron rattle to call for assistance,[63] was not adequate to handle the problems that Halifax offered.

> The upper streets were full of brothels. Grog-shops and dancing-houses were to be seen in every part of the town . . . The upper street (Brunswick) was known as 'Knock Him Down Street' in consequence of the affrays and even murders committed there. No person of character ventured to reside there; nearly all the buildings were occupied as brothels for the soldiers and sailors. The streets of this part of the town presented continually the disgusting sight of abandoned females of the lowest class in a state of drunkenness, bareheaded, without shoes, and in the most filthy and abominable condition.[64]

Such a lingering offence to public morality could not be tolerated indefinitely. Finally, Lieutenant-governor Sir John C. Sherbrooke, in his February 1815 speech to the Assembly, commented that the 'present state of the Police of Halifax, which, from the great increase in population, and other causes, appears to require some further regulation'. The Assembly apparently agreed that 'a proper attention to the regularity and general good order of the Community, and to the religious and moral conduct of the individuals which compose it',[65] was of importance and immediately struck a Committee to investigate. This Committee, assisted by commissioned magistrates like John Howe, predictably recommended the erection of a 'Bridewell or House of Correction' and 'the daily attendance of one Magistrate in some Public Office in Halifax, for managing the Police of the Town'.[66] The establishment of the jail and town court apparently did not solve the larger political issue. In 1825, the *Acadian Recorder* stated 'that no system of management can produce a police effective enough for the wants and adapted to the situation of such a Town as Halifax, unless it be by incorporation and the election of the magistracy',[67] — two issues that were to be very much the province of a younger Howe.

Duty to his church was also an important part of John Howe's daily life. He tried to follow the high ideal of living a good Christian life, placing great stress on deeds of charity. He also had become an elder of the Sandemanian congregation,[68] leading it in worship as they had no paid ministers. John Howe also served as a lay preacher to any other group who would accept his religious teachings. His religion extended beyond mere words, as 'It was not uncommon for him to take under his roof, penniless men in search of work, and to support them until they found it'.[69] He was also a frequent visitor to the prisoners at the Bridewell, going on foot, every Sunday afternoon to read and explain the Scriptures. He 'had a genuine interest in these unfortunate men. When they were released he took them under his care and helped them find work'.[70] Howe became disgusted with the appalling conditions that existed at the city jail and with the corruption of the officials who ran it. Son Joseph, later told how his father had finally left the place in disgust and refused to return.

John Howe was described as being 'a fine looking man — intelligent, courteous, and benevolent. He wrote well and, though having no taste for political disputation, spoke on religious subjects in a strain of simple, natural eloquence not often equalled and rarely excelled'.[71] But, he was a man of paradox as well. His sentiments were evidently not unlike the Quaker who said in a large situation: 'I may not strike thee but I will hold thee uncomfortably.' A man of peace, he launched himself into the cause of his King in two wars. A Sandemanian pacifist, he nevertheless could take exception to objectionable behavior, and did not always expect to have civic authorities to call upon. Returning home with his youngest son after a Sunday afternoon visit to the Bridewell, he came upon 'two young men polluting the Sabbath by fighting in the street'. Magistrate Howe ordered them to stop at once. On being told in impolite terms, to mind his own business, he handed his Bible to his son, and although no longer a young man, seized each by the collar, knocked their heads together and dropped them to the ground. Recovering his Bible, he admonished them to remember to keep the Sabbath in the future, and calmly continued his journey home.[72] Although a strong adherent to both his religious beliefs

47

and his civic responsibilities, he did not allow either to cloud his concept of justice or stand in the way of his practice of Christianity.

In 1817, at sixty-four years of age, 'in consequence of an apoplectic fit',[73] Howe resigned his positions as King's Printer and Deputy Postmaster General in favour of his eldest son, John Junior. That same year, Lord Dalhousie, then Lieutenant-governor of Nova Scotia commented in his diary on a chance meeting with Howe.

> In my walk today, Judge Stewart with me, we met Howe our Postmaster — a very sensible, well-informed and shrewd old man. He is just returned from a tour of Quebec, Montreal, New York and Boston. His conversation was so interesting that I cannot help sitting down immediately to make a Memorandum of it.

Dalhousie drew a picture of a man who was still vigorous, still interested, and as shrewd an observer as he had been ten years before. The Lieutenant-governor's 'Memorandum' included Howe's comments on the number of American merchants settling in Montreal, and the view that the St. Lawrence was 'at this moment as freely occupied and used by the American trade as is the Mississippi'. Howe also insisted that most of the immigrants to Upper Canada were simply passing through, stating that '. . . the far greater proportion of Artificers that come out with the sanction of Government to Canada do not stop a month before they proceed to the States'. Dalhousie also recorded Howe's meeting on the Plattsburg steamboat 'with a tall odd looking man, a Scotchman by his language — not more strange and eccentric in appearance than in his ideas and the view he took of all subjects in conversation'. Howe's chance acquaintance proved to be Robert Gourlay, 'the noted disturber of Upper Canada at present'.[74]

During his year of retirement, John Howe remained active. In 1819, he was again commissioned as a Justice of the Peace for Halifax County and also commissioned as a Justice of the Inferior Court of Common Pleas, Halifax District. In 1832, he accepted the additional responsibility of serving as a Health Warden, County Court House District, Halifax.

Throughout his life, Howe was occasionally involved with the affairs of the State, and always concerned with the state of affairs within his Province, but never had any connection with politics. In 1826, he broke with this habit and nominated S. G. W. Archibald as a candidate for the Legislative Assembly for the county of Halifax.[75] While it may well be improper to link Archibald's victory with the name of his nominator, there is little doubt that his connection with the respected John Howe did anything but assist his cause. Despite his retirement, Howe could not get too far from the printer's ink. His youngest son, Joseph, had become involved in the newspaper business, first with *The Acadian* and, in December, 1827, with *The Novascotian*. In an effort to give his paper a province-wide audience, he set out on his famous 'Rambles' throughout the province. During these absences, John Howe, with the assistance of his daughter-in-law, Susan Ann MacNab Howe, kept the presses rolling.[76] Among his other tasks, John Howe helped fill the pages of the *Novascotian* by writing editorials. His opinions, however, sometimes came into conflict with those of his absent son. During the war between Turkey and Russia, Howe's editorials favoured Russia. This view, when the issue had been independence of Greece, was in line with Imperial policy. The Czar's new war, however, was viewed with some alarm by Imperial officials as it could mean an extension of the Russian sphere of influence into the eastern Mediterranean. This new view was supported by Joseph Howe. On his return to Halifax, Joseph eased the situation by writing an editorial against war in general.

During his seventy-third year, John Howe finally applied to the British government for compensation for his service as a spy in 1808-1809. The money he hoped to receive was not for himself, but was to be used to extend the business interests of his sons.[77] John Howe, Junior, apparently went to England in 1826-27 on his own business and perhaps to press his father's claim. However, the 'Home Government' provided nothing. Likely, they felt that old warriors, like old wars, were best forgotten.

Howe continued to live in his simple cottage on the Northwest Arm during the years of his retirement. He 'rose at daybreak, in summer and winter; and was in the habit of reading and writing for hours before the rest of the family was astir'.[78] He wrote 'Christian Songs', some of which he sent to George Hutton in Dundee, Scotland; the home of Sandemanianism. He also 'devoted much of his time to writing on the Revelations' producing a 'large mass' of manuscript material which he never published. Howe also continued in his role as an elder and lay preacher within his Church. 'During the last four or five years of his life, he used to assemble members of his Church at a Mr. Reeve's about 6 miles from Halifax on the Sabbath Day, when he read the Bible and expounded the Scriptures to them as ably as he ever did.'[79]

John Howe's Halifax at the beginning of the third decade of the nineteenth century was a city of fifteen thousand inhabitants. As the military, economic and political centre of the province, it had an air of importance and business. Its public structures and elegant private residences were the centre of society, just as its free port was the centre of foreign trade. John Howe's home on the 'Arm' was little disturbed by the bustle of Halifax. This calm was temporarily broken, however, early in 1830, when the *Sir Charles Ogle,* the first steam-ship to make an appearance in Halifax Harbour, ' . . . steamed around Point Pleasant and proceeded up the Northwest Arm'.[80] John Howe, ' . . . one of the venerable fathers of the country . . . being accidently in his field', had his usual solitude broken by the chugging of the motor and 'by the three hearty cheers from the passengers on the deck . . . which were no less heartily returned by the good old gentleman'.[81]

John Howe's calm was to be broken by other less joyous, but equally noisy events. His youngest son, Joseph, was slowly but surely moving into a position of opposition to the establishment and becoming a voice for reform. 'There were many — and among them, old John Howe — who saw trouble in store for the editor of the *Novascotian* unless he curbed his zeal . . . '[82]. In 1835, trouble appeared. On the first day of that year, Joseph Howe had published an anonymous letter in his paper that 'accused the magistrates of Halifax of misconduct'. It alleged 'that during the lapse of thirty years, the magistracy and the police had, by one stratagem or other, taken from the pockets of the people, in overexactions, fines, and so-forth, a sum that would exceed in the gross amount £30,000.'[83] The establishment could not allow such a challenge to go unanswered. For publishing the letter, Joe Howe was charged with criminal libel. The trial was held 2 March 1835, before the Chief Justice and a special jury. Howe, pleading his own case, spoke for six and a quarter hours. He 'brought to light a mass of abuses which are without parallel, and which astonished the audience.'[84] Among them were memories of the situation at the Bridewell.

> I can recall a period when my father interested himself deeply for the welfare of the poor inmates of that prison', Howe told the court. He added pointedly; 'Though a magistrate himself, I mention his name with veneration . . . he never filched from them their daily bread, but he sought to impart to them the bread of life . . . he had nothing to do with (the other magistrates') dirty accounts and paltry peculations.[85]

The following morning, rejecting the publically stated personal opinion of Chief Justice Brenton Haliburton, the jury delivered their famous 'Not Guilty' verdict. The celebrations lasted for almost two days. Freedom of the press was established and Joe Howe launched on a long and distinguished public career.

Although no doubt a participant in the celebrations, to John Howe it must have been a bitter-sweet occasion. A Magistrate himself, the father of another and indeed considered by some as 'the Father of the Bench',[86] he was likely pleased to have these long-standing abuses revealed. At the same time, he must have considered the possible injustice of tarring every Magistrate with the same brush.

Perhaps this fear, and perhaps a desire to protect Joseph's victory, caused him to write one of a few letters he ever addressed to a newspaper. It objected to an earlier piece that had claimed that one 'Judge Sawers was the very man who, at the first, boldly and openly, and at his own risk, charged the Magistrates with the faults subsequently brought against them'. This claim, Howe completely rejected and regarded it as an attack upon himself. He wrote:

> I should certainly not, at my time of life, have written a line for a Newspaper, had not this attempt been made to claim credit for Mr. Sawers, for a lawless and impudent attack, upon a Court which was fairly and impartially performing its duties, as if he had been instrumental in detecting any of the fraudulent irregularities said to exist, the public shall not be so misled.

The dispute between Sawers and Howe grew out of a court case held in December 1831. Sawers was the legal counsel for Thomas Scutt, who was brought before the court 'for pelting the sentry on the Parade'.[87] Scutt was pronounced guilty of assault by the Jury, and Howe as senior Magistrate, fined him ten pounds.[88] Sawers, angered at the loss of this and one other case, apparently threatened the Jury members.[89] As a result, they decided that Sawers would not be allowed to appear before them until he apologized for 'publicly charging the Court with Acting with tyranny and injustice'. Sawers' indiscretion was followed by letters from Sawers and Scutt to John Howe, Jr., and John Howe, Esquire, 'calling into question their conduct as connected with their Public Capacities as Magistrates'. The court again retaliated by demanding an apology. Sawers, however, did have some friends in the Court. The issue was reintroduced on 10 March 1832, but without effect as three motions condemning Sawers were passed by an eleven to three margin. Again, on 12 March 1832, a motion to expunge the Sawers' affair from the books was introduced and defeated by an eight to one margin. Thereafter, the issue seemed to disappear. Sawers received an appointment as Justice of the Inferior Court of Common Pleas for the Eastern District and there the matter lay until 1835.[90]

John Howe's letter spawned many replies, some supporting his stand, and some in vehement opposition. One referred to Howe as gratifying 'the feelings of a family party'[91] and another spoke of 'that melancholy shew (sic) of enfeebled venom by old Mr. Howe'.[92] With this, Howe's supporters sprang into the unseemly fray. *Vox Populi* charged that all the negative letters were written by the same person,

> ... for I cannot bring myself to believe that there are
> three individuals in this Town well acquainted with
> Mr. John Howe, Sr., that can conscientiously reproach
> the veracity, integrity and honour of that gentleman.
> His age and grey hairs add weight and dignity to his
> magisterial functions. ... And when his accusers are
> driven so hard as to bring the infirmity of years, a
> charge against him, it is indeed a *dernier* resort, an
> unmanly subterfuge for a cowardly accusation.[93]

John Howe allowed the storm of this controversy to
wash around him without dignifying it with further comment.

The happiness over his son's legal victory, the joy of
another grandchild, the unpleasantness of the Sawers'
affair, and the contentment of the Christmas season that
followed, were the last events John Howe was to share
with his family. For two years his health had been a
source of worry to his sons. His eldest son, John, Jr.,
explained:

> Friendly as he always was to the poor, he seemed to
> think that he ought to devote the remaining portion of
> his life to the amelioration of their condition. He per-
> suaded a Gentleman to allow him to settle as many as
> he pleased on a large tract of land, ranging from 6 to
> 10 miles on the eastern side of Halifax Harbour. He or-
> dered Ploughs, Harrows, Spinning Wheels, etc. to be
> made and would have incurred a larger amount of obli-
> gation, had I have (sic) not watched his proceedings
> and prevented his orders from being carried into effect.

His family was often concerned because he was always 'riding about the country', often alone. 'He frequently met with accidents, but they had no effect on
preventing his excursions'. John Howe's last hours were
not with his family, but fittingly in the service of his
Church. He had ridden some six miles out of the city to
meet with fellow Sandemanians. 'He performed Divine
Service in the forenoon and afternoon and afterwards
chatted ... until 7 1/2 o'clock, when (as he said) he felt
tired and went to bed. The next morning the (Reeves)
Family found him a corpse'. His son thankfully added, 'I

am satisfied the melancholy change was unattended with pain'.[94] John Howe died, 'suddenly and without a struggle', on 27 December 1835, at 81 years of age. The *Acadian Recorder* wrote of him:

> Few men have ever departed from a community, leaving a more honourable fame behind, as citizens, or Christians, than the reputation which hallows Mr. Howe's name in Halifax. Justice, benevolence, and a high degree of piety, marked his course, and 'his works follow him' to the state of final reward.[95]

To Joseph, his more famous son, John Howe, that 'venerable being who has passed away'[96] was ever a source of inspiration and a fount of strength. Time and time again Joseph paid his respects to him:

> For thirty years he was my instructor, my play fellow, almost my daily companion. To him I owe my fondness for reading, my familiarity with the Bible, my knowledge of old Colonial and American incidents and characteristics. He left me nothing but his example and the memory of his many virtues, for all that he ever earned was given to the poor. He was too good for this world; but remembrance of his childlike simplicity, and truly Christian character, is never absent from my mind.[97]

From this, and the many other tributes he paid to his father, there can be little doubt of the. great influence John Howe had on his famous son. In their love of literature, their occupations, their prejudices, and in their willingness to serve their people, their careers ran parallel. To most, John Howe's life has been a footnote in the story of his son. But John Howe does not need to bask in reflected light, for his own life was full of adventure and intrigue, and marked by service to his King and to his God. Serve God and Honour the King — with this reading, the old Loyalist had charted his course, and although it often led him into troubled waters, he followed it to the end of his journey.

1. E. Alfred Jones, *The Loyalists of Massachusetts*, (London: The Saint Catherine Press, 1930), p. 122.
2. Terrence M. Punch and Allan E. Marble, 'The Family of John Howe, Hali-

fax, Loyalist and King's Printer', *The Nova Scotia Historical Quarterly*, v. 6, n. 3 (September, 1976), p. 317.

3. James H. Stark, *The Loyalists of Massachusetts and the Other Side of the American Revolution*, (Boston: Clarke, 1907), p. 361.

4. Charles St. C. Stayner, 'The Sandemanian Loyalists', *Collections of the Nova Scotia Historical Society*, v. 29, (1951), p. 99.

5. Isaiah Thomas, *The History of Printing in America*, v. II, (New York: Franklin, 1972), p. 25.

6. Jones, *Loyalists*, p. 122.

7. Thomas, *Printing II*, p. 27.

8. Joseph A. Chisholm, *The Speeches and Public Letters of Joseph Howe*, vol. II, (Halifax: Chronicle, 1909), p. 350.

9. Stark, *Loyalists*, p. 138, also see F.E. Crowell, 'New Englanders in Nova Scotia', Public Archives of Nova Scotia Scrapbook Collection MG 9 No. 109, pp. 132-133.

10. Wallace Brown, *The Good Americans: The Loyalists in the American Revolution*, New York: Morrow, 1969, p. 16.

11. Joseph Howe, 'Memo on my father', Joseph Howe Papers reel 22, Microfilm, Public Archives of Nova Scotia.

12. Harold G. Travis, 'The Spy that Hid in Weston', *The Weston Historical Society Bulletin*, XI, 3, (March, 1975), p. 3.

13. John Richard Alden, *The American Revolution 1775-1783*, (New York: Harper, 1954), p. 24.

14. Alden, *Revolution*, p. 39.

15. Howe, 'Memo', J.H.P. reel 22.

16. J.D. Logan, 'Old John Howe's Three R's', Public Archives of Nova Scotia Scrapbook Collection MG9 No. 43 (Halifax and Districts) p. 125.

17. Punch and Marble, 'John Howe', p. 318.

18. Alden, *Revolution*, p. 41.

19. Thomas H. Raddall, *Halifax: Warden of the North*, rev. ed., (Toronto: McClelland and Stewart, 1971), p. 79.

20. Stayner, 'Sandemanian', p. 99, also see Jones, *Loyalists*, p. 122.

21. Punch and Marble, 'John Howe', pp. 317-318.

22. Chisholm, *Speeches*, II, p. 350.

23. Joseph A. Chisholm, *Howe Letters*, typescript, Public Archives of Nova Scotia, p. 18.

24. James A. Roy, *Joseph Howe: A Study in Achievement and Frustration*, (Toronto: Macmillan, 1935), p. 2.

25. Stayner, 'Sandemanian', pp. 63-64, 77-78, 99-102.

26. Punch and Marble, 'John Howe', p. 317.

27. Raddall, *Halifax*, p. 96.

28. J.W. Regan, *Sketches and Traditions of the Northwest Arm*, (Halifax, 1908), p. 62.

29. Stark, *Loyalists*, p. 362.

30. Marie Tremaine, *A Bibliography of Canadian Imprints 1751-1800*, (Toronto: University of Toronto Press, 1952), p. 610; also see *Halifax Journal*, 'Masthead', p. 1.

31. D.C. Harvey, 'Newspapers of Nova Scotia, 1840-1867', *The Canadian Historical Review*, XXVI, 3 (September, 1945), p. 282.

32. Tremaine, *Imprints*, p. 611.

33. Joseph Howe, 'Memo', J.H.P. reel 22; also see Harvey, 'Newspapers', 284.

34. Fanning held a commission as Lieutenant-governor of Nova Scotia from 1783 to l786 but was not called upon to open it as the governor, John Parr, (1782-86), did not leave the colony. Macdonald writes that Howe, 'lived north of Governor Fanning with whom he was very intimate. These were the first two residences on the eastern side of the Northwest Arm. Parr often visited at the two houses, and was very friendly with postmaster Howe'. see James S. Macdonald, 'Memoir of Governor John Parr', *Collections of the Nova Scotia Historical Society*, 14, (1910), p. 63.

35. 'To the Public', *The Nova Scotia Magazine and Comprehensive Review of*

Literature, Politics and News (hereafter N.S.M.), II (July, 1790), p. A2 and 'Titlepage'.

36. N.S.M., (October, 1789), p. 270.
37. Punch and Marble, 'John Howe', p. 318.
38. Public Archives of Nova Scotia (hereafter P.A.N.S.), Commission Books, R.G. 1, vol. 172, p. 106.
39. Harvey, 'Newspapers', p. 284.
40. Chisholm, *Howe Letters,* p. 1, 5.
41. L.G. Campbell, *History of Sable Island before Confederation,* (Dalhousie University: Unpublished Master of Arts Thesis, 1962), *passim,* also see D. Brymer, ed., *Report on Canadian Archives, 1895,* (Ottawa: Queen's Printer, 1895), and L.G. Campbell, *Sable Island, Fatal and Fertile Crescent,* (Windsor, N.S.: Lancelot, 1974), *passim.* The unfortunate Mrs. Copeland was cast ashore by a storm and murdered by a wrecker for her ring. Her spirit roamed the island seeking restitution.
42. P.A.N.S., Commission Books, R.G.1., Vol. 172, p. 109.
43. P.A.N.S., Post Office Reports 1770-1817. Vertical Manuscript File.
44. C.M. Jephcott, *et. al., The Postal History of Nova Scotia and New Brunswick 1754-1867,* (Toronto: Sissons, 1964), p. 43.
45. Joseph Howe, 'Memo', J.H.P., reel 22, also see Jephcott, *Postal History,* p. 43.
46. Jephcott, *Postal History,* p. 52-56.
47. Theophrastus, 'Firewards for the Town of Halifax', *An Almanack for the Year of Our Lord, 1803,* (Halifax: John Howe, 1803), n.p.
48. P.A.N.S., Commission Books, R.G.1., vol. 172, pp. 140-142.
49. D.W. Parker, 'Secret Reports of John Howe, 1808, I', *The American Historical Review,* XVII, II, (January, 1912), p. 334.
50. D.W. Parker, 'Secret Report of John Howe', *The American Historical Review,* XVII, I, (October, 1911), p. 78; also see Marjory Whitelaw, ed., *The Dalhousie Journals,* (Canada: Oberon, 1978), pp. 102-103.
51. Chisholm, *Speeches,* II, p. 350.
52. J. MacKay Hitsman, *The Incredible War of 1812: A Military History,* (Toronto: University of Toronto Press, 1966), pp. 3-15, *passim.*
53. Hugh C. Barley, *America: The Framing of a Nation,* vol. 1 — to 1877, (Columbus, Ohio: Merrill, 1975), pp. 132-133.
54. W.S. MacNutt, *The Atlantic Provinces: The Emergence of Colonial Society 1712-1857,* (Toronto: McClelland abd Stewart, 1965), p. 133.
55. Parker, 'Secret Reports', I, p. 71-100, *passim.*
56. James Stuart Martell, *The Romance of Government House,* (rev. ed., Halifax: Nova Scotia Communications and Information Centre, 1979), p. 20, also see, Raddall, *Halifax,* p. 141.
57. Parker, 'Secret Reports', II, p. 338-354, *passim.*
58. Chisholm, *Speeches,* II, p. 350.
59. Parker, 'Secret Reports', I, p. 91.
60. Parker, 'Secret Reports', II, p. 340.
61. P.A.N.S. Commission Books, R.G.1., vol. 173, pp. 30-32, 9-17, 302-303.
62. Linda Levy, *Halifax Mail Star,* 10 October 1964.
63. Report of the Provincial Museum of Nova Scotia, 1927, (Halifax: King's Printer), p. 35.
64. Raddall, *Halifax,* pp. 150-151.
65. Government of Nova Scotia, *Journals and Proceedings of the House of Assembly 1815,* (Halifax: King's Printer, 1815), p. 5.
66. Nova Scotia, *Journals,* p. 113, 42.
67. *Acadian Recorder,* 12 November 1815, p. 3, col. 3..
68. Stayner, 'Sandemanian', p. 100.
69. H.R. Percy, *Joseph Howe,* (Don Mills: Fitzhenry and Whiteside, 1976), p. 3.
70. Percy, *Howe,* p. 4, 18.
71. Joseph A. Chisholm, *The Speeches and Public Letters of Joseph Howe,* vol. I, Halifax: Chronicle, 1909, p. 1.
72. Stayner, 'Sandemanian', p. 101, also see, Percy *Howe,* p. 4.

73. C. Bruce Fergusson, *Joseph Howe of Nova Scotia,* (Windsor, Nova Scotia: Lancelot, 1973), P. 15.
74. Whitelaw, ed., *Journals,* p. 102-103.
75. *Nova Scotian,* (Halifax, Nova Scotia), 3 May 1826, p. 178, col. 3.
76. Roy, *Frustration,* p. 24, also see, Percy, *Howe,* p. 11.
77. Fergusson, *Howe,* p. 15.
78. Roy, *Frustration,* p. 5.
79. *Letter,* John Howe Jr. to George Hutton, 23 May 1838, J.H.P., reel 22.
80. J.P. Martin, *The Story of Dartmouth,* (Dartmouth: For the Author, 1957), p. 165.
81. George Mullane, 'Footprints Around and About Bedford Basin: A District Brimful of Romantic Associations'; (reprinted from the *Acadian Recorder;* n.d.), p. 33.
82. Roy, *Frustration,* p. 48.
83. Fergusson, *Howe,* p. 64.
84. *Acadian Recorder,* (Halifax, N.S.) 7 March 1835.
85. Percy, *Howe;* p. 18.
86. *Letter,* Richard Tremaine to John Howe, Sr., *Novascotian,* 16 April 1835, p. 2.
87. *Letter,* John Howe, Sr. to Editor, *Novascotian,* 2 April 1835, pp. 2-3.
88. P.A.N.S., R.G. No. 34, Series 312, Quarter Sessions, Halifax County, 16 December 1831, and 20 December 1831.
89. *Letter,* Howe to Editor, *Novascotian,* 2 April 1835, pp. 2-3.
90. P.A.N.S., R.G. No. 34, Series 312, 5 Jan., 17 Jan., 6 March, 10 March, 12 March 1832.
91. *Letter,* Memo to John Howe Sr., *Acadian Recorder,* 2 May 1835, p. 2.
92. *Letter,* Investigator to John Howe Sr., *The Times,* (Halifax, N.S.), 2 May 1835, p. 2.
93. *Letter,* Vox Populi to Editor, *Acadian Recorder,* 2 May 1835, p. 2.
94. *Letter,* John Howe Jr. to Hutton, J.H.P., reel 22.
95. *Acadian Recorder,* Saturday 2 January 1836, p. 3.
96. Roy, *Frustration,* p. 58.
97. J. Chisholm, vol. 1, *Speeches,* p. 88.

South Aspect of Halifax, N.S., in 1780

Chapter 3

Francis Green

For Honour
& His King

by Phyllis R. Blakeley

Francis Green served in the British army during the 1758 capture of Louisbourg. He later became a merchant in Boston and fled the city in 1776 when the British troops were evacuated. His journey took him to Halifax, New York, London and back to Halifax where he served as High Sheriff of Halifax County. Like some other Loyalists, Francis Green was drawn back to his birthplace and spent the last years of his life in the United States.

Towards sunset on Monday afternoon on 4 July 1774, Francis Green, a merchant of Boston, drove into Windham in Connecticut on a business trip to collect some money from his debtors. While Green was walking along the street four strangers invited him to go into a nearby house to talk business. He told them to come to Carey's Tavern where he had taken a room. There the men asked whether his name was Francis Green and whether he had signed the Address to Governor Hutchinson.[1]

Green replied that he was and demanded their names and what further business they had with him. They answered that the town of Windham considered him an *Enemy to his Country* and ordered him to leave at once, but Green refused. In the meantime a mob had surrounded the house; now some put their heads into the open windows to listen to what was going on. That committee retired to talk to the clamorous crowd.

Another committee came into his room and told Green that he could tarry until six o'clock in the morning, but if he still lingered he might be tarred and feathered. Green assured them he would not go. At six o'clock the next morning the church bell rang, and a cannon fired but Green stubbornly refused to leave. One of the leaders offered to let him stay until four in the afternoon, but Green still said 'No!' The crowd surged into the tavern and upstairs, forced their way into his room and seized his bundles, papers, and baggage and threatened his life. Still obstinate, he warned them that he would report them to the magistrate. They shouted at each other but at last they went away. Green had been an officer in the army and had an unconscious air of command and a stubborn bravery to which they gave way. The Boston merchant stayed to breakfast and sent for various people he wished to do business with, and then drove off, assuring the ringleaders that he would 'take a proper notice of them'.

While he was on the road he learned that an express rider was sent ahead to excite the mob to attack him at Norwich. The 'friends of liberty' had assembled and agreed upon a signal the moment Green should make his entry into town. On his arrival on Wednesday morning at seven o'clock, Mr. Manning the grave-digger rang the meetinghouse bell, a cannon was fired, a drum beat and the mob assembled upon the plain to appoint a committee to wait upon Green to order him to depart the town within fifteen minutes. The Boston merchant was at the house of Samuel Huntington, his agent. Green answered that 'their Demand was very insolent, illegal and presumptuous to the highest degree, and he would not comply with it' and asked 'By what authority do you act?' They answered: 'The authority of the People'.

Green turned to Samuel Huntington, a magistrate and judge of the superior court and said: 'Sir, I demand of you as magistrate that Protection which every Subject employed in his lawful & necessary Business is entitled to — I repeat my Demand, and desire to know whether I may expect it'. Huntington made no answer so Green added: 'you know, Sir, I am here on my lawful Business and if I cannot receive my Protection, but must be obstructed in the collecting my Debts in this province, I will make a Complaint of your Government'.

Then Green went over to Lothrop's Tavern and ordered breakfast. Immediately the mob burst into the room crying out: 'The Time is up, Out with him, Out with him' and laid hold of him and forced him out of the house with great violence. About two hundred had gathered around a Cart to take him for tarring and feathering. Green struggled frantically and tried to strike them but they grabbed him shouting 'Into the Cart, Into the Cart with him'. One of the leaders intervened and insisted that Green be sent off in his own carriage. The crowd forced him roughly into his carriage and set his horses galloping and followed him with shouts and huzzas for a kilometre, pelting him with stones, sticks and mud and frightening his horses into a wilder gallop back towards Boston.

Francis Green returned to Boston to his wife and children and to complain about the breakdown of law and order to the Governor of Massachusetts, General Thomas Gage, who did lodge a complaint with the Governor of Connecticut but the mob was not punished. Green himself offered a reward of $100 for the capture of the five ring leaders. Green was moving on a path which was to lead him to exile in England and Nova Scotia for his loyalty to the British Constitution. Samuel Huntington had chosen the opposite course and was to be a delegate to the Continental Congress, Governor of the state of Connecticut, and to be remembered as one of those who signed the Declaration of Independence for the United States of America.

In 1774 Francis Green was 32 years old, born at Boston on 21 August 1742, the second son of Benjamin and Mary Pierce Green and a descendant of Percival Green who had come to Boston in 1635.[2] In his memorial to Lord George Germain he said 'That, derived from Ancestors emigrated from Great Britain, at the Settlement of New England, who (in an honourable Succession in public Stations in America) have transmitted to him the Principles of Loyalty to the Crown, and affections to the Nation . . . influenced by an invioable attachment to his most gracious Sovereign . . . . ' [3] His father was one of the New England force which besieged Louisbourg in 1745 and had accompanied General Sir William Pepperell as secretary to the expedition and remained there after the capture of the French fortress as commissary of stores, secretary and manager of finances. After Cape Breton was returned to the French, Benjamin Green moved to Halifax which had been founded in the summer of 1749 by Governor Edward Cornwallis with 2,400 settlers from England. Here Green served as provincial treasurer.

Mrs. Green moved from Boston to Halifax with her children, but Francis was sent to Boston to be educated at John Lovell's Latin School, from which he was admitted into Harvard College in July 1756. Francis boarded with President Holyoke in Cambridge. However, the year before his entrance to college his father had obtained an ensign's commission in the 40th Regiment from his friend General Charles Lawrence, then Governor of Nova Scotia and military commander, with the promise that Francis should have leave of absence until he completed his studies. War with France having broken out again, Lord Loudoun arrived in America as commander-in-chief of all the King's Forces in America, and ordered all the officers to join their corps. In 1757 Francis sailed to Halifax expecting a leave of absence but instead had to remain with the 40th.

Like most men of his generation in New England, Francis Green could boast that he had military service at Louisbourg — but it was in 1758 with a British regiment, the 40th — not with Pepperell in 1745. Loudoun's cabbage planting expedition did not attack the French fortress, but in April 1758 the 40th embarked for the siege of Louisbourg under the command of General Amherst by land and Admiral Boscawen by sea where 16 year old Francis' only injury was 'a slight contusion only, on his leg by a Stone'. Louisbourg had the finest fortifications in North America on a rugged promontory to the south of the spacious harbour and a seaport where 150 ships came annually from France, West Indies, Quebec, and the British colonies. There were impressive stone buildings such as the Chateau St. Louis, the barracks, the hospital, the convent, the church and houses — all burned or damaged by the British guns. While at Louisbourg, Lieutenant Green was commander of a fortified island at the entrance to the harbour for a little while. On 21 August the 40th was one of four regiments left to garrison Louisbourg and encamped on the slope while the embarkation began.

Francis must have often heard his father talk about the unhealthy climate of Louisbourg with so much cold, foggy weather and floating ice which choked the harbour in May. While on garrison duty at the bleak post of Louisbourg Francis amused himself by shooting, fishing and hunting, and taking part in assemblies and plays. He wrote in his reminisences: 'There was a very pretty Theatre there & the officers were the actors, *at their own expense. F.G.* was urged to take an active part in the *theatrical exhibitions* & performed several characters in *Tragedy & Comedy* (not without commendation)'.

In 1759 when General James Wolfe was at Louisbourg waiting for the fleet to assemble for the attack on Quebec, he formed an additional flank company called the light infantry company to serve with every battalion in the front line as part of his improved tactics for fighting the French. Francis Green was proud to be one of the officers chosen and was looking forward to 'going on the expedition to Canada with Gen. Wolfe' but because the garrison at Louisbourg was so weak only the grenadiers were embarked, and the 40th was left to another boring winter at Louisbourg. In August 1759, Lieutenant Green commanded a sloop of war of 10 guns and 40 soldiers which sailed from Louisbourg harbour, passed through the Gut of Canso, and relieved the garrison on the Island of St. John (now Prince Edward Island) with provisions and military stores. Off Canso they chased a suspicious vessel which turned out to be a trader from Boston instead of a French vessel.

In the spring of 1760 Green and his soldiers sailed to Quebec, and proceeded up the River St. Lawrence to join the forces of Major General James Murray on 17 August and surround Montreal until Canada surrendered on 7 September. In October the troops went into winter camp on the north side of the St. Lawrence, opposite Sorel. It was a cold winter for the river froze on the 11 November and ice and snow lasted until 14 April.

It had been decided to send the British troops to capture the French islands in the West Indies so in June 1761, the 40th travelled to Crown Point, both sides of Lake Champlain 'being a perfect wilderness'. Toward autumn they crossed Lake George to Ticonderoga, on to Albany, then descended in sloops to New York, to camp on Staten Island until the regiment sailed for Barbadoes in November. The French were surprised at Martinique and surrendered in January 1762. Green had commanded a detachment which led the attack on Mount Fortinson which drove the enemy from their trenches and took the mountain which overlooked Fort Royal, but his sergeant and several of his men were killed.

Orders came from England for an expedition to sail from Martinique to Havannah since Spain had entered the war. Green was chosen to go with Lieutenant-colonel James Grant of the 40th to Antigua where they purchased and hired 400 Blacks before joining the fleet to land on the island of Cuba on 7 June. The siege was a dreadful one because of the intense tropical heat, shortage of water, spoiled provisions and epidemics which incapacitated half the British forces. After the Spanish surrendered Moro Castle on 12 August 1762, the 40th Regiment was detained to garrison Havannah until the following June.

The next winter Green was lucky to be sent to Boston to recruit soldiers, and after the war ended he decided that he would leave the army to settle in Boston as a business man, as service in four campaigns had brought only slow promotion to first lieutenant. However, he travelled to Ireland with the 40th Regiment but sold out of the army in 1766, for commissions were then bought and sold in the British army although promotions could be made on the field in wartime campaigns. Sir William Howe later testified that Green had served as an officer in the 40th Regiment on service in America during the last war, 'in which he conducted himself with Gallantry & great Propriety' . . . .[4] Since he had been a veteran whose college career had been interrupted by war he applied for and received his degree at Harvard. Not until 1774 was he rewarded for his military service by a grant of 2032 acres near Pessody's or Pebody's River in New Hampshire.[5] He also owned 240 acres of uncultivated land at Stevens Town (later incorporated as Salisbury) which he had inherited from his uncle Joshua Pierce.

Presumably his family connections helped him to set up in business in Boston. On 18 October 1769 he married Susanna, daughter of Joseph Green and Ann Pierce Green, his double cousin, by whom he had five children, three of whom died in childhood. Francis had returned home to a scene of political and economic unrest, for the struggle had begun which was to create the United States of America. The resistance to the Stamp Act, to the act for compulsory billeting of troops, and to the enforcement of laws against smuggling had created an organization of protestors against the decrees of the British government. Green was still in the British Army during the Stamp Act riots when the mobs attacked the house of Chief Justice Thomas Hutchinson, who was also lieutenant-governor, and hewed down the doors with broad axes, and destroyed or stole everything of value, including priceless papers which he had collected for a history of the colony. Those who were arrested were released by another mob who forced the jailor to give up the keys.[6]

The Stamp Act was repealed on 18 March 1766 but a duty of three pence was placed on tea to reaffirm the right of the British government to tax the colonies. The tea duty in Britain was also lowered making the East India Tea competitive to smuggled Dutch Tea.[7] The agitation against the importation and use of tea had been kept up in the colonies and large public meetings were held at the Old South Meeting House in Boston attended by 2,000 out-of-towners from various parts of the Greater Boston area to decide what action should be taken to prevent the landing of the tea from the East India Company. The meeting broke up with a cry from Samuel Adams: 'This meeting can do nothing more to save the country!' and immediately about thirty men disguised as Indians made their way to the waterfront to throw overboard the cargoes of tea.

Francis Green was among those who condemned this lawless destruction of property and 'When the Cargoes of Tea were destroyed (in 1773) his political Conduct & Character provoked the Resentment of the Populace, and their Leaders'.[8]

Francis Green remained loyal to the British crown when many Massachusetts men did not because he had been an army officer and many army officers believed that they had taken an oath of loyalty to the King which must be obeyed. Although he was a Tory it must be remembered that in the 1760's and 1770's a large number of Tories supported the protest against the Stamp Act and also the cry of 'No Taxation Without Representation'. In his reminiscences he wrote:

> At the commencement of the American Revolt, which terminated in a successful Revolution, F.G. (although always a firm friend to, & advocate for Civil Liberty, and an avowed enemy to the pretended unlimited power of parliamentary taxation) having adhered to the old Constitution, in hopes of an honorable compromise, without recourse to arms, and being with his family in Boston . . . manifested an unequivocal attachment to the British Government, & strenuously opposed the Rise & Progress of the said Rebellion in America; nor hath He ever acknowledged or submitted to the authority or Pretensions of the usurpers in any Instance or Degree.[9]

To punish the people of Boston, the British Government passed the Boston Port Bill to close the harbour on 1 June 1774 to all vessels which wished to enter, and after the fourteenth all that remained could not depart. Word of the passage of the Boston Port Bill reached Massachusetts on 13 May along with the news that General Thomas Gage was appointed as Governor Hutchinson's successor. Before Hutchinson's departure to England, 120 merchants of Boston signed an address to him on 30 May 1774 in which they expressed approval of his general conduct.

The Port Bill had devastating effects on merchants such as Green although merchants at Salem and Marblehead offered wharf space. The bill brought disaster and hunger to Boston because practically all goods were carried by water and roads were impassable many months of the year. The address to Hutchinson said in part:

> We greatly deplore the calamities that are impending and will soon fall on this metropolis, by the operation of a late act of Parliament for shutting up the port on the first of next month ... Without meaning to arraign the justice of the British Parliament, we could humbly wish that this act had been couched with less rigor, and that the execution of it had been delayed to a more distant time ... Making restitution for damage done to the property of the East India Company, or to the property of any individual, by the outrage of the people, we acknowledge to be just; and though we have ever disavowed, and do now solemnly bear our testimony against such lawless proceedings, yet, considering ourselves as members of the same community, we are fully disposed to bear our proportion of those damages, whenever the sum and the manner of laying it can be ascertained.[10]

They asked Hutchinson to speak on their behalf when he arrived in England showing that these Tories still believed in petitions and lawful means and thought that the British Government would listen to them.

For the next seven years the Addressors were held up to their countrymen as traitors and enemies to their country and the ink was hardly dry upon the parchment before the persecution began against all those who would not recant publicly in a newspaper. There was a strong group in America, including Tories, who looked to closer union between the Mother Country and the colonies by giving the colonies a voice in the deliberations of the British Parliament. Another vocal group was demanding virtual autonomy for the colonies, with the only binding tie to Great Britain resting on the recognition of the King as the head of the Empire — as later took place in Canada.

Governor Thomas Gage, who was also military commander of British troops garrisoned in Boston, adjourned the House of Assembly of Massachusetts and ordered the next meeting at Salem on 7 June 1774. In the meantime Adams and James Warren made plans for calling a Continental Congress with delegates from all the colonies in America and making provision for supplying funds and munitions of war. On 17 June Gage sent his secretary to dissolve the Massachusetts Assembly, but the Rebels locked the door while the Assembly proceeded to adopt and sign the 'Solemn League and Covenant' in which all former non-importation agreements were concentrated and a committee appointed to send the covenant to every colony in America. Those who signed swore to cease all commerce with England until the 'late wicked acts of Parliament' should be repealed and the Massachusetts colony reinstated in all its rights, to abstain from the use of any British goods whatever and to avoid all commerce and traffic with those who refused to sign the League, and all those who refused should be held up to public scorn and indignation by the publication of their names.[11]

Many Tories and moderates had withdrawn from public meetings because of the violent plans to lead the colonies into revolution but some moderates were still attending town meetings in an attempt to stop the violence and were even elected to provincial congresses as delegates, but they were not organized effectively as the Whigs and independents were. Green emphasizes in his memorial that

> in June 1774, when he exerted himself publicly in several Town meetings to discourage & abolish the Committees of Correspondence, to suppress the 'Solemn League & Covenant' to promote, as an Act of Justice, an Agreement to pay for the Teas that had been destroyed, with other pacific Measures as the only Means in his opinion of preventing a civil War, — His public & unreserved Declarations & Endeavours on that Occasion he presumed are remember'd by most of the Boston Loyalists . . . '[12]

There can be no doubt that the incitement of crowds by popular leaders was breeding a hatred of the British Government among the common people. It was during this unrest that Francis Green went to Windham and Norwich to collect his bills and was attacked by the mob.

On his return to Boston he found that the Rebels, who called themselves Patriots or Sons of Liberty, had determined to prepare for war, and in this movement the provincial congress of Massachusetts took the lead ordering the purchase of ammunition and stores for an army of 15,000 men, and in training minute men. The Tories, or Loyalists as they began to be called, denounced the military program of the Whigs which would lead to civil war and insisted that the struggle be carried on constitutionally as civil war would destroy lives, property and established institutions.

In the spring of 1775 Gage had determined to stop the rebellion and seize or destroy the stores of the patriots at Concord and accordingly on the 18 April, he sent 800 British troops to Lexington and Concord.[13] Paul Revere and William Dawes escaped from Boston with warnings. The British troops had to retreat back to Boston without accomplishing their objective, to the consternation of the inhabitants of Boston who realized that British troops were not invincible. From 19 April Gage cut off all communication with the surrounding area and none were allowed to leave the city without his permission. This stopped the supply of provisions and fuel by land and few supplies came in by water.

The Committee of Safety learned that Gage had set the night of 18 June to take possession of Bunker Hill and Dorchester Heights. Two nights before the intended British move, the rebel provincials moved quietly to take over Breed's and Bunker Hill and by dawn on 17 June had thrown up entrenchments six feet high. Around noon, between two and three thousand picked men from the British army under the command of General Sir William Howe embarked in barges and landed at the foot of Breed's Hill. The inhabitants of Boston watched from every hill and roof in the city. Three times the brave British troops, burdened with heavy knapsacks, toiled up hill towards the redoubt in the heat of the summer, and whole platoons were mowed down by gunfire until the Americans ran out of ammunition. At last the British regained the Neck.[14]

By September 1775 General George Washington had arrived as commander-in-chief for the American Congress. Gage sailed to England on the 10 October 1775 leaving affairs in the hands of General William Howe. On 1 November 1775 Howe commissioned Francis Green as Captain of the 3rd Company of the Loyal Associated Volunteers and he was ordered to

> take charge of the District about Liberty Tree & the Lanes alleys & wharves adjacent & that by a constant patroling party from sunset to sunrise you prevent all Disorders within the District by either Signals, Fires, Thieves, Robers, house breakers or Rioters, Are to use for his troops any buildings in the centre of his district & apply to Town Major for Arms.[15]

The Liberty Tree was a large elm at the corner of Washington and Essex streets, named because under it the association called Sons of Liberty had held meetings during the summer of 1765. From the time of the Stamp Act excitement until armed possession of Boston by General Gage and his troops in 1774, that tree had been the rallying-place for the Rebels.[16] On the 19 November 1775, Green's wife Susanna died of puerperal or childbed fever, leaving three young children to the care of her grieving widower and the family servants.

The blockade of Boston continued. As part of his military duties Green was ordered by General Howe to alleviate the scarcity of fuel by pulling down some wooden buildings interspersed among those of brick, and the men in his company of Loyal Associated Volunteers were to be paid by those who received the wood. Fences were burned for fuel and trees cut down, including the Liberty Tree which provided fourteen cords of wood.[17] The Old South meeting house was used as a riding school, and Brattle Street Church, where Green had a pew which he had purchased for £44, was used as a barracks for the troops.

Howe who fortified Bunker Hill and Boston Neck proved to be a better general. That winter General George Washington had collected 17,000 men for the Continental Army and in March 1776 the American troops quietly marched to take possession of Dorchester

Heights. In the Continental Army were veterans who had fought against the French, and one of the engineers was Richard Gridley, who had been an engineer against the French at Louisbourg. The cannon on Dorchester Heights commanded the town of Boston on 5 March 1776, thus the British feared bombardment of Boston, and that their naval ships would be trapped in the harbour. The army and civilians alike were suffering severe shortages as shiploads of supplies had not arrived from Great Britain. Howe called a council of officers and on 7 March resolved to evacuate the town. This unbelievable news spread panic among the loyal citizens who had to prepare for a speedy departure. There were not enough ships but as much merchandise, household furniture and belongings of every kind as possible were loaded on board. Some destroyed what they could not take away and drunken soldiers broke open and pillaged many stores. Early on Sunday morning on 17 March,the embarkation of the British army and Loyalists commenced, but it was ten days before they sailed to Nova Scotia.[18]

Earlier Green had been entrusted by Sir William Howe with the care of all the arms which the inhabitants had been forced to deposit in the Town House and was 'verbally ordered at the Evacuation, to embark, & carry off as many as was practicable, which He did, & delivered them out, at Halifax, according to Directions, to such Loyalists as applied there, for on this Score He apprehends He may (unless indemnified) be liable to many private actions at Law, notwithstanding the Treaty of Peace —'[19]

Green accompanied the army to Halifax in March 1776 with 'Three (motherless) Infants & three Servants' and wrote that the

> Hurry and Confusion of that sudden unexpected Evacuation and his many avocations render'd it impossible to conduct his Concerns with any Certainty or Regularity, and therefore what Part either of the Goods of his own, or of others in his Hands at that time, or of his Household Furniture &c were left behind, lost, or embezzled He never absolutely knew, having never obtained Bills of Lading or Receipts for what were shipped, & having (in almost a State of Distraction),

71

Francis Green

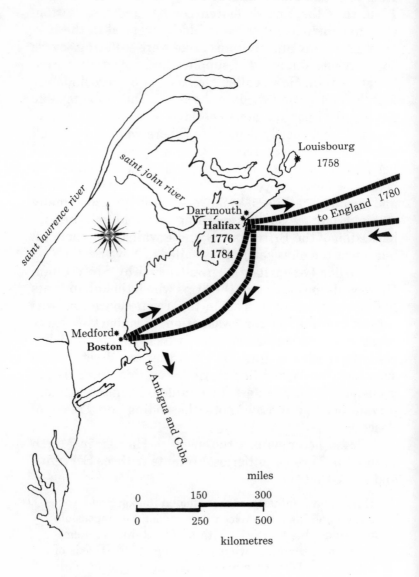

Louisbourg
1758

to England 1780

saint lawrence river

saint john river

Dartmouth
Halifax
1776
1784

Medford
Boston

to Antigua and Cuba

miles

0	150	300

0	250	500

kilometres

employ'd any Persons he could meet with to remove his Effects — When he arrived at Halifax, He collected from several Vessells what He could find, but believed besides what was left, that considerable Loss & Damage was sustained in what was thus hastily removed.—

That having found himself possess'd, of so much Property, as to enable him not to despair of immediate Subsistence, and flattering himself with the Hopes of a speed Return, (under the authority of the Crown to his native Place, where every Idea of Settlement & Comfort was fix'd) He entertained no Thoughts of ever making any application to Government for either Support or Compensation . . . [20]

Later he estimated that furniture left at Boston was worth £350 and heavy goods left there at £850, while the expenses of removing three children and three servants from Boston to Halifax, New York and England was another £300.[21]

At Halifax 10,000 British troops filled the barracks and bivouaced in tents on the hill still called Camp Hill. The loyal refugees complained bitterly about the soaring rents and high price of food, and hated the cold, foggy spring and the contrast with life in Boston. Therefore, those who could afford it sailed to England.

Green was luckier than the other refugees because his older brother Benjamin had succeeded his father as provincial treasurer of Nova Scotia, and his mother was living with her daughter Charlotte and her husband, the Honourable Henry Newton, who was collector of Customs at Halifax and a member of the Council of Nova Scotia. The Newtons were hospitable, and the Congregational minister from Yarmouth, the Reverend Jonathan Scott, wrote in his journal that 'good old Mrs. Green and her daughter, Mrs. Newton spoke the Language of Canaan, and appeared so meek, sober, spiritually and heavenly minded . . .' [22]

Some refugees remained in Halifax as they expected Boston to be recaptured, but after Sir William Howe captured New York they followed the British army there. New York City became the major British stronghold through the rest of the war with many refugees and troops and by 1781 had a population of 25,000. One quarter of the city's houses had been destroyed by fire soon after the British occupation, so lodgings were scarce and expensive because the army had first choice of what remained. Green followed the British army to New York in the spring of 1777 and offered his services to the commander-in-chief.

In the spring of 1778 Green and 'other loyal Refugees' equipped a private vessel of war, *Tryon*, of 16 guns with a crew of 72 men. This vessel kept cruising from the spring of 1778 to the autumn of 1780, sinking and capturing a number of rebel vessels but did not seem to make much money. In June 1778, *Tryon* brought a naval messenger to Lord Howe in New York with the first advice of the arrival of the French fleet of Count d'Estaing on the coast of America. On Christmas Day 1779, the *Tryon* attacked the ship *Thorn* (captured by the Rebels from the British Navy). In a bloody engagement the *Thorn* was so damaged as to be obliged to put into port. Captain George Sibblees of the *Tryon* was mortally wounded, many of the officers and men were killed, and the ship so damaged that she had to be sold for a small sum. Associated with Green as owner was Philip Dumaresq, a Boston commission merchant and agent for Jersey merchants involved in fishery. Green's estimate of loss on the *Tryon* was £4099.8. 5, including repairs in Antigua of £1777.17. 2 and £503 in legal fees.[23]

When the *Oliver Cromwell* was captured from the Rebels, Green was one of the first subscribers to equip the ship renamed the *Restoration* under the direction of George Leonard, who had also served in the Associated Loyalists of Boston and gone to Halifax with a household of nine. In 1779 Green equipped at his own expense, the *Carleton*, a vessel of war mounting 12 carriage guns, as one of the refugee fleet employed to protect the ports of Rhode Island and Martha's Vineyard and convoying supplies for the garrison until Rhode Island was evacuated. She convoyed wood fleets without pay from Lloyd's Neck, Long Island, through the Sound to New York at the request of the deputy barrack master general. When John McAlpine arrived in New York after having been freed as a prisoner, he made an agreement with Francis Green

74

to furnish fuel to the British army in New York. Later Francis Green found that the barrack master at New York was cramming 1,000 cords of wood in the carts so tightly that it was being measured as 800 cords when McAlpine was paid.[24]

But ill-luck still followed Francis Green. In his reminiscences he wrote that

his loss of property in New York was great for out of 5 ships and vessels not one escaped — all being uninsured, owing to the times — were all lost in one month, December 1779:

1. The *Tryon* an armed Brig (Half his own) of 16 Guns & 70 men on a voyage to the Spanish Main, had an engagement with a 20 gun ship & after a drawn Battle in which the Captain *Sibblees* was killed, & the most of his crew, she put into Antigua to refit from whence Drafts were made out & paid by F.G. for upwards of a thousand pound sterling & the vessel was afterward sold at *Tortola* for a small part of her cost.

2nd. The *Carleton* was cast away (with a valuable freight) on the back of Long Island [on her way to Charlestown, South Carolina].

3rd. A brig bound to Lisbon was captured —

4th. A sloop (*Jackall*) cast away on an Island near N.Y.

5th. The Brig *Windsor packet* frozen up with a Load of Fuel & c at Oyster Bay, Long Island & detained in the ice all that hard winter, on great expense, & so damaged as to be almost useless afterward. —

All this taking place within *one month* was rather remarkable, & verified the old well known adage 'Misfortunes seldom come alone'.[25]

Another disaster was the death of his four year old son Francis Erasmus 'by a shocking accident, . . . who was burned by his Cloaths catching Fire, in such a manner as to occasion his Death in a few hours'. These misfortunes persuaded him to move to England in the fall of 1780, and in July 1781 the Lords of Treasury granted him a temporary pension of £100 per annum, which was increased to £150 the next January.

In his petition from Hackney, London dated 1 December 1783 to the Commissioners appointed by the British Parliament to enquire into the 'Losses and Services of the American Loyalists' he stated that the allowance was not 'adequate to his Expenses, having two children [Susanna and Charles] of 12 and 11 years of Age, one of which is so circumstanced as to be *uncommonly* expensive'.[26] This was his son Charles who had been discovered to be deaf when he was six months old. Francis refused to subscribe to the popular belief that children were dumb because of a flaw in their vocal organs, but believed that they did not learn to speak because they were deaf. When Charles was eight years old his father sent him to Edinburgh to Braidwoods Academy for the Deaf and Dumb. Although some children had been instructed by private tutors, this was the first school in the British Empire for deaf children. Thomas Braidwood, a graduate of Edinburgh University, had started with one pupil, the son of a merchant in Leith, and after 1760 became famous as a teacher of the deaf and dumb. His school became a model and was featured by Sir Walter Scott in the *Heart of Midlothian* as 'Dumbiedykes'. In 1773 the school was visited by Dr. Samuel Johnson and his biographer Boswell described it in the *Journey to the Western Islands*.

Green said that Charles remained at Braidwoods Academy for eight years where he 'acquired the faculty of speech and *almost* perfect knowledge of language both oral and written, as well as *arithmetic, Geography* &c and was preeminent in the art of painting at 16'. Included in the papers submitted to the Loyalist Commission is a letter from 'Mr. Francis Greens son who is Deaf & Dumb' written in beautiful large handwriting to 'Miss Green Kensington House'.

My dear Sister,

I thank you for your Letter by Papa I could read it, I love to learn. I can read and speak pretty well. I was very happy to see my Papa. I love him very much, because he is always good, & kind to me. Will you write to me very often, pray? I will write you very often. I would be very happy to see you. Pray, will you accompany Papa when he comes to see me again? Pray do you love to learn? Do you like to live in London? Pray with whom do you live? I like Edinburgh very much. I hope you are very well my Papa tells me that you are grown tall, and learn to dance. — Do you remember *Molly* at New York? and *Birch Brinley*, & Mrs. Bean the School Mistress, and Mr. McAlpine. I remember them and all my Friends very well — Give my Compliments to Mr. and Mrs. Joy, and their Family at *London*.

I am
Your loving Brother
Charles Green[27]

Edinburgh
15th June 1781

Green was so impressed by his son's progress at Braidwoods that while in London he wrote and published a pamphlet in 1783 entitled VOX OCULIS SUBJECTA or a 'Dissertation on the curious, & important art of imparting Speech & the Knowledge of *Language* to the Deaf & Dumb, with a proposal for extending, and perpetuating the benefits thereof' by a Parent.[28] He took credit for helping to establish and encourage a public institution for the education of poor children who were deaf and dumb at Bermondsey near London under the patronage of the Duke of Buckingham. The London Asylum, the first public school for deaf and dumb, was founded in 1792 and Dr. Joseph Watson, its first principal was a nephew of Braidwood.

London had become a magnet for Loyal refugees escaping from America who could afford to pay their way across the Atlantic. As the civil war dragged on, most became bitter and disillusioned, for they had no influence on the activities of the British government and London was an expensive city to live in. One of the mercantile firms in London which helped the Massachusetts refugees was the firm of Lane and Fraser which had been trading for over two decades with New England and shipped goods to America, managed their funds, extended credit and arranged social activities. [29] By March 1784 Francis Green owed £2000 to Lane and Fraser and about £1400 to the widow of George Hayley of London.[30] Green had visited Europe, making an excursion to Belgium and Holland, and also travelled through half the counties of England and Scotland, including the Western Highlands.

One can imagine the fear and disbelief when the American refugees learned in August 1782 that the British government was prepared to give independence to the Thirteen American colonies. The Massachusetts Loyalists living in London gathered at Sir William Pepperell's home to discuss petitioning parliament for compensation for their losses of real, personal and business property. In September 1783 the commission appointed by the British Government to enquire into the losses and service of those 'who have suffered in their Rights, Properties, and Professions, during the late unhappy dissentions in America, in consequence of their Loyalty to his Majesty and Attachment to the British Government', advertised in the newspapers, instructing Loyalists to submit their claims for property loss to the commission's offices in Lincoln's Inn Fields.[31] The claims had to be submitted in quintuplicate which meant much copying of documents and deeds by hand, and letters of reference from prominent officials had to be collected and witnesses found who could testify to the loyalty of the claimant and to the extent and value of property lost or confiscated in America.

On 20 February, 1784 Green wrote to Charles Munro, secretary to the Commissioners, requesting an 'Audience of the Commissioners, as soon as possible, respecting my Loyalty, Services, & such Losses as I could ascertain' as it is 'my Intention to embark very soon for Nova Scotia'.[32] He included certificates about his loyalty, military services, and his property from Sir William Pepperell, Sir John Wentworth, former Governor of New Hampshire, who said: 'I have known the said Francis Green Esq. more than twelve years last past', General Thomas Gage, Sir William Howe, and William Franklin, Governor of New Jersey who had remained loyal to the Crown in contrast to his father Benjamin, who wrote he was 'well acquainted with the Memorialist Francis Green, Esqr. at New York, to which Place he came *after the evacuation of Boston.*' . . . [33]

For the hearing on 2 March 1784, Green could not

find any witnesses in London who had an intimate knowledge of his business or value of his house and lands. He called only one witness, the Reverend Samuel Peters, who said that when he came to Boston in 1774, he had found Mr. Green 'a Loyalist & an out Law . . . He knows nothing of his Lands . . . has heard that the House in which Mr. Green was a Partner was in great business & good Credit'.[34] The Commissioners studied documents carefully, and questioned the witnesses separately and in secret. They wanted to verify each individual entry on the schedules both as to fact and amount of loss. Francis was asked for details of how he acquired various property, what he had paid for it and its value. He had bought house, land and potash works in Connecticut at Pomfret on 4 July 1774 from Abel Clark for £300; at Stafford from Joshua Warner on 1 December 1772 for £52.2. 0; cultivated lands in Great Barrington in 1773 from John Harvey for £50; and uncultivated lands in Hebron taken over in 1772 for debt for £103.12. 10 and it was in 'hands of Mr. Samuel Huntington of Norwich, late President of Congress, who was his *Aty* in that Country'. He also had 300 acres in Parrys Town inherited from his grandfather and 240 acres in Stevens Town, both in New Hampshire, left to him by his uncle Joshua Pierce. He was also questioned over the ship building at Wells which he had taken over for a debt of £620.

Green included a long list of notes and bonds for money which he had lent to people or which they owed him as creditors for goods they had purchased. He not only asked for payment of the sums payable but for interest which he had not collected up to 31 December 1783 — making a total of £6086.4. 4. In another schedule that Green submitted he claimed £13,895 for lands, £8,933 for notes and bonds, £4300 for losses on his privateers and £7,300 for profits lost in seven years since he lost his business which with some miscellaneous items made total losses of over £36,300.[35]

The decision made by the Board in March 1784, on the understanding that Green would provide more documents about his property in America and how much had been confiscated, was that Francis Green was truly a Loyalist and was awarded an allowance of £150 per annum from the Treasury, and £40 for the sum he had expended on making a road on the 2,032 acres he had received in New Hampshire for his services as a veteran in the Seven Years' War — and which he had valued at twenty shillings an acre![36]

However, Green set off from Great Britain in June 1784 to Halifax, Nova Scotia without being aware that the Commissioners (whose deliberations were secret), had decided not to pay compensation for tracts of uncultivated land, any claims for rents or incomes lost during the war, or estimated income from trade. The British government finally paid compensation of £3,033,091 but this was only one-third of what Loyalists had claimed.[37]

In November 1784 Green was offered the position of High Sheriff for Halifax County by Chief Justice Finucane and was reappointed for three years. For months Provincial Secretary Richard Bulkeley and Sheriff Green had to superintend the streets for the safety and protection of the people, for the town was crowded with soldiers, sailors from transports and men-of-war as well as refugees, and riots were frequent and there was no police force.[38]

It was possible to live comfortably in Halifax if one were wealthy. Penelope Winslow wrote to Ward Chipman from Halifax on 2 April 1785:

> ... Your other friends are well, pursuing pleasure with ardour. Feasting, card playing & dancing is the great business of Life at Halifax, one eternal round — the votarys of pleasure complain of being fatigued & want variety of amusements. The new Imported Ladies continue to be the Belles. The Princes, Taylors & Halliburtons are totally eclipsed, and the Millers, Betsy and Matty Matthews, are the admiration of all the Beaus. The High Sheriff [Francis Green] has been sighing at the feet of Miss Miller. The world takes the liberty to condemn her as romantic for rejecting his hand. The Newtonian race, who you know are connected with Mr. Green, are mortified & have advised & it is said have prevailed with him to transfer his affections to Harriet Matthews. With this he readily complyed & found her not reluctant. The High Sheriff enjoys all the pomp of this pompous Town and you would, by the style & state

he take upon himself, swear he was born a Halifaxian — gives dinners two or three times a week & tomorrow evening all the Nobleese are to be entertained at his house, a Ball and supper superb. Charming doings is it not, don't you envy the gay circle? Everybody here has independent fortunes — at least of this I am sure that there is not a family in this place, that figures at all, can spend less than five or six hundred [pounds] a year.[39]

On 19 May 1785, 42 year old Francis Green was married in St. Paul's Anglican Church in Halifax to Harriet Mathews, daughter of the Honourable David Mathews. Green had known the Mathews family in New York where the lawyer David Mathews was Mayor while the British army controlled that city, and had been appointed by General Howe as assistant magistrate.[40] Mathews had a large family of twelve children and large estates which were confiscated. He had arrived from England at Halifax in November 1784 after a stormy voyage and had received a kind welcome from Governor John Parr. Mathews was counting on being appointed as Attorney-general of Nova Scotia and was bitterly disappointed when S.S. Blowers received the post. The Island of Cape Breton was being established as a separate government from Nova Scotia, and Mathews had to accept the position as attorney-general there, although after learning about the hardships of Abraham Cuyler's settlers that first winter in ruined houses in Louisbourg, without enough wood to burn or enough food, Mathews wrote: 'I shudder at the thought of carrying a family there'. By the summer of 1785 he had joined Governor J.F.W. DesBarres at Sydney, but complained that he could not supplement his low salary with outside fees because the 'distressed' residents of the Island could not pay for legal services. In June 1790 he said that the only fresh meat his family had eaten for three months was 'a little moose meat which at this season is extremely poor and bad'.[41] Yet he built a fine house at Point Amelia across the harbour and served as administrator of Cape Breton.

But misfortunes continued to follow Francis Green. He had difficulty collecting his fees as sheriff and Nathaniel Cary of Sherborn in Massachusetts sued him for a bill of exchange for £49.15 which he had endorsed in Boston on 10 March 1775. The original draft had been drawn by Walter Patterson, later Governor of Prince Edward Island and was dated 28 November 1774 at Pictou. Although Green protested that because of the confusion of the times in Boston he thought the bill had long ago been settled and that it should have been returned to Patterson, the jury made him pay.[42]

In July 1787 John Stairs recovered judgment against Francis Green, High Sheriff of the County of Halifax, for £31.17. 10 plus costs because Green was found negligent for letting a creditor of Stairs named Lovisay escape from jail. Green could not pay and had to sell one hundred acres of land in Dartmouth 'on the South side of the Main Road leading to Cole Harbour' which he had purchased in October 1784 from James Cavanagh.[43]

Since his position as High Sheriff was not renewed, Green retired from Halifax with his wife and infant daughter Harriet Mathews, together with his daughter Susanna and son Charles by his first marriage 'to his new uncultivated Lands in the Wilderness of this Province . . . yielding little more Benefit than those of House room & Fuel'.[44] Green and Theophilus Chamberlain had prepared a report on 'the new Settlements of Dartmouth (near Coal Harbour) and Lawrence Town' describing the quantities of shingles, boards and planks cut by three sawmills and the possibilities from the fisheries and raising cattle and said that the 'Loyalists in general are an Industrious people & very spirited in their endeavours to improve the Lands assigned them'.[45] They mentioned that there was an Iron Work in Dartmouth 'the Proprietors of which labor under great inconvenience on account of an Act of Parliament passed about 30 years ago, prohibiting the use of a *Tilt Hammer* in America' and asked to have the act repealed because a 'Tilt Hammer would enable the Proprietors of Iron Works to Plate Iron for Mill saws, Plow Shares &c &c'.

In the summer of 1788 Green received notice from Charles Munro that he must provide authentic proofs of confiscation and final loss of his estates before the Commissioners could pay compensation. Green wrote 'I *feel myself* dispossess'd of almost all my former Property & *very much injured and impoverished by my* attachment to the British Government notwithstanding that I know of *none of my Lands having been 'sold' by the States'*. [46] Unless he paid £192.14. 9 in state notes or £15.7. 8 in hard money immediately, as charges on his 1961 acres in Masons Patent he would lose his property.

In July 1789 Green was informed by his agent in London, Hodgson and Atkinson, Coleman Street, that the Commissioners of American Claims had ordered the reduction of his temporary allowance from £150 to £100 per annum and wrote 'That from a former State of Prosperity, & chearfull Prospects of Provision for his Family, He, by his Attachment to the British Government (previous to this unexpected Regulation) was reduced to a State of Poverty . . . ' and he asked for 'his Relief as a suffering Loyalist, & Friend to the British Government . . . '.[47] He included a certificate from John Halliburton, surgeon of H.M. Naval Hospital and practitioner 'of Physick & Surgery' dated Halifax 1 August 1789 that Francis Green 'hath within the last years made frequent application for Medical & Surgical assistance, owing to an impaired & Infirm State of Health, brought on (in my opinion) from the uncertain State of his Circumstance & the Embarrassed Situation in which he remains, respecting the state of his Claims . . . Dejection of Spirits . . . & some more than usual Exertion of Strength, in the Business of his Farm, occasioned a *Rupture*, for which he is under the Necessity of wearing a Truss . . . '.[48]

The final settlement of his claim did not provide 'Relief as a suffering Loyalist'. Francis Green of Massachusetts had claimed £1149, but the sum allowed by Commissioners was £912. But then the British Parliament had decided that the total amount was so large that only about one-third was to be paid out to Loyalists so the sum payable under the Act of Parliament to Green was £300 — and from this £5 was deducted on account of his pension![49] And remember that he had asked for £36,000.

One reason for the small amount paid to Green was that he owned so much uncultivated land and also that he could not obtain sufficient proofs for the confiscation of his property. However, Mary Beth Norton has pointed out in *The British-Americans* that a majority of refugee merchants received less than one-third return on their estimates of losses because of the decision of the Commission to exclude claims for uncollectable debts. George Erving, a Boston merchant, received only £500 on a claim of £20,000. The merchants protested that the agents and commissioners were lawyers, professional men and landowners who failed to understand that business was carried on by credit, and that they had lost their capital.[50]

Wallace Brown in *The King's Friends* learned from an analysis of 313 claims from Massachusetts for compensation, that 106 were from merchants and shopkeepers, the largest category;[51] 17% were professional men and 11% were farmers. Also 21% of all the awards in Massachusetts were for £500 or less, and 73% of the Loyalists were born in that state.

No wonder Francis' health failed, because he had suffered another tragedy when his son Charles, only seventeen, was drowned while shooting ducks at Cole Harbour on 29 August 1787. In 1789 another son Henry Francis was born, and two more daughters: Ann Winslow and Eliza Atkinson in 1791 and 1794 joined the Green family. Francis Green had moved his family to a farm at Preston, about four miles from Halifax but on the eastern side of the harbour to a property which he had inherited from his father. Here he built a fine house with a magnificent view of the countryside and the ocean — a mansion which is still remembered as Maroon Hall.[52] On 22 September 1794 his eldest daughter Susanna 'a most aimiable character' was married to Stephen Hall Binney by the rector of St. John's Anglican Church at Preston, where her father was one of the wardens.[53] For a time after the death of his brother Benjamin, Francis was joint treasurer for Nova Scotia with George Thesiger from 3 December 1793, until Sir John Wentworth, who had become lieutenant-governor of Nova Scotia, appointed his brother-in-law Benning Wentworth to succeed on 6 August 1794.[54]

In 1796 the Commissioners of Maroons from Jamaica arrived at Halifax with 600 Maroons who had been transported from Jamaica because of their guerrilla warfare. The Jamaican government planned to settle them in Nova Scotia and purchased lands and buildings at Preston and Cole Harbour for the Maroons. Francis Green sold his property and also his house, which was enlarged for the commissioners and as an administrative centre and named Maroon Hall.

And now finding himself without any *adequate* employment (the Judges of the Common Pleas having no Salary, & a *precarious* income by fees only) and also having always had a predilection for the Lands of his *ancestors, & his native country* which at that period was respectably federal & appeared to open its eyes to discern the folly of an alliance *with France*, & soon after declared it null and void, F. Green removed with his family and took up his residence at *Medford* [55], near *Boston* in June 1797.

There two more children were born to Harriet and Francis, Mary Hall in 1799 and Mathews Wylly in 1803.

The laws against Loyalists or Tories had been relaxed in the United States in the twenty-one years since Francis Green had sailed from Boston Harbour with his three motherless children. A considerable number of refugee Loyalists did return eventually to their old homes, and thirty-three of the claimants from Massachusetts later returned to the United States to live. The money he had received for his Preston property enabled him to set up in business in Boston as a marine insurance underwriter.

Again Green was unlucky in his business affairs. In 1798 and 1799 he

sustained pecuniary Losses, as an underwriter at Boston, & paid away $25,000 upwards of 10,000 of which were for french spoliations, robberies & shamefully unjust & *illegal* adjudications, under various, infamous pretences, for which a clear Demand on the Government of France existed for which, consequently, there *now* is a *just claim on the Government* of the U.S. which has been hitherto cruelly & basely evaded, & postponed by the anti federalists in Congress, and whether ever *Justice*, or Retribution to the various mercantile petitioners of the principal seaports will be

Green gave up underwriting and is reputed to have lived on his pension from the British. In memory of his son Charles, Francis filled some of his leisure hours at Medford 'with his humble endeavors to disseminate (in this country) the knowledge of the practibility of the important art of instructing the *Deaf & Dumb* to speak & *converse* intelligibly as well as educating them in the fullest manner'.[57] He published extracts from his translation of Abbe de L'Epee's letters (who had established the first school for deaf and dumb in Paris) in various Boston newspapers such as the New England *Palladium* in the hope that the United States would 'alleviate the *human misery* of the deaf and dumb'. He collected statistics to show that there were at least seventy children who could be instructed in Massachusetts and at least five hundred in the whole United States, but he became discouraged by the lack of progress although he is now recognized as one of the pioneers in the education of the deaf. Bitterly he wrote in 1806: 'But the *Philanthropy & Charity* of the present era seem to be elbowed off from the Stage, by the predominant speculations of the *Banking Mania*, & the universal *Lust of Lucre* . . . neither *Compassion Humanity* nor *Taste* are likely to avail!'[58]

In a summing up of his career in 1806 he wrote:

1st. F.G. has reason to be thankful, for an excellent constitution & a long & uninterrupted enjoyment of Health, for many years.

2nd. He has had the great Blessing, of experiencing in each of his *respectable* female companions, a *virtuous* amiable Wife, in whom '*his heart did always* safely confide'.

3rd. He has never been (even for an hour) *deprived of his Liberty*, nor ever been wounded, or maimed, either in his person, or Reputation, tho' oft' times expos'd to perils in battle, *Perils* by sea, & Land, as well as *perils* by false, envious & malicious brethren. Upon the whole, *checkered mediocrity* has been his Lot.[59]

He quoted from Pope:

'Honor & shame from no conditions rise,

Act well your part, there all the honor lies'.[60]

Throughout his long life, Francis Green had endeavoured to 'act well' his part. His loyalty resulted in material loss and inconvenience, but his 'honour', he believed, remained intact.

1. Public Record Office, Audit Office (London, U.K.), (afterwards cited as PRO A.O.), 13/45 p. 525. Memorials from Francis Green and other documents concerning claims for his losses as a Loyalist may be found in Audit Office Claims, American Loyalists, in PRO A.O. 13/45 pages 464-529 (PAC Micro B 2341) and A.O. 13/73, pages 714-725 (PAC Micro B2440).
2. Much of the information in this article is based on 'Genealogical and Biographical Anecdotes of the *Green* Family deduced from the first *American Generation* by Francis *Green* for his Childrens (sic) information. 1806. F.G. Being the only surviving male Branch of the *fourth* American Generation vide Genealogical Tree'. 25 pp handwritten in the Public Archives of Nova Scotia MG1 Vol. 332D; also article on Francis Green in the *Dictionary of American Biography*.
3. PRO A. O. 13/73 p. 721.
4. PRO A. O. 13/73 p. 723; A.O. 13/45 p. 482.
5. *Second Report of the Bureau of Archives for the Province of Ontario* 1904 Vol. II, p. 1209 (Toronto, 1905).
6. James H. Stark, THE LOYALISTS OF MASSACHUSETTS *And The Other Side of the American Revolution* (Boston, 1907) 40-1.
7. Stark, *op. cit.*, 47-49.
8. Edgar Rowe Snow, 'Boston Tea Party', *Amazing Sea Stories Never Told Before* (New York, 1954) 84-106.
9. Public Archives of Nova Scotia (afterwards cited as PANS) MG1 Vol. 332D, 13-14; PRO A.O. 13/45, 453 ff.
10. Stark, *op. cit.*, 123-125; Condon, Ann Gorman, 'Marching To a Different Drummer', RED, WHITE AND TRUE BLUE, *The Loyalists in the Revolution* ed. by Esmond Wright (New York, AMS Press, 1976), 4, 6, 18.
11. Lossing, B.J., *Pictorial Field Book of the Revolution* (New York, 1850), I, 509-510.
12. PRO A. O. 13/45, 453ff, Dec. 1, 1783.
13. Lossing I, 523-532.
14. Lossing I, 538-547.
15. PRO A. O. 13/45, 474-476.
16. Lossing I, 466, 583.
17. PRO A. O. 13/45 484ff; Lossing I, 583.
18. Lossing I, 580-583.
19. PRO A. O. 13/45, 454ff, 477ff. He made a meticulous list with names of makers and marks, number of muskets etc.
20. PRO A. O. 13/45, 455; Jones, E. Alfred, THE LOYALISTS OF MASSACHUSETTS Their Memorials, Petitions and Claims (London, England, 1930), 153-4.
21. PRO A. O. 13/45 p. 521 (dated Oct. 1782).
22. C.B. Fergusson, ed., *The Life of Jonathan Scott* (Bulletin No. 15 of the Public Archives of Nova Scotia) 41-2.
23. PRO A. O. 13/45 p. 492; Jones, *Loyalists of Massachusetts* 123-4, 153, 194-5.
24. T.M. Punch, 'Loyalists are Stuffy, eh?', *The Nova Scotia Historical Quarterly*, 8, No. 4, December 1978, p. 324.
25. In his schedule dated October 1782 in PRO A. O. 13/45 p. 512b he stated that he lost by *Tryon*, £2000; *Carleton*, £1600; *Jackall*, £400; *GeneralPatterson*, £200 and *Golden Pippin* £100 making total of £4300.

26. PRO A. O. 13/45, 453ff.
27. PRO A. O. 13/45, 518-519.
28. It was reprinted by the Boston Parents Education Association for Deaf Children in 1897 and there is a copy of this report in the library at the Public Archives of Nova Scotia.
29. Mary Beth Norton, THE BRITISH-AMERICANS — The Loyalist Exiles in England 1774-1789 (Boston, 1972), p. 77.
30. Ontario Archives Report 1904, II, p. 1209.
31. Ibid. I, p. 14.
32. PRO A.O. 13/73 p. 717.
33. PRO A. O. 13/73 p. 724b.
34. Ontario Archives Report 1904, II, p. 1210.
35. PRO A. O. 13/45 p. 469b.
36. Ontario Archives Report 1904, II, 1209-1210.
37. Norton, op. cit., 201, 216.
38. Collections of the Nova Scotia Historical Society, 12, 79.
39. Rev. W.O. Raymond, ed., WINSLOW PAPERS 1776-1826 (St. John, N.B., 1901), 288.
40. Lorenzo Sabine, Biographical Sketches of Loyalists of American Revolution II, 51-2; PANS RG1 Vol. 248 doc. 20; PRO C. O. 217/35 ff141-2; Robert J. Morgan, 'The Loyalists of Cape Breton', Dalhousie Review, 55, No. 1, Spring 1975, 1-15.
41. Norton, op. cit., p. 238.
42. PANS RG39 Series C Vol. 46 Nathaniel Cary vs. Francis Green (SC 1787).
43. PANS RG39 Series C Vol. 50 Stairs vs. Green, 1787; RG39 J Vol. 8; Nova Scotia Minutes of Executive Council March 1, August 3, 1787.
44. PRO A. O. 13/45 p. 510A.
45. PANS MS file Dartmouth-Description 1784.
46. PRO A. O. 13/45p. 498, 506.
47. PRO A. O. 13/45 p. 510.
48. PRO A. O. 13/45 p. 513.
49. PAC M14 A. O. 12/109ff 150-1 No. 262.
50. Norton, op. cit., 209, 219-220.
51. Wallace Brown, The King's Friends (Providence, R. I., 1965), 19-42, 294-298.
52. Mrs. William Lawson, History of THE TOWNSHIPS OF DARTMOUTH, PRESTON AND LAWRENCETOWN (Halifax, 1893), 177-178.
53. Nova Scotia Royal Gazette Sept. 23, 1794.
54. PANS RG1 Vol. 171, 73-4, 106.
55. PANS MG1, Vol. 332D, 17.
56. Ibid., 23.
57. Ibid., 18.
58. Ibid., 18-19.
59. Ibid., 24.
60. Ibid., 22.

Shelburne, N.S. with the Barracks in the background in 1789

Chapter 4

Joseph Durfee

Shelburne Pioneer

by Mary Archibald

Joseph Durfee was a merchant fleet owner in Rhode Island whose ships were well known in the West Indies and London. He worried about the escalating ill-will between the colonies and the mother-country. After serving the King in the conflict, he and many others had to flee north. In 1793 he was one of the Port Roseway Associates who established the city of Shelburne, Nova Scotia. Durfee spent the rest of his life playing various roles, from judge to lighthouse builder, in that Loyalist centre.

Late in the evening of 17 July 1769, a huge crowd had gathered on the beaches of Aquidneck Island, Narragansett Bay. Some had been there since early morning and had seen the British sloop *Liberty* seize a Rhode Island vessel bound for Newport. Many of them had been there when the boats had put out from shore carrying angry men across the water to the British customs ship. They had watched the men board the sloop and only minutes later had seen fires burst from the hold sending towering flames high into the summer sky. The crowd had gathered and waited for hours until the charred remains of the *Liberty* drifted ashore. Then, shouting and jostling each other, they had dragged the battered timbers together and made bonfires until all that remained of the *Liberty*, a symbol of British authority, was a huge pile of ashes, smoldering in the darkness.

Joseph Durfee stood apart from the crowd. He had been there since dawn and had watched each act of the drama from its opening scene to its tragic ending. As he sensed the mood of the crowd he had moved farther down the beach, found himself a resting place, and as the action quickened, leaned wearily against the huge rocks lining the shore. Now, when it seemed to be all over, he wondered aloud: 'How had the last four years led to this? What really had gone wrong between England and her American Colonies? What would be the next crisis?'

Lowering his head and hunching his shoulders, Joseph Durfee turned from the crowd still on the beach and started the long walk to his home on School Street. Although Joseph Durfee was only 35 years of age, that summer night in 1769 he walked like an old man.

Joseph Durfee's family had lived in Rhode Island for four generations. His great-grandfather, Thomas Durfee, had come to the colony to be part of the community established in 1639 by Roger Williams, who had fled Massachusetts to escape the intolerance of the Pilgrims who themselves had sought religious freedom in America. The Durfee family had prospered and had become highly respected throughout the colony. Joseph had made his own mark as a person concerned about the welfare[1] of his fellowmen. In 1758, he had been admitted as a freeman of Middleton, Rhode Island, and in 1766 had been made a member of the Fellowship Club of Newport, which had been established in 1752 by 19 seafaring men as a mutual aid association for distressed mariners and their families. Two-thirds of the members of the Fellowship Club of Newport were captains and commanders of vessels.

After his mother died and his father had married again, Joseph started his own business becoming part of the commercial growth that had made Newport one of the fastest growing ports on the Atlantic seaboard. He had built up a fleet of vessels that carried Rhode Island lumber and fish to the West Indies where these products were exchanged for rum and molasses which were then taken to London, sold in the market-place and replaced in the holds of the ships by enumerated commodities sent by London merchants to Boston and other towns in New England. Joseph had often sailed his own ships. In later years, when he had put into Boston he had sensed the growing unrest among the people.

The unrest had started six years before with the end of The Seven Years War in America. During the war, thousands of families had moved in from the countryside. When the war was over there was no work for so many people. Heavily in debt to business houses in London and burdened by the Poor Tax, the merchants of Boston felt themselves further burdened in 1765 when England passed The Stamp Act to help pay the cost of the war and the cost of maintaining troops on the foothills of the Allegheny Mountains to protect the colonies from the still-hostile Indians. In contrast and as stated in a proclamation in 1763, the King was to protect his Majesty's Indians by arranging for the orderly progression of settlement. Thus the Indians had a mixture of promises and attacks. The following year, after much agitation in the colonies and in England, the British Parliament repealed The Stamp Act but later passed the Townshend Duties which taxed paper, paint, glass and tea. The Boston merchants had formed themselves into clubs, had drawn up the 'Solemn League and Covenant for the Non-Importation of Goods', and had supported the 'Sons of Liberty' in their harassment of anyone who ignored the covenant or who cooperated with the British appointed customs officials. Rhode Island had reacted strongly to all those happenings. In 1765 she had been the only colony to refuse to allow stamp distributors within her borders and when Boston threatened violence against her stamp distributors, tiny Rhode Island had volunteered to send 10,000 men to help with the action!

But arson seemed too wild a reaction! Ann,[2] his wife was waiting for him. They talked long into the night as Joseph told her about that day's tragedy in Narragansett Bay. What should they do, stay in Newport or move to some other part of the colonies? They could not go back to Portsmouth where they had both been born as Mary, Joseph's stepmother, and Joseph could never get along in the same town as they had already had difficulties. Mary argued with Joseph and Ann that the colonies should not have to abide by The Navigation Acts, and that they should be able to import whatever they wished without paying duties to the government in England. 'England has not the right', she said, 'to impose taxes on the colonies in a parliament in which we have no representation. The war is over. We don't need the British army to defend us'.

As dawn came, Joseph and Ann fell asleep fearful of the future but undecided about what they should do to meet it. Perhaps this would all pass over and there would be no more violence. Perhaps the British Government would find a solution to the growing unrest in her colonies in America.

Two weeks after the burning of the *Liberty*, Francis Bernard, the hated Royal Governor of Massachusetts was recalled and replaced by Thomas Hutchinson who had been born in Massachusetts. Two months later a crowd of over one thousand people seized a sailor who had been one of the crew of the ill-fated *Liberty*, tarred and feathered him and then paraded him through the streets of Boston. Two years later, the King Street Riots (known as The Boston Massacre) broke out when Patrick Walker, an off-duty British soldier given a temporary job as a Boston ropemaker, was told to clean out the outhouses of the other workers. When he refused, he was knocked down, and his sword taken away, but he escaped to his barracks. By nine o'clock in the evening a fight broke out and crowds gathered around the barracks in which Walker was quartered. They threatened that if the soldiers did not come out they would burn down the buildings. One soldier did come out but was immediately knocked down by his officer. As Dirk Hoerder records in *Crowd Action in Revolutionary Massachusetts, 1765-1780:* 'Then the town bells began to ring'.[3]

The crowd decided to march to the Mainguard, headquarters for the customs officials. A group of soldiers, led by Captain Thomas Preston, followed, pushing their way through and drew themselves up in a defensive half-circle. Snowballs made around coal, ice and othe᛫ rubbish were hurled at the soldiers. When the soldiers levelled their guns, the crowd threatened to throw the sentry-box into the harbour. Men, armed with sticks, came running. A soldier was knocked down, his gun went off. The crowd yelled, 'FIRE!' The soldiers mistook the cry as an order from their officers. In the ensuing gunfire, four men were killed and eight wounded. More than half of the crowd that had gathered that March evening in 1771 were people without any property and on the poor relief of Boston.

After the King Street Riot, England cancelled The Townshend Duties — all but the tax on tea. The British troops were removed from the mainland to Castle Island. In the fall of 1772, Sam Adams and other Whig leaders set up the first Committees of Correspondence aimed at keeping the Patriots, as they called themselves, in communication with each other and at drawing up opposition to Britain's colonial policy.

The year after Sam Adams[4] formed the first Committees of Correspondence, a group of Bostonians, dressed as Indians, boarded three British ships laying in Boston harbour, lifted the hatches, broke open the casks carrying tea, tea, which even with the tax would have sold cheaper than the tea stored in the Boston merchants' warehouses, and pitched it into the harbour. After the 'Boston Tea Party' Britain closed the port of Boston and passed other acts 'intolerable' to the citizens of Massachusetts. General Gage was put in charge of the British army which returned to the capital of the Massachusetts Bay Colony. In May, 1775, the Second Continental Congress met at Philadelphia and named George Washington as Commander-in-chief of the Continental Army.

All this while Joseph Durfee was trying to maintain his business interests.

Brother Oliver — Newport November 19th 1774

Yours by Mr. Church of this Date I received and observed its contents as to taking a Mortgage will not Suit me if they have a mind to Sell it and paying part of the money Down and wait a Reasonable time with Interest for the Remainder if the price is agreeable I will wait on them about the affair but Mortgages are attended with Difficulty

I am your friend and Brother

Joseph Durfee

P.S. I have thought of a Branch of Business which I
think will be an advantage greatly to us Both. Come to
town tomorrow if you can.
J.D.

And early in 1775:

Brother Oliver — Newport Febr. 17, 1775

I did not think yesterday to tell you the widow Earl of
Portsmouth, Oliver Earls widow Thos. Borden told me
has Many hundred of Locost posts I advise you to go &
see her as Soon as you can Engage them on the Same
Terms as with Coggeshall they Engaging to Deliver
them at the Wharfe at Briston Ferry I could have them
fetched from there by water if you cant git them for the
same price you gave for those you have Bot see the
Lowest they will let them go for and give them an Answer Soon
Joseph Durfee
P.S. We want more them Engaged
100 post 7 feet
50 D feet 8 feet
Engage this if you can of Mrs Earl[5]

Two months later the situation in the Colonies exploded.

Knowing that many of the militia were Loyalists
determined to maintain the order established by the
British Army, some of the colonists formed themselves
into Minutemen to be ready, at a minute's notice, to go to
the aid of the Rebels. Hearing of a cache of arms belonging to the Minutemen at Concord, Massachusetts, General Gage dispatched some of his soldiers to Concord.
Paul Revere learned of the move and sent word to the
Minutemen. Although we do not know whose musket
went off first that day in April 1775, the shot was fired
that 'was heard round the world' and the American Revolution really began.

Violence broke out in many areas. There was riot-
ing and looting in towns all along the coast of New England. Joseph and Ann decided to move their family from
Newport. Daniel Goddard, their friend the cabinet-

maker from Dartmouth, Massachusetts, an inland town, suggested they go there. Accordingly they closed their house, shut down the business, harnessed their two horses, and took their five children to Dartmouth. It did not work as Daniel Goddard's parents became suspected of being Loyalist sympathizers. Joseph and Ann were harassed, and their children taunted by their playfellows. Early in 1776 they went back home.

In June of that same year, General Howe, who had replaced General Gage as Commander-in-chief of the British Forces in America returned from Halifax, Nova Scotia, where he had fled following the evacuation of Boston after the Patriots, or Rebels had seized Dorchester Heights and threatened the safety of the British Army. Most of the Loyalists of Boston had gone with the retreating troops to Halifax. The British and Loyalists landed on Staten Island, and in December, under the command of Sir Henry Clinton, occupied Newport. Second in command of the troops who landed at Newport was given to Sir Robert Pigot who had bravely led his men during the Battle of Breed's Hill — commonly called the Battle of Bunker Hill.

Sir Robert Pigot formed The Loyal Newport Associate and Joseph Durfee was made a Lieutenant under Colonel Watson. He put his sloop *Friendship*, and his schooners *Peggy* and *Dolphin* at the command of the British Army[6] and he was one of three men assigned the task of taking a census of the inhabitants of Newport, the object being to assess the potential of the town in case of an attack by the Rebels.

In 1777 the *Friendship* and her cargo was lost to American Privateers in the Gulf of Florida bound for Jamaica. The Loyalists had suffered many misfortunes in 1777, especially when the British and Loyalists were defeated at the Battle of Saratoga, a victory for the Rebels that brought France openly into the war against her traditional enemy.

In the summer of 1778, a French fleet carrying 4,000 soldiers crossed the Atlantic. On receiving intelligence that Sir Henry Clinton had removed to New York, Admiral d'Estaing, thinking New York harbour too shallow for this fleet decided to capture Newport. The result was the Battle of Aquidneck Island, the only battle of the Revolution fought on Rhode Island soil. Writing in *Decisive Battles of the American Revolution*,[7] Lt. Col. Joseph E. Mitchell, gives this version of the battle. When the French Admiral found he could not attack the British at New York he 'faced the question of what to do with the army of four thousand soldiers he had brought. All these allies could not be left idle after coming all the way from France to help the Americans in their revolution'. Sir Robert Pigot at Newport had only three thousand men. By August, General Sullivan, the leader of the Rebels, commanded a force of 10,000. Admiral Howe, a brother of General Howe, arrived off Newport with a larger British fleet. 'Fortunately for the French a great storm arose, dispersing both fleets'. Sullivan attacked, but when d'Estaing 'returned with his fleet and his troops, he refused to cooperate with General Sullivan and sailed away with his ships for Boston'. The result of the first efforts of the Americans and French to cooperate in their attempts to defeat the British and Loyalists 'resulted in a fiasco'.

The French presence, even though d'Estaing had gone to the West Indies, was very real. England decided to concentrate her forces at New York and, in the fall of 1779, evacuated Newport. Joseph and Ann and their five children, some of the twelve thousand Loyalists who would find refuge in New York City during the Revolution, took up their residence at No. 125 Water Street. The Rebels confiscated their property in Newport. That same year the *Peggy* 'ran ashore by accident at Point Judith and was seized and sold by the Americans'. The *Dolphin* was 'taken in the Sound' by American Privateers and 'carried to New London'.

Possibly Joseph spent Christmas, 1779, with his family, but certainly he was one of the eight thousand, five hundred men who sailed out of New York harbour the day after Christmas, bound to retake Charleston and bring the south back into the British Empire. The British and Loyalists landed about 48 kilometres below Charleston in February 1780, and waited for more men from New York and Savannah before starting their campaign to cut off the Wanda, Cooper and Ashley, the three

rivers that run west of Charleston and which would provide paths of escape for the Rebels if they decided to
abandon the city.

In March, the Loyalists crossed the Ashley River
and began their offensive from the Atlantic Ocean. Admiral Arbuthnot sent his frigates into Charleston harbour, which was guarded by Fort Moultrie on Sullivan's
Island and Fort Johnson on James Island. Joseph Durfee
was in charge of guiding the frigate 'over the bar and
past Fort Sullivan'. After the offensive he received the
'thanks of the General and a present of 50 Guineas' for
his service as a pilot.

The Loyalists advanced by land. Lieutenant-colonel
Banastre Tarleton and his British Legion, together with
Major Patrick Ferguson's American Volunteers and a
force of British regulars closed the Cooper River but
nearly a month passed before Fort Moultrie and then the
city of Charleston surrendered. The British and Loyalists captured over three hundred and ninety guns, desperately needed to offset the supplies being received by
the Rebels from their French allies.

After the capture of Charleston, the British and
Loyalists set up defence posts in the north of the colony
and by 20 May had defeated the last Continental unit in
South Carolina. Sir Henry Clinton sailed for New York
leaving General Cornwallis with more than eight thousand men to proceed into North Carolina and consolidate
the position of the British Empire in the southern colonies.

Many of the Loyalists stayed in Charleston, but not
Joseph Durfee. By early summer, he was back in New
York City, assisting Colonel Crosby, the Barrack-Master
in the manoeuvering of the hundreds of small craft that
were bringing supplies into the harbour for the thousands of refugees crowding the city. He held this position
for two years and received from Brook Watson a certificate for the faithful discharge of his duties as 'director of
vessels'.

During the latter months of 1780 and for the first
nine months of 1781 the Loyalists gathered in New York
City were jubilant. In 1778 the French navy had shown
itself to be uncooperative with the rebel forces; two years

later the British and Loyalist victories at Charleston had established a springboard for control of the south. It was only a matter of time, so they thought, before they would win the war, be able to go back to their homes and take up the life they had known before the Revolution.

This was not to be. Instead of taking up his final position inland, the British General Cornwallis massed his troops on the Yorktown Peninsula jutting out into Chesapeake Bay. During the early part of October 1781, the French Admiral DeGrasse took command of the waters off Yorktown, cutting off Cornwallis' supply-line by sea. General Lafayette and General Washington and their troops prevented the escape by land. On 19 October 1781, the very day that Sir Henry Clinton, a personal rival of General Cornwallis, sailed from New York with 8,000 men, the British and Loyalist forces surrendered at Yorktown to the French and Rebel armies. Even then, the British had thousands of men in America and could have continued the fight, but the people in England were tired of this expensive war in America. For example, the British were paying £40,280 a year just to support the loyalist refugees isolated in New York City.

The final blow to the Loyalists was the news of the terms of the peace agreed to in Paris by the British, French and American delegates. Neither the American Congress nor any of the new United States of America would guarantee the safety of the Loyalists should they return to the communities where they had made their homes before the Revolution.

Where could they go? Encouraged by Sir Andrew Snape Hamond, Lieutenant-governor of Nova Scotia, and his Council, and by Sir Guy Carleton, Commander-in-Chief of His Majesty's Forces in America, a group of Loyalists at New York decided to immigrate to Port Roseway on the south-western coast of Nova Scotia. There were good reasons for the choice of the location. Many of the Loyalists gathered at New York were from the Atlantic seaboard colonies and certainly Gideon White[8] and many other New Englanders, and quite possibly Joseph Durfee, had sailed the coast of Nova Scotia, often putting in at the fine harbour at Port Roseway which extends 13 kilometres in from the Atlantic Ocean.

The Port Roseway Associated Loyalists, as they called themselves, held their first meeting in November, 1782. Much of the leadership and preparation of the Association was due to the dedication and work of Joseph Durfee.[9] The association formed by the Loyalists bound for Port Roseway was a democratic society. All business was to be settled by 'a majority of votes of the Company Assembled'. A president would be elected at each meeting. The president's responsibilities would be 'to Regulate, direct and decide on the proper mode and manner of all Votes, and preserve Order and Attention to Business'. A committee was appointed to 'petition and transact all business relative to the Benefit and settlement of the new town and to make a report at every meeting'. Persons who wished to join the association could not join at the general meetings but had to 'attend for that purpose at the House of Captain Durfee, No. 125 Water Street, New Slip with Proper Recommendations from one of the original Association'. From the very beginning, Joseph Durfee was acknowledged as one of the leaders of the Port Roseway Associates. He was made a member of the committee to transact 'all business relative to the benefit and settlement of the new Town' and elected president at ten of the twenty-four meetings the Association held in New York City.

At the meeting held on 23 November 1782, it was decided to prepare a memorial to be presented to Sir Guy Carleton concerning 'the particulars of the Intentions of the Associated Loyalists' and to request 'protection and assistance and the abstract of such articles as would be absolutely necessary to complete the Emigration and the Intended Settlement at Port Roseway'. 'Mr. Durfee and Mr. Dole' were appointed to present the memorial.

The memorial was well received. James Dole and Joseph Pynchon were chosen as delegates to go to Halifax on behalf of their fellow associates. The delegates were to follow these instructions:

1. Seek the best council in the Province for grants and other matters affecting the Associates.
2. Inquire about the privileges granted former settlers.
3. Inquire about the instructions that had been re-

ceived from George III regarding the settling of the Loyalists.

4. Insist that the Association be allowed to nominate their own officers for the settlement at Port Roseway.

5. Be sure the titles to the grants the Loyalists would receive were 'exempt from Quit Rents, laid out and surveyed at Government expense, as many of them as possible on the sea coast and that they bring back to the Associates a copy of the lands that had been escheated'.

6. Ask for more land if they felt not enough had been set aside.

7. Be sure that the 'Fishing and Fowling' on the lands granted were reserved for the settlers.

8. Insist that there be no impressment ever for the Associated Loyalists.

9. Ask that a force by sea be assigned to protect the Associates.

10. Ask the Government and Council to sent 'Articles and Workmen to assist Us in forming our Settlement'.

11. Seek permission to embark from New York 'as early in the Spring as possible'.

12. Ask for orders that 'Every Inhabitant be obliged to perform due Cultivation of his lands'.

13. Ask Assistance of the Government in building roads.

14. Seek assurance that their claims in no way interface with their claims and demands for former losses and sufferings.

15. Present the following request:

'As in every infant Settlement, much depends on the Peace and Unanimity of the Internal and Commercial Interests Abroad — we request the Privilege of a Patent for a city be granted which would greatly prevent designing Men from Interrupting our Peace and Quiet and assist in Rendering the Port Roseway Associates a happy and Flourishing People'.

Early in the New Year, there was disquieting news. Governor John Parr replaced Sir Andrew Snape Hamond at Halifax and James Dole had communications difficulties with the new governor. In his letter to the Associates Joseph Pynchon chose to ignore the difficulties: 'We were favorably received on Your Account and much Applauded in coming as they waited with impatience for some to come . . .' However in March Captain Durfee reported to the Associates on Sir Guy Carleton's reply to the Memorial presented on behalf of the Associates and told them that the Commander-in-chief 'rather recants from his former Promises and absolutely Refuses any other Assistance than providing us with Vessels and Conveyances to take us there and provision for six months in the following manner — Men and boys upwards of 13 years of Age Full Allowance — NO RUM — Women half allowance and children one-fourth'. Captain Durfee and Mr. Dole reported that Brook Watson, the Commissary-General, had assured them that the transports would be ordered to remain until, 'We got shelter from the weather'.

Determined to continue with their plans, the Port Roseway Associates agreed that 'should a head of a Family be lost or die the family so left shall be entitled to the same share as though the head of a Family had arrived at the intended place of Settlement'. William Johnston, 'the son of William Johnston who was unfortunately killed in a late Battle with the Enemy', even though he was under age 'was to be allowed to go as an Associate and be entitled to all the privileges for the benefit of his father's family'.[10] At the 19 March meeting, the first steps were taken for the Associates to organize themselves for their departure from New York:

It being recommended by the Commander-in-Chief that we form ourselves into a Militia and that we immediately appoint proper persons as Captains and those Captains shall be authorized as Magistrates by him to determine & Settle all disputes that May arise in the body between Individuals or Others until the Government of the Province of Nova Scotia take place that each Company do consist of One Captain, Two Lieutenants, 4 Sergeants and 36 Rank and File.

As the time for departure drew near the Associators were ordered to inform the Commissary-General of the number in their family (including servants), their occupations and whether they were poor or needy. Their request that they be allowed to transport sixty horses to Port Roseway was refused by the Commissary-General

103

who asked, 'Where will You get the necessary forage?' While the requested tonnage of 30 tons of shipping for baggage was thought high, they were instructed to approach Admiral Digby who would be providing the transports.

On 24 March, Captain Durfee reported on the reply he had received from Sir Guy Carleton on the second memorial presented by the Associates:

> I waited on the Commander-in-chief agreeable to the request of the Committee.
>
> He asks that we be able to go as soon as possible. Transports will be ready and should lay at Port Roseway until we are under Cover and in an easy situation. He recommends that we apply to the Admiral for a Strong Convoy. Six months Provisions will be provided. The Commander particularly expresses that we should not be discouraged by the six months Provisions. It could not be supposed that Government would set a Number of People down there and say We will do Nothing YOU MAY STARVE. There is no doubt but if any are in want they will be supplied. The Commander-in-Chief has asked me to say Any who are dissatisfied had beter NOT GO if they can better themselves . . . .[11]

By the first of April the rules for joining the Association had become less strict. Each Captain was at liberty to fill up his company with fresh members 'if any of the Original Numbers fall off from their Association and that he be particularly careful in those Numbers he may admit into the Association'. Captain Durfee was 'particularly requested by the Body to hold the Subscription Book of this Association'. At the last meeting of the Associates held in New York, 12 April, the names of delinquents were read as were the farewell addresses to the admiral and to Sir Guy Carleton. It was agreed that 'the Meeting of this Association do adjourn until the Body arrive at Port Roseway'.

For two long weeks, Joseph Durfee was one of the thousands of people who worked on the waterfront at New York loading the small boats that plied back and forth between the docks and the transports riding at anchor in the harbour and on 27 April he and his family

Joseph Durfee

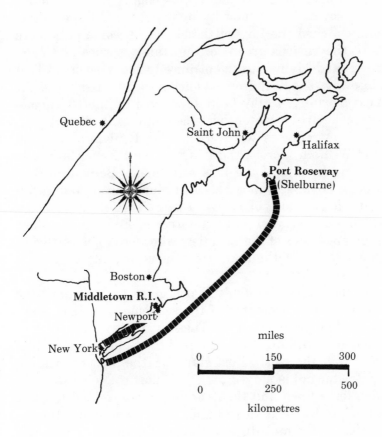

were part of the Spring Fleet bound for Port Roseway. The numbers of the emigrants had grown far beyond the plans of the first meeting in November 1782. In 'The Founding of Shelburne', W.O. Raymond tells us that instead of 16 companies, as the Associates had originally planned, there were 41 and that the total number in the companies alone amounted to 4,787 persons.

Seven days after they had left New York City, Joseph Durfee and his fellow passengers saw the black rocks covered with snow lining the shore at Cape Negro, and watched the blur of the skyline become punctured with the various greens of the stately spruce and fir of the island[12] lying at the entrance to the harbour at Port Roseway. The fleet dropped anchor for the night, and the next morning, 4 May 1783, proceeded up the 13 kilometres of deep blue water to let the immigrants disembark.

The refugees were greeted by Benjamin Marston and William Morris, the two men sent from Halifax to survey the site of the new settlement. Benjamin Marston, a Loyalist, was a native of Marblehead, Massachusetts, a graduate of Harvard in Science (though not a qualified surveyor) and a relative of Edward Winslow, Muster-Master of the Loyalists who were to be settled in Nova Scotia. William Morris, a surveyor, was a native of Halifax.

Benjamin Marston's Diary, gives us one version of the first fifteen months of the settlement at Port Roseway. He explains that on 'Tuesday, 6 May, Joseph Pynchon and William Morris advised the Captains and Chief Men that the North East Harbour [the present location of Shelburne] is judged to be the most convenient situation for a town and tis accordingly determined to fix it there'. In the next entry in his diary, he writes of the objection of 'the multitude to the location because they say tis a rough uneven piece of land — so they propose to mend the matter by choosing three men from every company to do the matter over again'.

Joseph Durfee must have been concerned over the confusion among the Loyalists on their arrival at Port Roseway. He had given up a spacious home, a thriving business and the land where his family had lived for four generations in protest against the violence of the American Revolution. Now, in his new home, all around him were multitudes of people, arguments and endless confusion. The government of Nova Scotia had not sent any supplies to Port Roseway for the Loyalists; no land had been cleared and even the decision concerning the site for the town had been left until the arrival of the refugees!

Gradually order began to come out of chaos. On 9 May, King Street, the first street of the new town was laid out; it was decided that the town should consist of five parallel streets, 60 feet wide crossed by others at right angles, each square of the town to contain 16 lots, 60 feet in front and 120 feet in depth, and that the space between Water Street and the shore should be cut by lanes and divided into small lots, so that each Associate might have a town and a water lot as well as a 50 acre lot on some part of the harbour, or on one of the rivers in the neighbourhood of the new settlement. Parties from different companies went on shore in regular order and accompanied either Benjamin Marston or William Morris to clear spots on which the tents they had brought with them might be pitched. As soon as possible huts were built and the tents put up and a hut or a tent with a stand of arms and a certain quantity of ammunition alloted to each family. The lots were drawn, Joseph Durfee received Town Lot. No. 12, Letter C. North Division (the division north of King Street), Water Lot No. 32, Letter C. South Division and 500 acres on the western side of Port Roseway harbour.

In August, 1783, Governor Parr came from Halifax in the *Sophie* to land at the foot of King Street 'under a general discharge of all the cannon on the Shore'. All the inhabitants turned out; both sides of the street were lined by men under arms. In a short speech the Governor gave the new settlement its present name of Shelburne and 'then admidst general cheering and discharge of cannon drank the King's health, prosperity to Shelburne and to the Loyalists'. He appointed five Justices of the Peace — one was Joseph Durfee — and after administering the oath of office to the Justices and taking part in various celebrations, the Governor returned to Halifax.

After the Governor's visit, the settlement began to

experience difficulties. In January 1783, the Associates who were planning to go to Port Roseway had specifically instructed their agents at Halifax to request that their settlement be incorporated as a city. During his August visit to Port Roseway, Governor Parr hesitated to comply with their request, promising only to consult the Attorney General as 'his right by virtue of his commission to grant the required charter'. This hesitation was only one of the many disappointments the Loyalists received after their arrival in Nova Scotia. As late as the spring of 1784 it was still necessary for people required to appear before the Court of Sessions to journey to Liverpool for the administering of justice at Shelburne. One can easily imagine the disregard for the laws of the land and the growing violence until a Court of Sessions was actually established at Shelburne.

By this time, thousands more people had come to the settlement. Almost immediately after the arrival of the 'Spring Fleet', people thronged to Port Roseway to be part of what they thought would be a vibrant metropolis. On 29 June 1783, Benjamin Marston noted, 'The past days I have been laying out town lots for newcomers'. On 12 July, he wrote that 'the people yesterday drew for their 50 acre lots . . . they wish to engross this whole grant into the hands of the few who came in the first fleet, hoping the distress of their fellow Loyalists, who must leave New York will oblige them to make purchase', and on 17 July, 'Two vessels arrived this afternoon'. In August more than 1,500 Free Black Loyalists came to Shelburne from Halifax and, by the Governor's orders were settled on the northwest arm of Shelburne Harbour. Refugees came all summer and in August Sir Guy Carleton wrote George Washington of the refugees still in New York City: 'Their safety depends upon my moving them'.

As T. Watson Smith writes in 'The Loyalists at Shelburne'[13] the removal from New York was made in haste. On 15 September about 12,000 Loyalists embarked from New York City; over five thousand of them came to Shelburne. Most of these people were disbanded soldiers, members of the British and Loyalist Regiments. Dr. C. Bruce Fergusson places the maximum population of Shelburne in 1784 at 16,000.

In the spring of 1784, a Court of Sessions was established at Shelburne and Joseph Durfee was appointed Judge of the Court of Common Pleas. But it was too late. All that winter discontent had smoldered among the disbanded soldiers, most of whom had spent the months since their arrival aboard the transports that had brought them and were anchored in the Cove,[14] so close to each other that planks provided walk-ways for the people crowded beneath the decks of the ships. The people on shore also had a hard winter. In January of 1783, Joseph Pynchon had shown real foresight when he advised 'each family should bring all the stoves it can procure for it may be possible that all the chimneys cannot be built by winter. In such cases every family with a little cooking shed adjoining the back door and a stove in the sleeping room may be comfortable during one winter'.

In July 1784, the discontent that had built up during the winter and the early spring and summer broke out in riots. The disbanded soldiers overturned more than 20 houses belonging to the Black Loyalists who had taken up land in the north of the town claiming that 'they the Negroes worked for less pay than they the soldiers'. This was Nova Scotia's first race riot, but, as James W. St. Clair Walker explains in *The Black Loyalists*, 'The incident is important not so much as an illustration of racial hostility than as an indication of how serious was the economic predicament of those Nova Scotians who had not received land on which to support themselves'.[15]

By the summer of 1784, Joseph Durfee had many problems. The Port Roseway Associates were having a most difficult time in their new homeland. Added to his local responsibilities, he was troubled by personal communication he received from his former home in Newport, Rhode Island which informed him that 'Father deceased in April last . . . ', and reminded him of his duty to share the cost of his late father's maintenance.

And I Doubt not you are Very Sensible that You Ought to pay half of it, as the Law Compels you as much as one to Support him while he Required it, as we Were the Only two Children that were Able and I have ever Expected that You would Neither have Demanded Your Small Note or the Mortgage Which You had Against my father's House and Lot, but would have made Over the Mortgage to me, as both Mortgage & Note were Not Equal to Your part of the Expence in Supporting father. I Now Request that You will Make just Proposal, You in Good Conscience Shall Think Right & Justice to be Done, through the Blessing of God the Mortgage had Narrowly Escaped Confiscation as I was Town Clerk in Middleton and had the Records in my hands Three Years.[16]

Shelburne flourished, in spite of the many refugees who came and then moved on to other parts of Nova Scotia, to the new province of New Brunswick, to England, to 'Canada' or who had returned to their former homes in the United States of America. Places of business lined Water Street, the main street of the settlement. Dozens of vessels sailed back and forth between Shelburne and the West Indies, between Shelburne and England and between Shelburne and various ports in the United States of America. It is not documented what business Joseph Durfee carried on at his Water Lot, Lot. No. 32, Letter C. South Division, but the records in the Shelburne Municipal Court House carry this information:

> 12 December 1797 — Joseph Durfee and Ann his wife, Grantor, 11 Pounds for Water Lot 32 and all the Buildings, Improvements thereon sold to Frances Wood, Butcher, Grantor.

On 20 July 1786, The House of Assembly at Halifax had granted £500 to build a lighthouse at the entrance to Shelburne harbour. Joseph Durfee, David Thomson and Stephen Skinner were eventually appointed the commissioners.[17]

In his diary of 1795, Reverend James Munro of Antigonish, Nova Scotia, describes the lighthouse which was constructed by 1792:

> Upon McNutts Island aforesaid is now built an excellent Light House which is not exceeded or even equalled on the continent of america It is built upon a

110

solid rock. Its height from the surface of the water to the foundation is seventy five feet, from the foundation to the top is 92 feet making in all 165 in height. Its form is octogon or eight sided figure about 10 feet each square at the bottom or base gradually decreasing to the top, built of Stone in the Strongest manner. Hath two lights. The upper and lower. The lower hath three Lamps, the upper 9 all properly placed so that the whole of them shall face the windows. In each Lamp there are twelve lights, so that the whole make 12 Lamps and 144 lights. And from its great Height from the lamps well trimmed gives an excellent light which hath been seen at the distance of Seven yea even at the distance of ten Leagues off. It appears to be well kept which every thing of the kind ought to be seeing so much depends on them.[18]

By 1788 Joseph Durfee and his family had moved to their 500 acre lot on the west side of Shelburne harbour. By this time Joseph was fifty-four years old, Anne's age is unknown, but Robert, their only son was 30, Hannah 28, Mary 26, Ann 22, and Elizabeth was 20. One of their neighbours, Alexander Houston from Glasgow, 'North Britain', kept a diary which gives some insight into their daily life.

June 24, 1788, A Cloudy warm morning. Some rain and Wind at South West with some thunder. Messrs. Hughes, Wilkins, Durfee and Cunningham came to Mrs. Elvens. Mr. Parker was over in the evening Nothing new, only fine growing weather.

Saty September 27, 1788, A moderate morng. Wind at N. No Frost not yet cold turns out very warm. I was at Durfees with some shingles did get my hay cut and did see Mr. Johnston. A fine night Warm Mrs. Elvens was over late about Vincents letter.

Saty October 11, 1788, a dull cloudy morng. wind at SE blows fresh I was at Capn Durfees did go and warn some of the Negroes to work on the road and did call at Mr. Johnstones does blow fresh in the evening from SE.

Mony October 13, 1788, a clear morng. wind at N. Blows fresh and cold — frizing after the sun is up did go down with Mr. Johnston and agree with Capn Durfee about a Bridge was at Silbys and Walders about Mrs. Elvens.

Wednesy Novr 19, 1788, A dull hazy Morng. calm with some rain did go and finish our Bridge and got paid for it from Js. Durfee and did Engage to make another on Hughes Lot.[19]

Joseph Durfee lived 12 more years and then died at his home on Shelburne harbour '21 March, 1801, after a few days' illness'. Part of his obituary reads:

. . . at the close of the Revolutionary War he removed to Shelburne with his family and the wreck of his property and sat himself down upon a tract of uncultivated land. The same industry and perseverance which had uniformly distinguished him soon rendered him an example to that infant settlement. Few men possessed a more manly and independent mind, exhibited more striking traits of industry, or have quitted life more generally and universally regretted.

There is no record of Ann Durfee's death and only a few details of the rest of Joseph Durfee's family due to a lack of early church records.

While the Associated Loyalists bound for Port Roseway were still in New York, at one of their meetings they discussed the possibility of taking a member of the Anglican Clergy with them to the new city they hoped to found in the Nova Scotian wilderness. Their minutes record that they decided to postpone their decision until they conferred with their agents who were then in Halifax. In his essay 'The Loyalists at Shelburne', Dr. T. Watson Smith suggests that while in Halifax, James Dole, one of those agents, boasted that the Associated Loyalists would establish their settlement without 'the hierarchy of the church'. In his 'History of the Church of England at Shelburne', W.O. Raymond wrote that before leaving New York, some of the Associates had invited Mr. George Panton, former rector of Trenton, New Jersey, who had served as chaplain of the Prince of Wales American Volunteers to come with them and that Mr. Panton had received the approval of the Society for the Propagation of the Gospel in Foreign Parts, whose headquarters were in England. For reasons of health Mr.

Panton did not sail in the 'Spring Fleet'. After their arrival at Port Roseway, some 125 of the Associates invited Dr. William Walter, former rector of Trinity Church in Boston who had served as chaplain of the 3rd Battalion of DeLancey Brigade to join them in Shelburne. In the resulting controversy between the two ministers, 'Joseph Durfee, the president of the Association' and other leading men resolved to stand by Mr. Panton, 'claiming he had the prior right to their consideration'.[20] Even the executive of the Association was divided in their loyalties with John Miller, the secretary while the Loyalists were in New York, supporting Dr. Walter. The controversy went on for years and was responsible for many people leaving Shelburne. Mr. Panton, who came to Shelburne late in 1783, took his records with him when he retired to Philadelphia.

The family line that Joseph Durfee established continues to contribute to their native province drawing inspiration from their founding father.[21]

Joseph Durfee was an idealist. He believed that difficulties whether they were between members of a family or between members of a family of nations could be settled without resorting to violence. After the American Revolution he dreamed of a new life in a new land that was still within the benevolence of the British Empire. When that new life and that new land were caught up in a violence not of their own making, he retired to the quiet of the countryside where he spent his last days lending his talents as they were needed and as they would help his neighbours.

1. The Newport Historical Society, Newport, Rhode Island has been most helpful in my research into the early life of Joseph Durfee. The genealogical data on his life comes from Wm. F. Reed's Descendants of Thomas Durfee of Portsmouth, Rhode Island, Volume 1, published in 1902. The Newport Historical Society tells us that 'The Durfees were probably of Huguenot descent', and provided the information of the Fellowship Club established in 1752.
2. *Ibid.* Ann Lawton Durfee was the daughter of Jeremiah whose parents were born in Portsmouth. 'The first Lawtons here were two brothers who came from England in the 17th century'.
3. Dirk Hoerder, *Crowd Action in Revolutionary Massachusetts 1765-1780*,(New York: Academic Press, 1977). The burning of the *Liberty* is recounted in *Crowd Action in Revolutionary Massachusetts, 1765-1780*, as is this version of 'The Boston Massacre'.

4. The role of Sam Adams in the American Revolution is well known. What is not so well known is that (as Dirk Hoerder tells us) in 1765 Sam Adams was £8,000 behind in his local tax collections.

5. Copies of the Durfee letters of 1774, 1775, and 1784 were sent me by the Newport Historical Society.

6. The account of Joseph Durfee's vessels and his part in the American Revolution are taken from his memorial presented to the Commissioners appointed to hear the claims of the Loyalists. The Memorial was published in the *Report of the Bureau of Archives for the Province of Ontario for 1904*, and in the *Shelburne Coast Guard, 20 October, 1932*.

7. Lt. Col. Joseph Mitchell, *Decisive Battles of the American Revolution*, (Greenwich, Conn., Fawcett Publications, 1962).

8. Mary Archibald, *Gideon White, Loyalist*, (Shelburne: Shelburne Historical Society, 1975).

9. Neil McKinnon, 'The Loyalists, A Different People', *The Ethnics of Nova Scotia*, (Port Credit, Ontario, The Scribblers Press, 1978).

10. Public Archives of Canada, The Minute Book of the Port Roseway Associates, copied at Shelburne County Museum. MG10, BII-1-14, Vol. 1, 1782.

11. W.O. Raymond, 'The Founding of Shelburne', St. John: *New Brunswick Historical Society Collections, 8.*

12. McNutt's Island, named for Alexander McNutt lies at the entrance to Shelburne Harbour. In 1764, he was given 100,000 acres in the vicinity but lost his grant because of his inability to bring in the necessary settlers. Before the coming of the Loyalists, McNutt applied for assistance to the Massachusetts Assembly for 14 families still at Port Roseway. When the Port Roseway Associates sailed up the harbour, some of these families were probably living on the island or at the mouth of the harbour.

13. T.W. Smith, 'The Loyalists at Shelburne', Halifax: *Nova Scotia Historical Society Collections,* VI, pp. 54-89.

14. 'The Cove' refers to Bell's Cove lying in the south of the town. It was named for Joseph Bell, Loyalist, whose house still stands in Shelburne, Nova Scotia.

15. James W. St. C. Walker, *The Black Loyalists*, (Halifax: Dalhousie University Press, 1976), P. 49.

16. Newport Historical Society.

17. In 1784, David Thompson was granted a Wharf Lot, a Town Lot and 100 acres on the East Side of Port Roseway Harbour. Stephen Skinner was a Major with the New Jersey Volunteers during the Revolution. He came to Shelburne in 1787 and died in Shelburne in 1808.

18. Rev. James Monro, 'History and Description and State of the Southern and Western Townships of Nova Scotia in 1795'. *Report of the Trustees of the Public Archives of Nova Scotia*, (Halifax: Public Archives of Nova Scotia, 1947), p. 45.

19. Personal papers Isabel Baker, Shelburne, Nova Scotia.

20. W.O. Raymond, 'The History of the Church of England at Shelburne', St. John: *New Brunswick Historical Society Collections*, No. 8, 1909.

21. Marjorie Bruce Records, Shelburne, Nova Scotia. There is a record of Joseph Durfee's son Robert. In 1800 Captain Robert Durfee shipped on the Privateer *Nelson*, out of Shelburne as 'Surgeon', and later that same year sold his share in the privateer to Edward Brinley, who had come to Shelburne in 1783 as the Commissariat. Captain Robert Durfee's son Joseph was baptized in 1811 and Joseph's daughter, Servilla, married James Purvis McGill, a descendant of David McGill from Sutherlandshire, Scotland, who came to Shelburne in the fall of 1783. Servilla Durfee McGill's daughter, Mary Prescott, was born in 1871 and married Robert Irwin, a descendant of John Irwin of Armagh, Ireland, who fought at Saratoga in 1777 and came to Shelburne in 1783 as a corporal with the 40th Regiment.Robert Irwin was a strong figure in the political life of Nova Scotia, becoming Speaker of the Assembly and in 1929 Lieutenant-governor of

the Province. When their Majesties, King George VI and his wife, Queen Elizabeth, visited Nova Scotia in 1939, Joseph Durfee's great, great, granddaughter, Mary Prescott McGill Durfee was their hostess.

Fort Johnson in what is now New York state

Chapter 5

Molly Brant

Mohawk Heroine

by Helen Caister Robinson

Molly Brant, leading matron of the Society of Mohawk Nations, was 'probably the most politically active woman Loyalist to come to Canada'. Her importance was due to her ability to keep the Mohawk and others of the Six Nations people loyal to the King. She was capable of such influence because of her position in the powerful matrilineal society of the Mohawk, because of the strength of her personality and also because she was a sister of Chief Joseph Brant and the widow of Sir William Johnson. Forced from her home in the Mohawk Valley, she moved with her people to British territory (southern Ontario) serving them and the Crown throughout her active life.

On an August morning in 1777 a handsome Indian woman emerged from the Manor House at Fort Johnson, in the British colony of New York, and strode purposefully down the hill to the Mohawk river. Stepping into the canoe beached there, she knelt and began to paddle toward the opposite bank. 'Her features were fine and beautiful, her complexion clear and olive-tinted. Her black hair, drawn straight back from a low smooth brow, was fastened in flat plaits at the back of her well-formed head'.[1] Unruly strands, loosened by the breeze, strayed across her face, and she brushed them back impatiently. The woman was Molly Brant, 41 years old, the Mohawk widow of Sir William Johnson.

In 1744 King George II of England had appointed William Johnson Superintendent of Indian Affairs for the Northern District. Born in Ireland, educated as a lawyer, he had come to America to manage the Mohawk Valley estates of his uncle, Admiral Sir Peter Warren of New York. Sir Peter's words of advice to him upon his arrival, 'Keep well with all mankind. Act with honour and honesty; don't be notional as some of our countrymen are, often foolishly',[2] were taken seriously. He did indeed keep well with all mankind. During his 38 years in The Valley he was friend alike to the Indians and the English and Dutch settlers who lived there. He was host many times to prominent men from London, New York, and Boston who came to discuss matters of importance with him, and who, with their wives, lingered to enjoy his hospitality for extended periods. In his time he probably commanded more authority, and wielded more influence than any man in the colonies. The Six Nations Indians, for whose welfare he was responsible, valued his friendship so highly that they adopted him as a brother, naming him 'Warragheyagey'.[3] That was no mean honour. The proud and powerful confederacy of Iroquois or Six Nations Indians had inhabited the Mohawk Valley for more than 200 years and considered the lands they occupied theirs by inherent right. Their intense hatred of the French began with their first confrontation on the north shore of the St. Lawrence river when Samuel de Champlain assisted their enemies, the Huron and Algonquin tribes. By the Treaty of Utrecht, signed in 1713, they were recognised as British subjects. William Johnson's association with them fostered that friendship, and during the French and Indian wars they declared themselves allies of the King, and joined with the local militia to fight on the side of the British.

By 1777 the colonies were embroiled in the War of American Independence. Friends of long standing had in many instances become enemies. Neighbour no longer fraternized with neighbour as one by one each man had made his decision to embrace the cause of the Rebels or remain loyal to King George III. For Molly Brant the decision was a simple one. During his lifetime Sir William was an ardent Loyalist, and she knew that had he lived he would have counselled her people to support the King, and his politics became hers. It was her duty, she believed to urge her people to remain loyal.

At the landing-place below the home of her neighbour, Nicholas Herkimer, Molly drew her canoe up on shore and climbed the path to his rambling brick house, her knee-length skirt swinging rhythmically above deerskin leggings, the beads on her moccasins agleam in the sun. Like many other families in The Valley the Herkimer brothers, long time friends and neighbours of Sir William Johnson and Molly Brant, were divided in their loyalties. George Herkimer remained a staunch Loyalist while his brother Nicholas became a general in the rebel army.

Alerted by a light in the window of Nicholas Herkimer's house, a Mohawk sentry, on guard at the stockades that surrounded Fort Johnson, had watched the General ride away at daybreak at the head of a large body of rebel militia. When Molly was informed she determined to learn his destination and plans. How? A Mohawk Matron she had her own methods. She would question, and if necessary threaten the Oneida wench who had been sharing the General's bed since the death of his wife. And because she was Molly Brant, and a prominent member of the powerful matrilineal society of Six Nations women, she would learn the truth. The Oneida woman would not dare lie to her even though the Oneida tribes had broken from the Six Nations confederacy to join the Rebels.

Soon after she returned to the Manor House an Indian runner was on his way to the rebel-held Fort Stanwix,[4] farther down the river. There, her brother Joseph, with a band of Mohawk braves, and Sir William Johnson's son, Sir John, in command of The King's Royal Regiment of New York,[5] together with John Butler with 60 Loyalists before he formed his corps of Rangers, and Colonel Barry St. Leger, and a company of British regulars were laying siege to the fort. Capture of Fort Stanwix was particularly important to the British cause since it was in the path of Colonel St. Leger's planned march to Albany to meet the main body of regulars under General John Burgoyne, newly appointed commander of the British forces. Molly's messenger advised Joseph that General Herkimer was on the march with reinforcements for the beleaguered Fort Stanwix garrison. The route he followed would lead him through the thickly wooded Oriskany ravines on a road that was barely a cart path. Immediately, Joseph and his warriors, and Sir John Johnson and his men hid themselves among the trees to attack General Herkimer's militia as they made their way through that narrow passage. The ambush was successful but the death toll was heavy, and General Herkimer was severely injured before he was forced to retreat. Although the Loyalist and British forces outnumbered the rebel garrison at Fort Stanwix by three to one Colonel St. Leger decided to withdraw his men without capturing the fort. Several circumstances influenced his decision. He needed heavy guns and Burgoyne's orders were to reinforce the main army on the Hudson. A message, which proved to be false, informed him that General Benedict Arnold was approaching Fort Stanwix with a large detachment of rebel militia. Secondly, while the Indians were fighting in the Oriskany ravines soldiers from the fort raided their camp, stole their clothing and other possessions. Angered by the theft, disgruntled by the lack of action on the part of the British regulars, many of the warriors vanished into the woods and did not return.

Molly Brant's message to Joseph at Fort Stanwix was one of several pieces of vital information she is believed to have given the Loyalists and British during the war. It is known that she supplied important news to General Sir William Howe when the British defeated the Rebel General George Washington at the battle of Long Island, 27 August 1776, the battle in which Molly's son, Lieutenant Peter Warren Johnson was killed. Some historians speculate that her purpose in remaining at Fort Johnson was to be in a position to relay significant information to the Loyalist forces, information she would have received from reliable Indian sources.

The Six Nations Indians were a matrilineal society, the blood line and clan affiliation descending through the mother. Molly was the granddaughter of the young

Mohawk chief who went to England in 1710, and upon being presented to Queen Anne asked that she send a missionary to his people in the Mohawk Valley. His request resulted in the establishment of Queen Anne's Royal Chapel of the Mohawks at Fort Hunter. There is some doubt as to whether Molly and Joseph were the children or step-children of Nickus Brant, chief of the Upper Canajoharie Castle,[6] although Molly and Joseph regarded him as their father. Educated first at the village school, and later at a private seminary for young ladies at Schnectady, Molly was quite familiar with the social customs and graces of English girls.

At the age of sixteen she caught the attention of Colonel William Johnson during a military muster on the grounds of his estate at Fort Johnson. He had been already twice married, first to Catherine Weissenberg, who bore him three children, and then after her death, by Mohawk ceremony to Molly's Aunt Caroline, niece of King Hendrick, powerful first chief of the Mohawk Nation. Caroline died during the birth of her third child. Attracted by Molly's fresh beauty and high spirits, William Johnson married her, by Mohawk custom first, and years later by a ceremony in the Episcopal church at Fort Hunter. Established in her own apartments in the Manor House at Fort Johnson, her training in an English school stood her in good stead. Quickly learning her role as mistress of William Johnson's home she became immensely capable, systematically managed both household and servants, and ordered needed supplies and materials from the New York and Boston shops. She was a gracious hostess to Sir William's many guests, and enjoyed the friendship of the women who accompanied their husbands. In love with Sir William throughout their twenty-two years of marriage, she was completely happy. Her insistence upon mothering her Aunt Caroline's children endeared her to her people, and her decision, taken with Sir William's consent, to keep the name of Molly Brant in order to retain her eligibility to become a member of the Society of Six Nations Matrons, won her the lasting respect of the Mohawks and strengthened the bond between them and Sir William. Had she taken the name of Johnson she would have forfeited her right to membership in that powerful matrilineal society.

Although many Loyalists had already fled the Mohawk Valley Molly remained at the Manor House secure in the belief that the Mohawks who guarded the Fort Johnson stockades would protect her. Rumours of acts of violence, instances of the tar and feathering of Loyalists, the burning and looting of their property served to increase her anger against the Rebels, and consolidated her determination to aid the British cause. But Molly was quick to sense an increasing hostility toward her as the weeks passed. Settlers in The Valley refused to sell her corn or grain. Although regarded as a wealthy women she had no ready money. Knowing that she and her household must live off the land she instructed her overseer to make certain that larger crops of grain and vegetables were planted. She and Joseph's wife, Catherine, who was living with her during his absence, spun the wool sheared from the sheep, carded and wove it into material for clothing for her family and the members of her household staff. Soon after the battle of Oriskany she was actively harassed by members of the Oneida tribes. Cows were stolen from her fields, her overseer was killed, and there was an abortive attempt to kidnap her son George. The Manor House was invaded by Oneidas and Rebels and her prized possessions destroyed. Fearful then for the safety of her children, angered by what she termed personal insults, she, Catherine and their families fled to the Cayuga village whose chief was her cousin and would, she said, protect her.

Following the British defeat at Saratoga, 17 October 1777, Molly was urged to go to Fort Niagara. Major John Butler, commander of Butler's Rangers, was well aware of the influence she had among her people, as was the Canadian Governor, General Frederick Haldimand. Because of the power she could exercise over the Mohawks in particular, her safety was important. In a letter to her, Major Butler wrote that a house would be provided for her within the compound at Fort Niagara where she would have military protection. The Cayuga village was no longer a secure place in which to live. Major Butler, who had been a friend of Sir William Johnson, reasoned that since the Indians were being forced out of

The Valley by the Rebels, and would seek refuge at Fort
Niagara, the presence of Molly Brant would be his best
insurance that her people would remain loyal to the
Crown.

Molly declined the invitation. Housed among the
Cayugas she was closer to her people, and in a better position to obtain information for the Loyalists. And she
hoped every day to hear some news of her son, Peter
Warren. Peter had left his school in New York to join the
British army at the beginning of the war. She knew he
had been involved in aborting the rebel Colonel Ethan
Allen's attempt to take Montreal, 25 September 1775,
and that he had taken Allen prisoner. But the only letter
she had received from him after Sir William's death was
written just prior to the battle of Long Island. However,
at Major Butler's continued insistence she eventually
went to Fort Niagara. In part it was concern for the
safety of her children, in part a burning desire to see the
Rebels defeated, and the traitorous Oneidas punished
that motivated her to accept Major Butler's invitation. In
her brother Joseph's absence, she knew her people would
need her counsel and encouragement.

Upon her arrival late in 1777, Major Butler made
haste to urge Molly to remind her people of their pledge
of loyalty to the King. Observing her angry reaction to
his news that all property previously owned by Loyalists
had been confiscated by the Rebel government he felt
certain he could count on her cooperation.

Scarcely had she settled into her new home when a
long line of Mohawks straggled into Fort Niagara, Nickus Brant and her mother among them. Although the
Superintendent of Indians, Colonel Guy Johnson, son-in-
law of Sir William, was present to greet them it was
Molly who was able to inspire them with some vestige of
hope. Standing beside him in the damp and frigid
weather of late November, her shoulders wrapped in a
protective crimson blanket, she spoke to them as Mohawk to Mohawk. When the war was over, when the
Rebels were defeated, their lands would be restored to
them and they could live at peace again. Joseph, when in
England, had received the King's promise. Dejected
shoulders lifted as she spoke, eyes glimmered with new

hope, there was a certain eagerness in their movements as each family set about building a temporary shelter. They listened and were agreed that Molly Brant spoke with the wisdom of their departed brother, Warragheyagey. Thus was her role established. The Mohawks who had little confidence in Guy Johnson would heed her counsel. It would be her responsibility to dispel the fears of her people, and urge the young braves to join her brother Joseph in the war against the Rebels.

Unable to carry more than a minimum of clothing with them on their flight from Fort Johnson, Molly and her family were now in urgent need of wearing apparel. Writing to Sir William's other son-in-law, Daniel Claus, in charge of the supply depot for the Canadian government's Indian Department at Montreal, she said she was penniless, and enclosed a list of articles necessary for the comfort of her family. Colonel Claus had great respect for Molly, and was perhaps more aware than any other Loyalist of her tremendous influence with the Six Nations people. When he wrote to the Canadian Governor on her behalf General Haldimand instructed him to give Molly Brant whatever she asked for, and said he would grant her £25 for immediate living expenses. Daniel Claus spoke to Joseph Brant also about his sister's penniless situation. Brant, in turn, wrote to Messrs. Taylor and Duffin, at Fort Niagara to ask that 'Molly Brant be given anything she wants'[7] from their store, and that they advance £30 to her, 'These items to be charged to Joseph Brant's private account'.[8]

In Molly Brant's letter to Colonel Claus acknowledging receipt of the items sent she wrote, 'Everything has come safe except the pair of gold earrings which I have not been able to find. We have a report of Joseph having had a brush with the Rebels, but do not know at what place. I am much obliged for the care and attention in sending me up those very necessary articles. I should be very glad if you have any accounts from New York that you would let me know them. I hope the time is very near when we shall all return to our habitations in the Mohawk Valley. I am Dear Sir ever affectionately yours, Molly Brant'.[9] In spite of her changed mode of living, and the fact that she now wore Indian dress rather than the

124

lavish gowns that had been a part of her life at Johnson Hall she felt a need to have a pair of gold earrings.

In acknowledging receipt of a second box of presents sent by Colonel Claus in the autumn of 1778, in which were included the gold earrings, she said, 'The manner in which I live here is very expensive to me, being obliged to keep in a manner open house to those Indians who have any weight in the Six Nations Confederacy'.[10]

Daniel Claus had a genuine liking for Molly. Acknowledging the power he knew she could wield with her people, he wrote to his brother-in-law, Sir John Johnson, 'A Joseph and Mary Brant will outdo fifty Butlers in managing and keeping the Indians firm. One word from Mary Brant is more taken notice of by the Five Nations than a thousand from the white man without exception'.[11] And so her importance in the eyes of government officials grew.

The winter of 1778 was a difficult one for the Mohawks who had fled to Fort Niagara. The huts they built were inadequate against the intense cold. Food was scarce, and the surrounding forests had long since been depleted of any abundance of game. When would the war cease? When would they be able to return to the Mohawk Valley? they asked. And neither Molly nor her brother Joseph could give them a positive answer.

By the spring of 1779 Molly had become concerned about the problem of educating her children. Her son, Peter Warren, had been at school in New York before the war began, her older daughters, Elizabeth and Magdalen at a private seminary for young ladies at Schnectady, and their education was considered to be complete. But she knew that Sir William would have expected her to see that her second son George, and her four younger daughters received the schooling due them as his children. In desperation she wrote to Daniel Claus and asked him to recommend appropriate schools for them. But when she informed Colonel Butler of her plan to take her children to Montreal he insisted that she must remain at Fort Niagara to control her people during his absence. He was about to lead his Rangers to Newtown[12] where he would join her brother Joseph, and Sir John Johnson in an attempt to block the advance of the Rebels into

Seneca territory.

Assuring him that the Mohawks could be depended upon to remain loyal, she watched him depart. When his company of Rangers had vanished into the distance she called together those women who belonged to the Society of Six Nations Matrons. She informed them that she must go to Montreal for a time in order to carry out Warragheyagey's wishes for the education of his children, and commanded them to urge their men, constantly, to help the King win the war. On the following day she obtained passage for herself, her seven children and three servants on a ship bound for Carleton Island. Having been instructed by General Haldimand to see to her comfort, Daniel Claus met her when she reached Montreal, and informed her that suitable educational arrangements for her children had been made on her behalf.

He had expected that she would remain permanently at Montreal, but Molly insisted she must go back to Fort Niagara in order that she might 'use her influence with the other members of the Society in urging the young warriors to fight against the Rebels'.[13] Upon learning that Colonel Claus could not arrange transportation for her without the consent of the Canadian Governor she angrily suggested that the Governor must be unaware 'that she would be going to Niagara to further the cause of the King, and that it would be a most inconvenient and uncomfortable journey for her to undertake'.[14]

Governor Haldimand, however, gave immediate approval for her journey. In a letter of instruction to Colonel Guy Johnson the Governor wrote, 'I have acquainted Colonel Claus that Miss Molly is to act as she sees best, and you or Colonel Claus will give her such presents as you may think necessary, and when she goes provide for her journey as it seems to be a political one'.[15]

Molly's journey up river was a dismal one as she was depressed by news of the death of her mother, whose unfailing belief that Molly and Joseph were destined to be leaders of their people had inspired them. Arriving at Carleton Island she was advised by Captain Alexander Fraser, the Indian agent, that all ships going to Fort Niagara were being reserved for troops, Indian warriors and supplies. It would be impossible for her to continue her journey. Her temper flared at first, but she agreed to remain when the Colonel asked for her assistance in managing the young braves gathered there. At his request she addressed the assembled warriors. He felt more assured of her ability to manage them as he observed the authoritative tone in which she commanded them to await her brother Joseph's arrival before launching the attack they contemplated on rebel communities in New York and Pennsylvania. Although angry following the Loyalist defeat at Newtown, and eager to retaliate for the destruction of the Seneca villages, they agreed to wait.[16] Molly was quick to observe the relief in Colonel Fraser's eyes. She was aware also of the added deference with which he treated her after the incident, and her feeling of self-importance grew. When he asked for her continued cooperation she came to a quick decision. Although she was established in less than comfortable quarters within the barracks she would remain there as long as her presence was required.

Observing that the Indians complained of unfair treatment received from Colonel Guy Johnson, a man for whom she had little liking, she wrote to Daniel Claus. 'The Indians are a good deal dissatisfied on account of the Colonel's hasty temper which I hope he will soon drop. Otherwise it may be disadvantageous. I need not tell you that whatever he promised or told them ought to be performed'.[17]

In spite of the seriousness of the war she enjoyed the winter at Carleton Island. Young officers attached to the barracks sought the company of her older daughters, Elizabeth and Magdalen. While maintaining strict chaperonage over her girls she thrived in the atmosphere of gaiety and laughter that prevailed during the young men's visits. When Dr. Robert Kerr, a young army surgeon, fell in love with Elizabeth, Molly willingly gave her consent to their marriage, pleased that her daughter would marry well, certain that Sir William would have approved.

While in Montreal again in the spring of 1780 to arrange for the schooling of a younger daughter, whose education like that of her sisters was being financed by the government, she was visited by Sir John Johnson. He informed her that it had been established beyond doubt that her son, Peter Warren, had been killed in action during the battle of Long Island. She did not cry or wail as the Mohawks usually did on the death of a family member. Four years had passed. It was too late for mourning. Instead, the news strengthened her determination to see the Rebels defeated. Consequently, when Captain Fraser wrote to ask Daniel Claus to persuade her to return to Carleton Island as quickly as possible, she went the moment that transportation was provided.

Never entirely certain that the Indians could be depended upon to remain constant, government officials counted on the Brants to foster loyalty. The war was not going well. More than ever it was vital to the British to retain the friendship of the Indians, and Molly Brant, foremost matron of the powerful Society of Mohawk Matrons must therefore be treated with tact and diplomacy because her influence over her people was so great. When she complained to Colonel Claus about the inadequacy of her accommodation within the barracks a house was provided for her in 1783 near the ruins of Fort Frontenac.

Eager to participate in the war, her son George left his school in the summer of 1781 and joined her brother Joseph and his Mohawk braves in raiding rebel villages in New York state. Joseph had brought her news of the death of their father Nickus Brant, and when the raiding party had gone from Carleton Island she felt bereft and desolate. She would have liked to go to Fort Niagara, but when Captain Fraser reminded her of her promise to control her people she abandoned all thoughts of leaving Carleton Island. She was becoming more and more aware of her worth to the English and more conscious of her personal power.

When the British General Lord Cornwallis was hemmed in at Yorktown in Virginia, and forced to surrender 19 October 1781 the war began to wind down. Five days later, unaware of the calamitous turn of events in Virginia, Joseph Brant and Sir John Johnson led a devastating raid on Johnstown, home of Johnson Hall where Molly and Sir William had lived in the days when there was peace in the Mohawk Valley. But as soon as news of the cessation of fighting in June 1782 reached the Canadian Governor, an order was issued forbidding further raids. At Carleton Island, Captain Fraser persuaded Molly that her continuing presence would be doubly necessary to keep the young braves in check.

When the terms of the peace treaty, negotiated in Paris, were made known consternation spread among the Indians. The British had betrayed them. How could the King give the Indian lands to the Rebels when they were not his to give, they asked. The young warriors at Carleton Island angrily threatened retaliation. In desperation, Captain Fraser begged Molly to try to placate them. Shocked by the news, she refused at first, but after some persuasion agreed to command them to withhold any action until the truth of the announcement could be verified.

On his way to Quebec to confer with General Haldimand about the implications the treaty had for the displaced Mohawks, Joseph Brant stopped at Carleton Island. Worried, haggard from lack of sleep, he and Molly talked late into the night about what they must do if the Canadian Governor confirmed the rumour that the Indian lands were forfeit. They agreed that General Haldimand must be made to understand that their people were deeply disturbed and very angry, and unable to understand why the British had forgotten them. In the meantime Molly would make certain that the Carleton Island Indians made no further raids on rebel villages. When he had gone she sent her son George to Fort Niagara with a message to the Six Nations Matrons there urging them to counsel their men to curb their tempers until Joseph returned from Quebec. She was certain they would obey her.

General Haldimand was extremely anxious to appease the Mohawks. Assurance of their continuing loyalty was equally as important to the British now as it had been during the war. Without that assurance there would never be complete freedom from fear of an Indian uprising. Without the friendship of the Mohawks the future of the Canadian colony would be unsettled. Their influence on other tribes on either side of the new border was tremendous. At whatever cost, the friendship of the Indians, nurtured so carefully in his time by Sir William Johnson, must be preserved. To succeed they would need the full cooperation of Molly and Joseph Brant.

Unable to await confirmation from London, General Haldimand in desperation took it upon himself to grant lands to the Mohawks along the shore of Lake Ontario at the Bay of Quinte. Later, further lands were given them along the Grand River in southwestern Ontario. A government surveyor, marking individual lots at the Bay of Quinte, allotted acreage to Molly Brant and her children in compensation for the estates she had forfeited in the Mohawk Valley. She was given lands also at Fredericksburgh and at Fort Niagara.

When the boundary of the new republic was established, Fort Haldimand, on Carleton Island, and some forty-four other British-held forts along the Lakes and down the Ohio and Mississippi rivers, including Niagara, Detroit and Mackinac, were found to be on the American side of the boundary. Because of the failure of the Americans to make payment for Loyalist lands confiscated during the war, many of the forts were not relinquished until two years after Jay's Treaty, signed 15 November 1794, confirmed their transfer. But the Carleton Island fort was reduced in 1783. British troops stationed there moved to the Canadian mainland at Cataraqui,[18] and Molly Brant moved with them. By order of the Canadian Governor two houses were to be built near the fort, one for her and one for the use of Joseph's family, 'so that they might be comfortably housed while he was absent on government business'.[19] The cost of educating her children had been defrayed by the Canadian government, and now a permanent residence was provided for her, and in addition to the lands granted her she would receive an annual pension of £100. In a letter to Joseph Brant, dated 27 May 1783, at Quebec, Governor Haldimand wrote, 'In consideration of the early and strong attachment of your sister, Mrs. Molly Brant, and of the zealous interest and service manifested by her and her family to the King's government, I have thought fit to grant unto her a pension of £100. currency a year, which as far as it depends upon me shall be continued to her, the said pension to be paid to her quarterly by Brigadier General Sir John Johnson to commence from the date of Brigadier General Sir John Johnson's appointment as Superintendent General and Inspector General of Indian Affairs, 14 March 1782'.[20]

When the Mohawks were granted further territory along the Grand River, and many of them were settled there by her brother Joseph, she was invited to join them. She refused, preferring to remain at Cataraqui; as Superintendent of Indian Affairs Sir John was responsible for the welfare of her people, but she knew that the Mohawks did not entirely trust him. Arrogant as a young man, insensitive to their problems, he had discouraged their visits when he first moved into Johnson Hall after his father's death. The impression of his indifference lingered in the minds of many. In consequence, Molly felt it her duty to make certain that those of her people who settled at the Bay of Quinte were dealt with fairly by him. There were other reasons too for her decision. A town was beginning to develop at Cataraqui and a school was being built. Several Loyalists from the Mohawk Valley had settled near the fort. Her dear friend, the Reverend John Stuart, who for some years served her people as missionary at Queen Anne's Royal Chapel of the Mohawks at Fort Hunter, had fled to Cataraqui during the war, and was pursuing his duties as missionary there. His friendship, which had become a source of great comfort to her, undoubtedly influenced her decision to make Cataraqui her permanent home. The commander of the local garrison was noticeably relieved when he was informed of her decision. The young braves who loitered in the streets, with no particular occupation to interest them, were becoming increasingly restless. He hoped Molly Brant would be able to reason with them, hold them in check until they became reconciled to the loss of their former hunting grounds, and settled down to live at peace in their new country. On instructions from General Haldimand he gave her anything she asked for.

Angry words were exchanged between Molly and other members of the Society of Mohawk Matrons over the disposition of the communion silver that had been a part of the furnishings of Queen Anne's Royal Chapel of the Mohawks at Fort Hunter. Saved during the early days of the war, by Joseph Brant and their cousin John Deserontyou, and safely hidden, it had been carried to Fort Niagara in the arms of one of the matrons. When they moved to the Grand River the Fort Niagara matrons claimed the silver. But Molly disagreed with them. John Deserontyou and his band of Mohawks had chosen to settle at Cataraqui, and since he had shared with her brother the responsibilty for safe preservation of Queen Anne's gift, half of it must go to Cataraqui also. Leader of the Society, she was able to have her way. Four pieces only went to the Grand River. Four other pieces were claimed by Molly to be displayed in the church she was certain would soon be built at Cataraqui.[21]

Molly's house at Cataraqui was adequate for her needs. Her two youngest daughters were still at school. Elizabeth had married Dr. Robert Kerr and was living at Fort Niagara and George was employed as an accountant in the office of the Department of Indian Affairs at Montreal. Magdalen, Margaret and Susannah alone remained with their mother.

On his way to England in the autumn of 1785, Joseph stopped at Cataraqui to discuss with Molly his concern for the Indians in the Ohio Valley. The Miamis, the Shawnees and Delawares were in conflict with the government of the new republic over their lands, large slices of which were being claimed for an expanding white population. Skirmishes against the whites were occurring. The angry Western tribes considered the Ohio hunting grounds theirs by inherent right. But white settlers from the former British colonies saw the Ohio territory as theirs to explore and settle, and began to stake claims there, and clear the land for settlement. Now that the war had ended, the western tribes were resisting the onslaught of American settlers in the way they knew best, by night attack on villages and skirmishes with the American soldiers, while endeavouring to gather the tribes together for outright confrontation.

Both Molly and Joseph Brant agreed that the Mohawks and other Six Nations tribes who had moved to Canada must be restrained from actively helping their relatives in the Ohio Valley. They were allies of the

King, and England was now at peace with the United States. Joseph had a dream which he hoped would become reality, a dream that was part of the reason for his trip to England. He hoped to be able to unite all the tribes on both sides of the border into one great confederacy strong enough to bargain with governments without the need of bloodshed. If he could enlist the sympathies of the men at Whitehall in his scheme he thought it might work.

Molly made no mention to Joseph of a letter she had received in the ship's mail. The communication, from the office of the United States Land Commission, stated that her signature was required for transfer to the United States government of lands in Philadelphia Bush that were registered in her name. Her daughter Elizabeth, and her son George had each inherited land adjoining hers, and must establish their claim to the property.[22] The suggestion was made that if she would return to the Mohawk Valley she might find it to her advantage to remain there. Molly's curiosity was aroused. What ulterior motive lay behind the invitation? When Joseph had gone she wrote to George, at Montreal, and asked him to return to Cataraqui. The following spring he accompanied her to Fort Niagara to talk with Elizabeth and Dr. Robert Kerr. She had been angry when some months earlier Joseph was forced by the United States Commissioners to sign legal documents that would transfer all Mohawk lands, including certain properties owned by her, into the possession of the new government. Now she questioned whether her lands at Philadelphia Bush were indeed forfeit since no mention had been made of the property in the earlier transfer. It was agreed that she, George and the Kerrs should make the journey. She did not tell her children about the special invitation she had received from the Commissioners. Until she learned what was wanted of her she would mention it to no one lest it be thought that she was disloyal to the King. She intended also to observe, if possible, the extent of the unrest that existed among the Indians who remained under the jurisdiction of the government of the new republic.

At Philadelphia Bush she learned that the commissioner with whom she must confer was Philip Schuyler,

Molly Brant

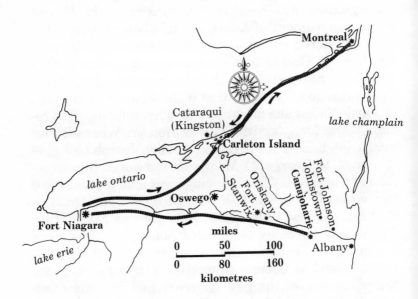

Montreal

lake champlain

Cataraqui
(Kingston)

Carleton Island

lake ontario

Oriskany
Fort
Stanwix

Fort Johnson
Johnstown
Canajoharie

Oswego

Fort Niagara

lake erie

miles

0	50	100

0	80	160

kilometres

Albany

son of a man who had been one of Sir William Johnson's closest friends. He informed her that her property was forfeit, but the lands her children had inherited from their father had not been confiscated because they were minors at that time. Upon signing transfer papers they would be reimbursed in full for the value of the property. Angry, but rigidly polite to the Schuylers, Molly left the area as soon as arrangements were completed. The devastation she saw on her journey through The Valley left her sad and depressed. At Schnectady, she was warmly welcomed by government officials who had heard of her power over the Mohawks, and knew of the esteem in which she was held by the Canadian Governor. In an endeavour to enlist her help in dealing with the Indians in the Ohio Valley she was offered funds, through the office of the New York Commissioner, that would more than compensate her for the loss of her property if she would return permanently to the United States. It was hoped that she would use her influence with the rebellious Indian tribes. Convinced that the dissatisfaction of the Western tribes was real and justified, aware that they were being exploited by white men in their hurry to obtain land in the Ohio Valley, aware also that she was being offered a bribe, she became angry and refused to be a part of the bargaining. She would not, she declared, set foot again on American soil.

Returning to Canada, she went directly to Montreal to talk with Colonel Claus. Shocked by her news, Daniel Claus commended her for refusing the bribe. Lord Dorchester, who had replaced General Haldimand as governor, had been assured, Claus said, that Molly Brant could be depended upon to persuade her people to remain at peace. And each time she was in communication with Sir John Johnson he urged her to make very certain the Mohawks did not go to the assistance of their relatives along the Ohio. She did not need his urging. She was in frequent touch with Joseph who went back and forth across the border in his effort to band all the tribes together in one large confederacy that would be powerful enough to bargain peacefully with any government. To him it was of supreme importance that the Mohawks keep the peace.

Molly was untiring in her efforts to support her brother in his struggle to promote a confederacy of all tribes, travelling to Fort Niagara and the Grand River to impress upon other members of the Society of Six Nations Matrons the advantages such a union would have for all the Indian people. At the Grand River there was criticism of both Molly and her brother by some of the younger Mohawks. They were denounced as traitors, censured for their acceptance of special government favours. Intensely disturbed by the faultfinding, Molly angrily demanded to know what they expected of her. Had they lost faith in the Head of the Society of Matrons? Calmed by the older women, her leadership reaffirmed, she returned to Cataraqui to find that a new commanding officer had succeeded Colonel Fraser. She took an immediate dislike to him. Lacking the diplomacy of Colonel Fraser, perhaps unaware of her importance to the government, he irritated her by his haughty, abrupt manner. Many clashes took place between them before he was removed to another post.

After a devastating crop failure in the summer of 1787 starvation became almost a way of life in parts of Canada. Before the government rations to Loyalists and Indians, discontinued after three years issuance, could be redistributed there was hunger in every household. Molly felt great concern for her people during that winter. She brewed medicinal potions from dried herbs, and she and her older daughters went in and out of many homes to minister to the sick, and share their meagre rations with those whose need seemed greater than theirs. As the story of her service to those stricken spread to Fort Niagara and the Grand River members of the Society of Six Nations Matrons congratulated themselves on their choice of a leader.

Molly Brant's influence over her people, her skill in keeping the braves under control, and the love and esteem the Cataraqui Mohawks held for her did not go unnoticed by government officials and Loyalists in the area. The men at Whitehall, informed by reports from the Canadian Governor, considered her to be a person of particular importance to their plans for the Canadian colony. With Daniel Claus' departure for England, and his subsequent death there, Sir John Johnson depended more and more on her cooperation in dealing with her people.

Upon being introduced to Colonel John Graves Simcoe and his lady, at a reception given in their honour, when they visited Cataraqui on the way to Niagara-on-the-Lake, she observed the portly new lieutenant-governor with particular interest. Aware that Sir William's son, Sir John had been named as a possible candidate for the post of lieutenant-governor of the infant province of Upper Canada, her feelings about Colonel Simcoe were mixed. Overweight, his face devoid of animation, he seemed dull and sullen as he stood erect in his immaculate colonel's uniform to greet the assembled townspeople. The Mohawks had often thought Sir John arrogant in his manner toward them. How would they react to this man, she wondered.

Molly was also present, with her daughters, at the opening ceremonies of the first parliament of Upper Canada. Her brother Joseph was at Niagara for the ceremonies also. Newly returned from a conference with United States President, George Washington, at Philadelphia, he was on his way to a grand council of Indians at Sandusky where he would present President Washington's proposals for a new boundary for the Indian lands along the Ohio river. In conference with Molly the conditions offered the Western Indians were discussed.

President Washington had asked Joseph Brant's cooperation in persuading the Western tribes to subscribe to the Fort Harmar treaty of 1789, already signed by some of them, which gave the Americans the valuable strip of land situated between the Ohio and Muskingum rivers in the Ohio valley. Joseph had little real confidence that the warring Miamis and Shawnees, after twice repulsing American troops, could be persuaded to give up the Muskingum strip. But he reasoned that if the lands beyond the Muskingum were guaranteed unconditionally to the Indians by the government of the United States, surrender of the strip between the rivers would be a small price to pay for a lasting peace. He had agreed to present the President's proposal to the Western tribes at Sandusky, because it was a guarantee against further encroachment by white settlers. But Molly had no faith in President Washington's promises. In her opinion the narrower boundary was merely the beginning of further inroads on Indian lands. She did not trust the Americans, and was certain Joseph's mission would be a futile one.

She was at Fort Niagara again the following summer when three United States commissioners were guests at Navy Hall, the lieutenant-governor's residence, while conferring with Colonel Simcoe and Joseph Brant before being escorted by Brant to a further council with the Western tribes at Sandusky. At this council Joseph hoped to convince the Indians that they should accept the President's proposal.

Chaperoning her daughters in their ball gowns, at a ball given in honour of the Americans, Molly attended in native costume, jacket and knee-length skirt, and leggings, her moccasins decorated with colourful beads. Her dislike of the Americans caused her to appear sullen and morose, and prompted one of the commissioners, General Benjamin Lincoln, to make a comment in his daily journal. 'These ladies possessed great ingenuity and industry and have great merit, for the education they have acquired is owing principally to their own industry as their father, Sir William Johnson, was dead, and the mother retained the manners and dress of her tribe'.[23] How little he knew of the real Molly Brant! She waited anxiously at Fort Niagara until Joseph and the commissioners returned. And when they came she did not need their words to tell her the outcome of the mission. In their haggard faces she read the news of defeat, and in her brother's a quiet despair. Drunk with power, having twice defeated the Americans, the Miamis had refused to bargain with the commissioners, and denounced Joseph Brant as a traitor.

Molly returned to Cataraqui in the autumn alone except for her servants. With the exception of Mary, who lived with Margaret and her husband, all her daughters had married. Lonely in her silent house, she went about the village, visiting the sick among her people, and teaching the Indian women to fashion garments from the woollen blankets issued to them by the Department of

Indian Affairs. Deeply religious, she derived spiritual strength from her weekly attendance at service in the new Anglican church, sitting in a pew reserved for her use. Around her were men and women she had known in the Mohawk Valley in the days when Sir William Johnson was alive, and she was mistress of Johnson Hall. She had agitated for, and given generously to the fund that paid the cost of building the first church at Cataraqui.[24]

She was at the Grand River toward the end of the summer of 1795, when a runner brought word of General Anthony Wayne's victory over the Miami tribes at Fallen Timbers. Unable to understand why the British commander, still occupying Fort Miami, had refused to shelter the defeated Indians at the fort, she mourned the useless death of so many braves. Weary, plagued by rheumatism, she returned to Cataraqui on the ship, *Mississauga*, the guest of the Lieutenant-governor's lady, Elizabeth Simcoe.

Brooding constantly over the uncertain fate of the Western Indians, the acquisition by the United States government of the disputed hunting grounds in the Ohio Valley, Molly's health began to deteriorate. Before spring returned she knew that her joints had become too stiff with rheumatism to allow her to kneel to plant her garden. When medicines failed to relieve the condition she moved to the home of her daughter Magdalen, now married to John Ferguson. Welcomed as an honoured member of the household, her health improved. John Ferguson was a member of the legislature for Upper Canada, and it was inevitable that among the friends who frequented his household conversation should revolve around politics, the doubtful wisdom of the men at Whitehall, and the impatience of the Americans to occupy the forts along the border from which the British were so reluctant to withdraw. More than ten years had passed since the Treaty of Paris had allotted to the Americans some 44 British-held forts along the lakes and down the Ohio and Mississippi rivers. But the British still held the posts, awaiting payment to the Loyalists for their confiscated lands. Molly was in her element as a participant in such discussions.

After she had been living in her daughter's home for

several weeks she began to notice that the Indians did not visit her as they had when she lived alone. Searching for a reason, she sent for her cousin John Deserontyou. He arrived in a sullen temper to accuse both Joseph and herself of being traitors to their race, and of furthering their own ends by fraternization with the English. The Mohawks no longer had faith in the Brants, he said. Well aware of the jealousy of her brother Joseph that smouldered in John Deserontyou's heart, Molly listened in silence until he had finished. In a cold rage, she addressed him formally. Would the Head of the Society of Six Nations Matrons, the Elder Sister of the Mohawks betray her people? She demanded retraction of his words to all with whom he had spoken ill of either Joseph or Molly Brant. If he refused she would take steps to make him regret his words. When he left her she was convinced he would cause no further trouble.

Molly's health began to deteriorate early in the new year; before spring returned she was gravely ill. Late in April 1796, in her sixty-first year, Molly Brant died. Her feelings of prejudice against the Rebels were strong when the War of American Independence began, and were magnified into a personal hatred by her forced flight from the Mohawk Valley. In Canada, she became almost fanatically loyal to the King, and as Head of the Society of Six Nations Matrons was able to persuade her people to remain loyal also. Her loyalty stemmed in part from the visit of her grandfather to the Court of Queen Anne of England in 1710, a visit that led to the Queen's special interest in the Mohawks. It was a loyalty fostered also by her long association with Sir William Johnson, a man who was most emphatically British. Her ability to control her people, to work with her brother Joseph to diffuse their anger during the difficult months following the announcement of the terms of the Treaty of Paris, by which their lands in the Mohawk Valley were ceded to the Americans, caused the Canadian Governor, and the men at Whitehall to regard her as a woman of considerable importance to the well-being of Canada. Fearful always of an Indian uprising in Canada, wary also of the intentions of the aggressive new neighbour to the south, government officials regarded her as a woman of considerable importance to the welfare of the Canadian colony.

When the bell in the tower of St. George's Anglican church at Cataraqui began to toll on that April afternoon in 1796, business men of the town, members of the provincial legislature, and officials from the Canadian government gathered to honour the woman many had known first in the Mohawk Valley as the Indian wife of Sir William Johnson. In her role of counsellor to her people they had not only respected her, but also sometimes feared her because of the influence she could and did exert over the Indians. Officers from Fort Frontenac filed past the wooden coffin with heads bowed. Mississauga chiefs gathered outside the church, hesitant to join the invited guests, while Chief John Deserontyou's Bay of Quinte Mohawks, and others from the Grand River filed inside to take their designated places as mourners. While they listened to the words of her friend the Reverend John Stuart, in the minds of many was a question. Who would replace her as counsellor to her people? The Mohawk woman who came penniless to Fort Niagara during the War of American Independence to find that the Canadian Governor was prepared to supply her with a house and funds, and defray the cost of educating her children, the woman whom the British government found it 'expedient to humour' would no longer be there to demand a fair deal for her people, and no longer encourage their loyalty to the Crown.

Molly Brant 'was buried, under her maiden name, without a stone to mark her grave, in the Protestant Loyalists' lot which in time came to be called St. Paul's burial ground and is now St. George's Anglican cemetery in Kingston, Ontario'.[25] She was probably the most politically active Loyalist woman to come to Canada.

1. Jeptha R. Simms, *Frontiermen of Old New York*, (Albany, N.Y.: George C. Riggs, 1882), Vol. I, p. 202; Helen Caister Robinson, *Mistress Molly, The Brown Lady: Portrait of Molly Brant* (Toronto: Dundurn Press, 1980).
2. *Ibid.*,
3. Warragheyagey means 'Man of business'.
4. Now Rome, New York State.
5. The King's Royal Regiment of New York (familiarly known as the Royal Greens).
6. Upper Canajoharie castle was the fortified Mohawk village built at the junction of Canajoharie creek and the Mohawk River, one of three Mohawk villages along the Mohawk. Canajoharie means 'boiling pot', or 'the pot that washes itself' see Simms, *op. cit.*, I, p. 28.

7. Public Archives of Canada, The Claus Papers, Vol. 2.
8. *Ibid.*
9. *Ibid.*
10. *Ibid.*
11. *Ibid.*
12. Now Elmira, New York State.
13. PAC, The Claus Papers Vol. 2.
14. H. Pearson Gundy, 'Molly Brant, Loyalist', *Ontario Historical* Society Papers and Records, XLV, No. 1 (1953), 97-108.
15. PAC, The Claus Papers, Vol. 2.
16. Mary Beacock Fryer, *King's Men* (Toronto: Dundurn Press, 1980), pp. 149-155, describes the devastation of the Iroquois villages by the rebel Sullivan expedition.
17. PAC, The Claus Papers, Vol. 2.
18. Now Kingston, Ontario.
19. Jean Johnston, 'Molly Brant, Mohawk Matron', *Ontario History*, LVI, No. 2 (June 1964), pp. 105-124.
20. PAC, The Joseph Brant Papers; Jean Johnston, *op. cit.*
21. Mabel Dunham, *The Grand River.* p. 62.
22. Public Archives of Ontario, Upper Canada Land Petitions, F3, No. 41, 1797; Gundy, *op. cit.*
23. From the private journal of General Benjamin Franklin in Marjorie Freeman Campbell, *Niagara* (Toronto: Ryerson, 1958).
24. She had a house in Kingston, where she was a benefactor of St. George's Church. Richard A. Preston, *Kingston Before the War of 1812.* (Toronto: The Champlain Society for the Government of Ontario, 1959).
25. James A. Roy, Kingston, *The King's Town* (Toronto: McClelland & Stewart, 1952).

Ward Chipman

Chapter 6

Ward Chipman, Senior

A Founding Father
of New Brunswick

by Darrel Butler

Ward Chipman Sr. was Harvard educated and seemed destined to a life of comfort and security when the Revolution sent him into exile. After filling various positions in England and America, he helped establish the new loyalist colony of New Brunswick. As a Member of the Assembly, Solicitor-General, Judge, and Provincial Administrator, for his service on international commissions to set borders between American and British territories, and to negotiate the Treaty of Ghent, Ward Chipman Sr. is justly remembered as a founder of New Brunswick.

There was an angry mood about Boston and the surrounding countryside on 1 September 1774. Early that Thursday morning, at half past four, two hundred British soldiers boarded thirteen boats, and proceeded up the Mistic River. They landed at Temple's farm and marched to the powder house on quarry-hill in Charlestown where they confiscated two hundred and fifty half barrels of rebel-stored gun powder. Enraged crowds of rebel sympathizers gathered throughout Middlesex County to organize a demonstration of several thousand people on the next day. However, a large mob, consisting of 'mostly boys and negroes' collected around the elegant house of Attorney-General Jonathan Sewall on that Thursday evening. Considering the turmoil of the day and the reputation of violent demonstrations, this must have been a particularly frightening situation for the Sewall family. A shot rang out from the upstairs of the house and the crowd attacked the building. After breaking some windows and causing some other damage, the mob dispersed. Sewall and his family, shaken by the incident, fled to Boston.[1]

Among the fleeing members of this family was the promising young protegé of Sewall named Ward Chipman. Chipman joined Sewall in a flight which would end over five thousand kilometres away in London, England. But he would soon return to fight for his King and the cause that he believed in, at the cost of personal gain and, eventually, at the cost of necessary influence in political circles. This would be the pattern of the rest of his life as he became one of the founders of the colony of New Brunswick.

Ward, born on 30 July 1754, was the fourth son born to John and Rebecca Chipman. John Chipman was a prominent lawyer living in Marblehead, Massachusetts, and his family had deep roots in the colony. His father had graduated from Harvard in 1711 and was, for many years, the pastor of the Second Church at Beverley. In legal and social circles, the family was highly respected. John, himself, had attended Harvard and graduated in 1738. Ward's mother's family was equally prominent in Massachusetts society. Her father was Reverend John Brown of Haverhill. Her mother was Joanna Cotton, a great-granddaughter of Reverend John Cotton of Boston. John and Rebecca were married in 1744, and they had a total of twelve children during their marriage but only six would survive to adulthood. Of these six, four were daughters and the other son, John, born in 1763, left the colonies for England during Ward's senior year at Harvard.

Naturally, Ward as oldest surviving son would follow his father in the hallowed halls of Harvard. At the age of twelve, the boy was about two years younger than the average age of the freshmen class of 1766.[2] He was a

146

good student and appeared to have adapted well to college life. The daily activities of students at this time were strict and a typical day began at 6:30 a.m. when the boys awoke. Then they had about one half hour to get dressed and studied for an hour by candlelight before breakfast at eight o'clock. From nine o'clock until one o'clock the students performed their recitations. Then it was dinner and free time until three o'clock, at which time they had to study for two more hours. They were allowed to go to sleep after nine o'clock.[3] Obedience was not always forthcoming from the students and there were demonstrations. In 1768, Ward joined one hundred and fifty-four other students in leaving their dinner tables and going out into the courtyard to scream their protests over the rancid butter used by the cooks.[4] This was the only such protest in which Chipman participated.

This year was significant to the young student for a far greater reason. John Chipman was arguing a case before the Superior Court at Falmouth when he fell victim to a stroke and died. This left Ward and his family with no support and threatened the boy's university career. At this critical time an old friend and colleague of John Chipman, Jonathan Sewall, intervened. Sewall was a prominent member of the Massachusetts Bar and was Attorney-General and Judge Commissary Deputy and Surrogate of the Vice-Admirality Court for the colonies of Quebec, Newfoundland and Nova Scotia.[5] He and several other lawyers supported Ward until his graduation in 1770. Since the standing of students within the class depended upon social and not upon academic status, Ward was sixth in position — well ahead of Samuel Adams.

Immediately after his graduation, Ward Chipman accepted the position of Precepter of the free school at Roxbury. However, he was soon bored of teaching and turned to legal studies under the guidance of Sewall and Daniel Leonard, an eminent Boston lawyer. Chipman began to repay his debt to Sewall by tutoring his two sons — Jonathan Jr., and Stephen, thus becoming more and more a member of the Sewall family and Jonathan Sr., became his mentor.

During these days the events which were shaping

the American Revolution began to unfold. Ward Chipman's reaction to the political uproar must have been influenced by Jonathan Sewall. By this time Sewall's opinions of the situation were formed and well known in Boston. He was a former intimate of John Adams and these two legal minds had argued political issues during the 1760's in the Boston newspapers.[6] It may have been his support of the governor in these articles which earned Sewall his appointment of Attorney-General. Thus, when on the evening of 1 September 1774, the mob gathered outside of Sewall's elegant residence in Cambridge Chipman had helped defend the Attorney-General's home and was, by that time, as strong a Tory as Sewall or Daniel Leonard. Chipman became a target for rebel abuse in 1775 when he signed the Loyal Petition to General Gage.

Life in Boston during the early months of the War of Independence was particularly grim. The death toll from the Battle of Bunker Hill was high and funerals so common that, according to Sewall, 'you met as many dead folks as live ones in Boston streets'.[7] This, plus food shortages and the crowding of refugees, citizens, and British troops, created enormous tensions and strains. Petty crimes increased and atrocities against Whigs, or rebel sympathizers, were frequent. Boston was a city under seige and not a pleasant place to live. For Chipman and the Sewalls, the situation was intolerable and they fled first to Halifax and then to London. Sewall arrived in the imperial capital by late summer, 1775[8] and Chipman was in the city by early June, 1776[9] both surviving the hazardous two month sea voyage.

Over the course of the war between seven and eight thousand Loyalists sought refuge in London. They came with high expectations of being welcomed by a sympathetic population; of being sought out by a government interested in their advice on the war; and, for some, of achieving influence in political circles to better themselves. Instead, they were isolated as a fringe group, and to a large extent ignored. There were two basic reasons for this: first, the English population was not united in its opinion of the revolution as many sympathized with the political philosophies of the Rebels, and second, the

Loyalists were always thought to be temporary refugees. Not until after the defeat in the battle of Saratoga, October, 1777, was it perceived that they might not soon return to their colonial homes. Many of the Loyalists also held this belief that they would quickly be back in the colonies and this caused considerable financial problems for them. Unemployment was compounded by their not having made arrangements before they fled and by living in the most expensive city in the world. Unable to find employment, they turned to the government for compensation for their allegiance. Politically, however, they had little or no influence. The Lord North Administration did not seek their advice on the war nor on how to handle the Rebels. However, the government did assist many refugees with grants and extended the salary of colonel officials while in exile. By 1777 a system was established by which a standard stipend of £100 was paid, with mandamus councillors receiving £200 and other civil servants up to £500. Refugees, who were not upper class or who did not have office, were given £40 to £80. In 1777 the cost of this system was £58,500 and 1778 was £68,500.[10] Such an expense generated ill feelings towards the Loyalists.

Confronted with this ill feeling from the main English society and reinforced by a desire to keep together, the Loyalists established themselves in 'colonial ghettoes'. Based upon the colony from which they fled, refugees gathered in certain areas of the capital and in specific coffee houses. For example, many Massachusetts Loyalists took lodgings near St. James Park.[11] Within each colonial division, the social barriers of the home society were transferred to London. Thus, the Massachusetts colonists divided themselves into three levels — the élite of Governor Hutchinson and his officials, the professionals and minor government officials, and the remaining poorer class.

Jonathan Sewall and Ward Chipman belonged to the second group. In the late summer of 1775, Sewall had joined a group of fellow Massachusetts men, including the famous artist John Copley, to form a social club for weekly dinner meetings. In September 1776, this was reorganized into the 'Club of Brompton Row'. Chipman, who had arrived in London that summer and who would have been receiving a government pension, joined this new version along with such prominent colonists as Daniel Leonard, Colonel John Chandler, Harrison Gray Junior, and S. Sampson Blowers. Everyone lived on Brompton, a road on the west side of London, and they met every third evening to play cards. Although it was a social club with little political influence, it did provide an opportunity for new and renewed friendships. Many of Chipman's acquaintances through this club would influence his later life.

Chipman's life in London was probably not satisfactory. It cost at least £100 per annum for an individual to survive in the city. By this time, his tastes were definitely upper class and very expensive to maintain in the city so that having enough money would have been a problem for him. He was, however, able to secure the position of Deputy Muster-Master General of His Majesty's Provincial Forces for New York from Sir William Howe, and so he returned to America by the summer of 1777. He had succeeded to this position upon the resignation of Ebenezer Bridgham, formerly a Boston merchant.[12] The Muster-Master General was Edward Winslow, a fellow Massachusetts Loyalist and an old friend. Chipman's duties were to muster the provincial forces, or Loyalist Regiments, six times a year and to adjust and certify every 'abstract for pay of the commissioned, non-commissioned, and private men'.[13] The growth of regiments as the war progressed necessitated the appointment of deputies in several areas. Thus, in a largely administrative position, Chipman would travel about the New York countryside inspecting troops, but he would not see the battlefield.

However, he was involved in some dangerous situations. During the evening of 13 June 1778, he joined Daniel Murray, Reverend George Panton, and Joshua Upham for an evening at Winslow's house in New Utrecht Town. At midnight a party of 25 rebel soldiers landed below the house. They marched past it and went into Flat Bush where they kidnapped Major James Moncreiffe and Mr. Bache. They attacked the Mayor, but he escaped. The rebels then returned to their landing by a new road which was only 200 metres from Winslow's house. The Muster-Master General and his friends knew nothing of the raid and chatted the evening away. Whether the Rebels had been frightened off by the Major of Flat Bush or whether they did not know who lived in the house is not known, but for some reason they did not attack the party. Winslow breathed a sigh of relief when he discovered his good fortune for 'Not a single charge of powder or ball had I in my house'.[14]

Chipman's position brought with it a salary of £500 per year. This allowed the young man to indulge in a life-style which he felt was suited to his social position. His former mentor became concerned about his excesses and, in April, 1782, chastised him for not putting any money aside for future needs writing: . . . 'permit my friendship to suggest that at your time of life you ought out of that sum to be laying up something'.[15] The phrase 'at your time of life' was particularly apt for Ward Chipman. By this time, the English had realized that they could not win the war with their former colonies and were beginning to sue for peace. The uncertainty of the future was uppermost in everyone's mind and there ensued a scramble for influence with political leaders. By this time Chipman was in a position to compete in this struggle. His circle of friends included not only Sewall and Daniel Leonard, but also Gabriel Ludlow, Beverly Robinson, Edward Winslow, Benjamin Thompson and other prominent Loyalists. His position also brought him in contact with Sir Guy Carleton, who had replaced Sir Henry Clinton as Commander-in-Chief of His Majesty's forces in North America in May, 1782.

Early in 1783, Ward Chipman began to prepare for his life after the war. In the spring Benjamin Thompson went to England and in June presented Lord North with memorials from Edward Winslow and Chipman requesting a half-pay pension at the end of the war.[16] Thompson's confirming letter to Chipman shows the circle of friends who were working together:

> Make my compliments to Colonels Ludlow, Robinson, Cruger — if he is at New York, and to all my old friends. Believe me ever my dear Chip — [17]

The fortunes of this circle rose sharply during the summer. Carleton sent the enterprising Brigadier-General Henry E. Fox to be his Commander-in-Chief in Halifax to oversee the establishment of the Loyalists sent to Nova Scotia. Fox was not only the brother of Charles James Fox, a popular English politician, but also an intimate friend of Edward Winslow who had been sent to Nova Scotia the year before to seek land for settlement for the refugees. Chipman, through George Duncan Ludlow, persuaded Fox to appoint Winslow as his secretary.[18]

Many prominent Loyalists, particularly within Chipman's New York circle believed that they had personally sacrificed and struggled for their King and Empire while the people of Halifax and Nova Scotia had profited from the war. More importantly, they saw Governor Parr and his administration as being firmly entrenched leaving little room for them to have any influence. They lobbied for a separate Loyalist colony north of the Bay of Fundy. Support for this movement grew as conflicts arose between Governor Parr and the refugees who arrived in his colony throughout 1783. Thus Sir Guy Carleton was drawn into the situation and he questioned the motives of the governor in a letter to Whitehall. Fox also supported a separation when he returned to England.[19]

As evacuation of Loyalists was carried out during the summer of 1783, many of the prominent Tories sailed for England to increase their political influence. However, before they left, fifty-five signed a petition stating that they intended to settle in Nova Scotia and, because of their social position, they requested the same number of acres as granted to a field-officer of the army. The petition was circulated in New York, Saint John, and London and caused tremendous excitement and resentment.[20] Chipman signed this petition to 'have as many strings to my Bow as I could'.[21] However, he soon regretted having done so when he found out that some who had signed it were not really Loyalists but opportunists. But the damage was done and this petition would come back to haunt him in the future.

Chipman did not leave New York as early as many of his friends. He had been appointed secretary of a commission investigating claims for supplies furnished to the British army during the war. Thus he stayed for the surrender of the city to the American Troops which he described in a letter to Edward Winslow, dated 29 November 1783:

> About 12 o'clock on Tuesday the 25th inst., all our Troops were paraded on the wide ground before the Provost, where they remained till the Americans about 1 o'clock marched in thro-Queen-Street and Wall-Street to the Broad-way, when they wheeled off to the hay-wharf and embarked immediately and fell down to Staten Island. I walked out and saw the American Troops under General Knox march in, and was one of the last on shore in the city; it really occasioned most painful sensations and I tho't Sir Guy, who was upon parade, looked unusually dejected . . . I have passed two days since in the City to which I returned upon finding all was peace and quiet. A more shabby ungentleman-like looking crew than the new Inhabitants are I never saw, tho' I met with no insult or molestation. The Council for sixty days, which is invested with supreme authority for that term is sitting; . . . I had the satisfaction also of seeing General Washington, who is really a good looking genteel fellow. Scarce any of our friends or any man of respectabilty remains at New York they are principally embarked for England.[22]

Chipman, too, was setting his sails for England. He explained his reasons for doing so as 'I consider the present by far the most important period of my life, and am determined to exert every faculty to get myself forward'.[23]

Chipman's future hung on the question of the new colony north of the Bay of Fundy and who would be its new governor. The first choice was Brigadier-General Fox. This was very favourable to Winslow and Chipman, who expected key, lucrative appointments in the new administration. Ward was hoping for the position of Attorney-General, and at one point, Carleton had recommended him to Fox for it. But Fox eventually declined to serve as Governor because he was not certain that Carleton would become Governor General of British North

America. The next choice was Brigadier Musgrave, who similarly refused. Third choice was Sir Guy's brother, Thomas Carleton, who accepted after he was assured of being soon transferred to Quebec.

This left Chipman and Winslow on the fringe of the administration. They had little influence with Thomas Carleton and received relatively minor council positions with low salaries. Winslow was Surrogate General and Chipman was Solicitor-General. Chipman lamented 'I have totally failed in all my pursuits and prospects in coming to England, most heartily regret that I did not go immediately to Halifax from New York'.[24] The salary for his position was so low that he received more from his half-pay pension and so declined any salary for serving as Solicitor-General. He sailed with Carleton to New Brunswick in August, 1784.

When Chipman arrived in the new colony of New Brunswick he landed at its principal town, Saint John. Here there were over 1,500 framed houses and 400 log cabins sitting on ground to which the families had no legal right. Many of the Loyalists were actually waiting to go up river to establish themselves, but delays from the old Nova Scotia Assembly had kept them at the mouth of the river. These people looked to the new Governor and Council to solve their problems.

Carleton established his government in Saint John and set about organizing his colony and aiding its citizens as much as possible. Chipman, as a member of the council, met the challenge and demonstrated his enormous capacities for hard work by performing the duties of Attorney-General from November 1784 to May 1785, as well as his own as Solicitor-General. In addition he prepared the charter for the incorporation of Saint John as a city. As a result of his work, he was made the first recorder of the new City Council in May, 1785. During February of that same year, Chipman had been admitted to the colonial bar. In May, Jonathan Sewall sent his oldest son, Jonathan Junior to study law under Chipman. Repaying his debt to his former mentor, Chipman took the young man into his office and provided for him over several years. On 30 June 1785, he opened his law firm in Saint John. Although young Jonathan Junior would

154

Ward Chipman Senior

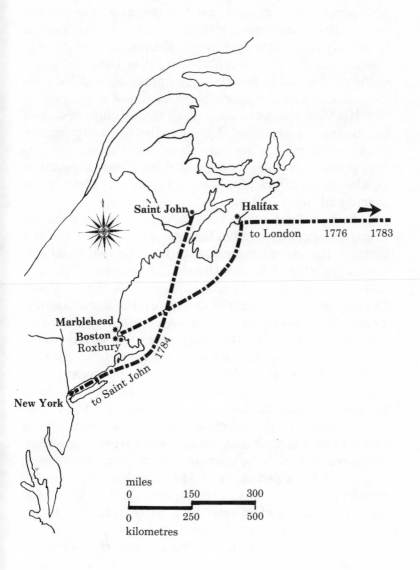

Saint John

Halifax

to London   1776   1783

Marblehead
Boston
Roxbury

1784

to Saint John

New York

miles
0   150   300

0   250   500
kilometres

say that the firm had 'as great a share of business as any practitioner in Saint John', it was not very lucrative and often did not provide much income.

On 10 October 1785, *The Royal Gazette* carried a proclamation calling for a general election. Carleton and his council had organized the new colony and set its administrative machinery in motion. But now they needed to establish the last remaining element of the government — an elected assembly — to ratify their decisions. Carleton wanted to have a strong party of 'worthy' gentlemen who would support the government in the assembly. His view was consistent with the original design of the colony which called for a balanced society with a small aristocracy. This opinion meant that it was not only proper but also necessary that members of the council also be members of the assembly as was already the practice in Great Britain.

In New Brunswick, Ward Chipman entered the political struggle as a candidate for Saint John City and County. His chief running mate was the man who had been appointed Attorney-General, Jonathan Bliss. The other four government candidates were William Pagan, Christopher Billop, John McGeorge and Stanton Hagard. Their opponents in the local area were led by Tertullus Dickenson. However, the most vocal opposition which was heard throughout the province came from Dickenson's brother-in-law, Elias Hardy. Hardy organized a group who opposed not only Carleton and his administration, but also the basic idea of favour for the Loyalists. He attacked the agents of the Loyalists and capitalized on the fact that most agents were New Englanders while many Loyalists, particularly in Saint John, were from New York and other middle colonies. Chipman obviously came under fire for being from Boston, but worse still came the cry of no votes for a 'Fifty-fiver'. His signature was coming back to haunt him.

The central issue in the election was whether members of the council should run for elected seats. Hardy and his fellows argued that it was against the traditions of colonial legislatures. The assembly was to be a check on the executive power in the form of the governor and council. The government men returned the argument that the contemporary British ministry had ministers in its elected assembly.

As the campaign continued the voters of Saint John became more and more divided. On the night of 9 November, amid the excitement of the election, Sheriff William Oliver moved the poll from McPherson's Tavern in the area of Dickenson's supporters, to Mallard's Tavern which was considered in the area of support for Bliss and Chipman. A gang organized itself around McPherson's Tavern and marched to Mallard's where fighting broke out and windows were broken. The troops stationed at Fort Howe were called out and arrested the leaders of the opposition party.

When the voting was over, Dickenson and his supporters had defeated Ward Chipman and Jonathan Bliss. Carleton was concerned as the election had gone well for him in every other area except Saint John. Since the public would not elect his candidates, then they would have to be brought into the assembly another way. Therefore, Bliss and Chipman demanded a scrutiny of the votes and when the opposition party members did not show up to defend their votes, Sheriff Oliver declared the governor's men elected. It was not a fair play and would be remembered by the voters of Saint John when Ward Chipman offered in future elections.

By this time, Chipman was not facing his problems alone for on 24 October 1786, he had married Elizabeth Hazen. She was a member of one of the more prominent families of the new city, whose father, William Hazen, had helped organize the prosperous firm of Simonds, Hazen and White on the Saint John River in the 1760's. Elizabeth, noted for her 'discretion, amiable disposition, good sense and cleverness', was a perfect balance to Chipman's excessiveness.

The couple moved into Chipman's house, which had formerly been the house of Daniel Leonard and was Governor Carleton's first residence. Although it was a fine house with a front terrace, the couple found it draughty, and decided to build another house. They purchased a plot of land two hundred feet by four hundred feet from the firm of Simonds, Hazen and White for £70 and commissioned the construction of the house.

As the work on his house progressed, Chipman became very concerned about his abilities to meet the increasing financial commitments. His law practice was fast winning him a reputation of being one of the foremost lawyers in the colony, but it was not prosperous and often his clients could not pay him. He received no salary for being Solicitor-General, and, as an election promise, he had refused any for serving in the Assembly. He did have his half-pay pension of £91 per annum and also received a salary of £50 for being secretary of the Society for the Propagation of the Gospel Indian School in Sussex. He had acquired the latter position while serving as a member of a commission headed by Carleton for the establishment of Indian schools throughout New Brunswick under the guidance of the missionary arm of the Church of England. Starting ambitiously and opening several schools in various areas, the only school left by 1794 was the one in Sussex.

Chipman looked to other ventures to develop his income and joined his wife's family in establishing a much needed grist mill in the city. He obtained capital for his share by writing to his sister, Elizabeth who had become the wife of a wealthy Salem merchant, William Gray. Chipman had a legitimate claim upon his sister for he had deeded all of the family property to them at the outbreak of the Revolution. He and Gray were close friends and the capital was quickly sent to Saint John.

The grist mill prospered due to benefits received from exemptions in trade laws. Trade with the United States was restricted except in essential commodities such as grain, which would not be grown in sufficient quantities in New Brunswick. The mill sold wheat, rye and buckwheat flour which were produced from local farmers. Its mainstay was Indian corn, which was largely imported from New England, particularly from William Gray.[25] But disaster struck in 1789, when Carleton permitted the importation of Indian meal, which forced the closure of the mill.[26]

Chipman's personal life during these years was focused on two things. First was his son, Ward Junior, who was born 10 July 1787 and was his father's chief joy. The second was his garden, which not only assisted the household budget, but also brought him much local respect as a gardener.

In 1792, one term of the assembly ended, elections were called and once again Ward Chipman was offered as a candidate for Saint John. Unfortunately, memories were still lingering from the bitter results of the 1786 campaign. The years between the elections were not economically prosperous and Carleton and his government had lost favour throughout the province. Worse still for Chipman was the selection of Fredericton over Saint John as capital of New Brunswick. The financial centre had been passed over for a small rural village, primarily because the port city was militarily difficult to defend. As Chipman had supported Carleton's decision, his chances for re-election were hopeless.

Severely defeated in his home town, Chipman and his supporters looked to other centres and since elections were held on different days in various areas, election was still possible. He preferred Fredericton, but it was too late to change voters' minds. Friends submitted his name in Northumberland County and he won handily. Chipman wanted to be the Speaker in the new assembly, but the opposition was too strong and he did not receive the appointment.

After the election, financial concerns were again uppermost in his mind. As he hoped to receive the position of Paymaster for the New Brunswick Regiment, which was formed in 1793, he wrote his old friend Edward Winslow. Winslow quickly answered that the commanding officer would actually be Beverly Robinson, who would favour his brother with the position.[27]

In 1791, Canada, New Brunswick's sister colony to the west, was divided into two separate colonies, Upper Canada and Lower Canada. Upon the advice of Jonathan Sewall Junior, who had become Solicitor-General in Quebec, Chipman sought the position of Chief Justice of Upper Canada. Chipman's influence in London had, however, dwindled to only the representation provided by New Brunswick's agent, Mr. Knox. Still, he was optimistic:

I will not, I cannot believe that after all my services

159

and the sacrifices for the public, and the exertions I am disposed to make, if there should be an opportunity, that I must linger out a life of mortification and disappointment without a competence for present subsistence or a prospect against any unseen accident.[28]

He was definitely frustrated. He had had a brilliant legal future in New England only to have it dashed by the Revolution. He had hoped for a prestigious position in the model colony of New Brunswick only to have lost it. Instead of enjoying the lucrative life of a wealthy lawyer, he had to save pennies. Again he was to be frustrated because the position went to William Osgoode, an English lawyer.

While this was occurring, other events were taking place in which Chipman would take a leading role. The treaty between the United States and Great Britain which recognized the former's existence, established the boundary between Maine and New Brunswick as being the Saint Croix River. Unfortunately, there were three rivers flowing into the Passamaquoddy Bay and which river was the Saint Croix was unclear. This confusion led to several international issues. The Treaty of Amity, Commerce and Navigation of 1794, or Jay's Treaty, laid the ground for the settlement of the problem. It set up a commission to hear the arguments of both governments. The Americans selected James Sullivan, an historian from the District of Maine, as their representative. Carleton selected Ward Chipman as an agent for his government.

This position was important to Chipman as it provided him with an opportunity to use all of his skills to represent his adopted colony on an international stage at a very critical time in its growing life. Since the commission would be meeting in New England as well as in New Brunswick, it would provide him with an opportunity to see his sisters and their families again. Even more importantly, it put him in a financially secure position for at least two years with an annual salary of £971. The meetings of the commission began in Boston in June 1796, and then moved to Halifax, St. Andrews, Boston and Providence. Sullivan argued that the treaty makers had intended to select the first major river west of the Saint John River which would be the Magaguadavic River. The testimony of John Adams and John Jay did not totally confirm Sullivan's argument and left him in a rather weak position.

Chipman's task was to identify the true Saint Croix River, which was considered the real boundary. To do this he needed a copy of the writings of Samuel de Champlain, who had spent the winter of 1604 on Dochet's Island in the mouth of the river. The Colonial Office searched the length of Great Britain, finally obtained a copy in Edinburgh, and necessary information was forwarded to Chipman. After an initial presentation to the commission meeting in St. Andrews, he was forced to hire Robert Pagan to conduct excavations on Dochet's Island and unearth the remains of Champlain's buildings. This ensured the success of his final argument in the autumn of 1797.

The next stage of the negotiations was to settle upon the boundary at the source of the Saint Croix River, to prevent further boundary problems. There were several factors to consider in the negotiations, including the fact that there were American settlements in the disputed territory and that New Brunswick had to have a good overland route to Canada, unsevered by American territory. Finally, a compromise was agreed upon with the northern branch of the Schoodiac taken as the boundary with a line running due north. This border line gave the Americans the settlements that they wanted and the people of New Brunswick received the Madawaska villages and obtained a greater stretch of the Saint John River. With his work on the commission completed, Chipman returned to Saint John. His success on the international stage earned him considerable respect, especially in London. Ward received the appreciation of both the Duke of Portland, the British Secretary of State for the Colonies, and King George III.

He had received the international recognition which he had sought, but it did not solve his continuing financial problems. A year after the end of the boundary commission he was again complaining that 'Business has, if possible, decreased, and more frequently than otherwise

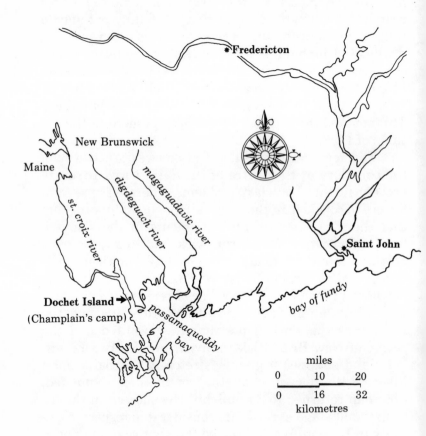

I find myself in debt at the end of the year'.[29] Thus the next five years were very difficult financially for Chipman and by 1805 he found his business to be at a virtual standstill. In the same year the British Consul at Boston died. Ward Chipman was interested in the position for it would have given him an excuse to return to his family in Massachusetts just at the time when his son was attending Harvard. His chances for obtaining the position were very slim; however, one of his best friends, Thomas Coffin, was in London and in a position to influence his appointment. Unfortunately, the number of applications was considerable and he could not compete with the direct influence which others had.

The following year Chipman was appointed a member of the Provincial Council, which did not bring a substantial salary with it and did little to alleviate his financial problems. It did, though, honourably acknowledge his legal abilities and his contribution to the province. By the fall of 1808 his income was £200 per annum, which he felt was not sufficient to maintain himself in the style he preferred. However, there was renewed hope for advancement when on 1 November, Joshua Upham, assistant Judge of the Supreme Court, died in England and by the death of Chief Justice George Duncan Ludlow in Springhill on 13 November. The salary for these two positions had recently been increased from £300 to £500 and from £500 to £700 respectively. Although either position would have certainly helped his personal finances, the Chief Justice position was more attractive.

Chipman immediately wrote to Thomas Coffin in England and enclosed a memorial and letters for the Duke of Kent. He also sought the support of the Governor, General Hunter, but again he was not the only applicant. Jonathan Bliss, who had been appointed Attorney-General over Chipman and who was an old courtroom opponent, also submitted his name for the position of Chief Justice. Bliss also wrote Hunter, who passed both names onto the Colonial Office for their consideration. The Attorney-General likewise wrote to his old friend the Earl of Liverpool for his influence. Since the Earl had recently died, his son sent the letter on to Lord Castlercagh with a request that Bliss be appointed.

In the end the Attorney-General was the victor. Ward Chipman was not totally passed over, for he was appointed a Puisne Judge to replace Upham.

At the end of the War of 1812, Chipman was again called into the service of his King. Because of his work on the international boundary commission, he was asked to represent New Brunswick and Great Britain at the negotiating table for the Treaty of Ghent. Chipman was now sixty-one and was in ill health with frequent attacks of gout. He hesitated to accept the honour because he felt he might not be able to maintain physically the pace of debate which would be required. He had his son, Ward Junior, appointed as his assistant and then was ready to negotiate the treaty. Chipman worked very diligently on the negotiations but left much of the work to his son.

In the twilight of his life, Ward Chipman might have been looking forward to a peaceful retirement in his gardens. He certainly deserved such a situation as he had worked extremely hard, and often unselfishly for the people and government of his province. His skills as a gardener were honoured when he was admitted as an honourary member to the Massachusetts Society for Promoting Agriculture in 1818. His son had a talented legal mind and a promising political career. However, Chipman did not retire and became caught up in one of the most controversial issues of his life which began in 1817 when General George Stacy Smythe became the Lieutenant-governor of the Colony. Smythe came into a government in which many judges were also members of the executive and legislative councils. The Lieutenant-governor, irritated by this situation, sought ways to free himself from the judges and their influence. Ward Chipman and his son, surrounded by old friends and former law students, were in the centre of the opposition to Smythe. As this controversy was enveloping Smythe died on 27 March 1823. An interim chief administrator would have to be selected until a new Lieutenant-governor was appointed. George Leonard, who lived in Sussex was the senior member of the council, and was expected to be the next chief administrator. Unfortunately, Leonard refused to accept the position citing ill health as the reason. The next in line, Christopher Billopp, who lived in Saint John, called upon the council to meet him in the port city. The majority of councillors were hesitant because of Billopp's age, which was eighty-five and because of his refusal to come to Fredericton. The majority then called upon the third senior councillor, Ward Chipman, who accepted the position.

In Saint John, Billopp was enraged so a rival party — at times almost a rival government — formed in the port city. He issued a proclamation in a local newspaper announcing that he had taken over the government. An address of loyalty to Billopp was drawn up and circulated but few people signed it. The biggest problem was that Billopp could challenge all laws passed by the legislature. Since this included important shipping legislation, Chipman wrote to the Colonial Office to have the dispute with his Saint John rival settled. The answer from Lord Bathurst supported Chipman, but criticized the council for by-passing Billopp.

Chipman continued to administer the colony until his death on 9 February 1824. Throughout his term he provided firm guidance to the government. He also took advantage of his control of political patronage as he aided his friends, relations and supporters by appointing them to minor offices. His death marked the passing of an era as he was the last of the original council members. The colony to which he had dedicated so much of his life had grown and changed for the generation of Loyalist refugees was giving way to its children.

Ward Chipman Sr., was given an enormous state funeral befitting his contributions to New Brunswick. He had helped organize its government, wrote the charter of its principal city, fought for its boundaries, been active in its school system and had risen to the forefront in its judicial system. He had indeed earned the epitaph of being one of New Brunswick's founding fathers.

1. *Boston Gazette and Country Advocate*, September 5, 1774, p. 2, c. 2.
2. Patricia A. Ryder, *Ward Chipman, United Empire Loyalist*, (M.A. Thesis, University of New Brunswick, 1958), p. 3.
3. David Whitney, *Colonial Spirit of '76*, p. 54.
4. Ryder, *Chipman*, p. 3.
5. E. Alfred Jones, *The Loyalists of Massachusetts*, (Baltimore, 1969), p. 258.
6. Robert J. Taylor (Ed.), *Papers of John Adams*, (Cambridge, Massachusetts, 1977), I, pp. 174-176.
7. Jonathan Sewall to Thomas Robie, July 15, 1775, *Massachusetts Historical Society, Proceedings*, Second Series, X, p. 414.
8. Mary Beth Norton, *The British Americans: The Loyalist Exiles in England, 1774-1789*, (Toronto: Little, Brown, 1972), p. 76.
9. Edward Gray, 'Ward Chipman, Loyalist', *Massachusetts Historical Society, Proceedings*, LIV, p. 333.
10. Norton, *British Americans*, pp. 54-55.
11. *Ibid.*, pp. 65-68.
12. W.O. Raymond, ed. *Winslow Papers 1776-1826*, (St. John, 1901), pp. 16 and 32-33.
13. *Ibid.*, p. 33.
14. *Ibid.*, p. 29.
15. *Ibid.*, p. 76.
16. *Ibid.*, p. 89.
17. *Ibid.*, p. 90
18. *Ibid.*, 91-92.
19. W.S. MacNutt, *New Brunswick, A History: 1784-1867*, (Toronto: Macmillan 1963), p. 43.
20. Lorenzo Sabine, *Biographical Sketches of Loyalists of the American Revolution*, (Boston, 1864), II, p. 429.
21. Raymond, *Winslow Papers*, p. 111.
22. *Ibid*, 152-153.
23. *Ibid.*, p. 153.
24. *Ibid.*, p. 209.
25. PAC. Lawrence Collection, Vol. II, Chipman to William Gray, 12 Dec. 1787.
26. Raymond, *Winslow Papers*, p. 372.
27. *Ibid.*, 401-402.
28. Joseph Wilson Lawrence, *The Judges of New Brunswick and Their Times*, (Saint John, 1907), p. 190.
29. *Ibid.*, p. 197.

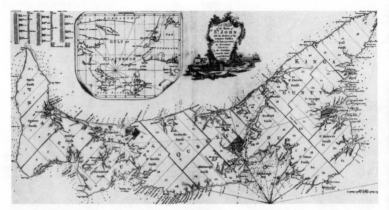

Captain Samuel Holland's map of Prince Edward Island in 1775, then called Island St. John

Chapter 7

William Schurman

of Bedeque
Prince Edward Island

by Donald Wetmore

William Schurman of both Dutch and French ancestry, was a prosperous farmer-merchant of New Rochelle, New York when the hostilities of the American Revolution forced him to leave his homeland. First he sailed with his family to Shelburne, Nova Scotia, but that township seemed too crowded for Schurman. So he soon moved his growing family to the wilderness of Prince Edward Island where his strengths and talents let him establish a place for himself and his descendents — even today.

On a chilly day in September, 1783, the wind blustered up along the Atlantic coast of Nova Scotia, and William Schurman tightened his fists over the ship's wheel. He was watching for rocks and shoals off the entrance to Canso Gut, unmarked on the primitive chart he followed. He had listened to warnings from Shelburne mariners of how perilous these could be, and he had too much at stake to risk another disaster of any kind. Determined, controlled, praying, he steered into the swell of the waves.

At sea now for three days since he had left Shelburne, he planned to reach the Island of St. John by the next evening. The Gut of Canso, between Cape Breton and mainland Nova Scotia, was a night shelter, and from there he had a direct run. He thought about the island for a moment which in 1798 would be re-named Prince Edward Island. As he had been there the year before and liked it, he was now seeking it again as a place to settle his family — to start a new life. He was forty and homeless. Old to be starting a new life, but he had to try.

Elizabeth, bent over in the bow of the schooner, happily nestled her arms around Benjamin and baby, Caleb. How blessed he was to have two sons already from his second wife. When Jane died, six years ago, Elizabeth had offered her love and help. They married soon after, and the boys were the first children of the new marriage. He was equally proud of the three sons Jane had given him: Peter, his eldest, now busy with the lines, Isaac aged nine, and the youngster Jacob, squirming on the lap of gentle Sook, teasing Sook by pulling her hair over her kind black face.

He had never regretted bringing his two black servants, Sook and old Bill, especially Sook whom he could seldom bring himself to call Susannah, her right name. For her part, Sook seemed glad to be a member of the family. Bill was different, apt to be grouchy, but in these disastrous times an extra hand was necessary and the black man earned his keep well enough. Bill and Peter were working together now. Thirteen-year-old Peter liked to learn from Bill the new ways of doing chores, and how to handle sails.

He remembered Jane's second child and his only daughter with a pang of regret. He wanted Mary with him now. Yet back in New Rochelle, Jane's sisters had urged him to leave her there, saying that the unknown wilds of Nova Scotia and the massing at Port Roseway of settlers, soldiers, sailors, labourers, adventurers, would be no place for a girl of twelve. Perhaps they'd been right; Mary would become a new American, enjoying a sheltered life with her mother's people, the Bonnets, in New Rochelle. Thankfully he had his five boys and Elizabeth with him now.

The remembrance of New Rochelle upset him as he had hated all his recent life in that town. He hated the political disputes and the Revolution that had followed.

He quickly put aside these thoughts and turned his eyes toward the low points of land they were nearing. Benjamin had seen them too, and was wagging chubby fingers at them.

Larboard stretched a spit of conifers and sand and Schurman wondered how far it might reach under water. Up to now he could see no hazards on his left. But granite ledges ran out from Janvrin Island on the opposite side, ugly rocks with vicious spume foaming over them. He recalled having seen these when he had gone through the Gut the previous year. He would steer clear as best he could and trust his ship and his family to the sand. He sent Peter forward to drop the dipsey lead.

Suddenly the wind shifted and a violent blast strained all his sails. The flying jibs rattled, the schooner shot forward, and he shouted to Bill to reef the topsails. The noise of the shrieking canvas and the hiss of the waves bursting along the gunnels terrified the children. Gathering them together Elizabeth and Sook got them to lie flat, then lay on top of them, holding on to each other. Schurman braced himself for he had never had much faith in his seamanship. The schooner might capsize or they could be blown against the Janvrin ledges. Yet he had one hope which Providence answered as this freak wind blew steady and never veered. Roaring from abaft, it pushed straight against the schooner's stern, and persisted only long enough to speed them past the entrance to Canso Gut into the narrow strait sheltered by hills and cliffs. Here the roaring sound faded, and here the family found a quiet haven for the night.

That evening, with the children and servants asleep below, Elizabeth and William huddled aft over a brazier of cinders. They had kindled a fire to make hot tea for all, and, as they finished the dregs, Elizabeth noticed how the wind sparked the cinders mottling her husband's face. She was amused; sometimes she saw him as a pirate, sometimes a satisfied Dutch patroon. She did not think he was either of these, perhaps a little of each, but a good deal of his own self.

He was not tall, but he had physical strength and a stolid form which he had inherited from his father Jacob, who had died in New Rochelle just before they had left.

Father Jacob had also passed on a determined streak of the autocratic patroon. This gratified Elizabeth; she acknowledged that in times like these a man could not rise far without decision and stubborn confidence, perhaps the best of Dutch qualities. And she appreciated his French side as well. His dark tanned face and his black eyes in the image of his mother, Jane Parcot, the energy and verve, the dreams — these attributes delighted her. The mix, she thought, made him special. Sometimes as he talked he wove French and Dutch idioms through an accented, amusing English. When he became excited he might say 'dis' and 'dat', 'ma foi' and 'verhip' all in one sentence. And that was when she liked him best. He often spoke French, for when he was growing up it was a common language in New Rochelle. She remembered how she had had to cope, because her parents, the Hyatts, had encouraged her to learn both languages.[1]

Now as they were committed to English and about to settle on an unknown island, Elizabeth sighed, but not unhappily. She picked up her mugs, William poured water over the cinders, and they went aft into their little cabin to sleep. They had come a long way; more significantly, they had made their own decision — a bold break with the past. With thousands of others they had been harassed and chased out of the new American Republic, had been forced to give up long loved homes, friends, lands, relatives and security, because they wanted to continue to live under the order and safety of British rule.

Still this decision had been a hard one for William. All of the Dutch Hugenot Schurmans had maintained an established way of life, and most of them had been prosperous for many years. Back in 1650 his ancestors had helped settle New Amsterdam, and later moved to nearby New Rochelle to join the French Hugenots there. In New Rochelle for over a century, they had continued to prosper at farming and trade. Before the Revolution William had been a merchant-farmer of means and property with five slaves, and, even when in his youthful twenties, ranked fourteenth among the 104 ratepayers in the town.

All this he had had to give up, and did. And because

he did, he and his family slept that night on a little coastal schooner in the empty Gut of Canso.[2]

When the thirteen colonies declared themselves independent of Great Britain, war became inevitable, and one third of the colonials faced seven years of bewildered anxiety. They were the Conservatives, the despised Tories, the Loyalists.

These Loyalists might have saved themselves, for they could have signed an oath of fidelity, but they would not. Many felt that to support the rebel cause would put them on the side of the losers as they expected Great Britain to win that war. But, as the conflict began to spread, they began to understand the terrible consequence of neutrality and indecision. 'As the times became more unsettled, as free speech was abolished, as mobbings and burnings, destruction and confiscation of property became common, the conservatives looked with horror on what might be in store for the colonies ... British tyranny plus British law and order began to seem preferable to turning fortunes and families over to mobs which stole and tarred and feathered'.[3]

William Schurman had tried to remain neutral. He despised mob rule but understood the ideals of the rebel leaders; he deplored England's autocracy but respected its benevolence. He had many friends among the New York City Tories, and in New Rochelle some 300 of his neighbours, including his brother Jacob, signed a protest against the Continental Congress. If he was ever to declare himself it would have to be soon. Dutch practicality and his brother, Jacob, kept prodding him to support England.

William made his choice on 16 November 1776. Jane, his first wife, had started the day by urging him to be careful; she was nervous and frightened, carrying the baby that would be little Jacob, the child whose birth would cause her death. She tried to restrain him but he and brother Jacob set off early on their horses, heading across the county towards the Hudson River. Along the way they were joined by neighbours and residents from nearby towns. The word had spread that Fort Washington,[4] between the Harlem and Hudson rivers, was under siege by General Howe; it might be the Rebels last stand. As they approached the Harlem they could hear gunfire, so they raced forward.

The Rebels had lined up infantry defence outside the fort, and, before the sun rose, Colonel Magaw, their commander, had demolished their bridge over the Harlem River to the fort. On the previous night, however, the British had secreted 30 flat boats on the Harlem and easily crossed. Soon they surrounded the fort and Howe called on Magaw to surrender. The offer was refused. The local townsmen, their thoughts with the hard-pressed soldiers, watched and waited silently. Suddenly they heard an explosion. The fort was being fired on from all sides. The rebel infantry stationed out front fled through the gates. Clouds of smoke billowed through the November air, the sound of musket fire cracked across the river. This deadly barrage continued for five hours until Magaw gave up and surrendered his entire garrison, nearly 3,000 men. It was 'the severest blow which the American arms had yet sustained'; it was to usher in a whole series of reverses and a winter of deepest gloom for Washington.[5]

William had no doubts now. He felt enough confidence that when the republican congress set up local committees to gather signatures of those sympathetic to their cause, he said openly that he would not sign. Brother Jacob said no, too. Both soon suffered a shock as the committee and many of their friends branded them traitors. This was a new and horrifying word to William. Jacob gave vent in a fiery reply, and continued to express his anger in public. The committee warned Jacob, and warned him again. Then Jacob was arrested, manacled and taken to a dungeon, his wife and children scattered, his farm, livestock, and his household goods confiscated. He spent the next two years in a succession of gaols and escaped only after the war had ended. His fate preyed on William's mind like a nightmare.[6]

The days grew worse when Jane died. Her sisters and their husbands offered little comfort, they were against him, they sided with Congress. Gratefully he accepted Elizabeth's understanding. During the next few years in New Rochelle he tolerated a strange existence. He could make no plans, see no future and even the news of the war killed his hopes. By 1780, when Benjamin was born, it was clear that Washington would win. Now he had five children to guide and shield — all born into a time of turmoil. Nightly he prayed they might live in a time of plenty. But he saw no hope, he could give them neither land nor money nor influence. His dream of establishing for them a benefic patroon estate had ended. Every day he was being pressured to leave the country for the safety of his wife and children.

Then he and Elizabeth made their decisive choice. They would leave their home and build another way of life. They moved into New York City to be among Tory friends, and there he learned about the Board of Associated Loyalists.[7]

By early 1782 England had abandoned — with the exception of New York City — all the posts she still held in the rebelling colonies. By April, England with a new ministry under Lord Rockingham was ready to discuss peace.

Sir Guy Carleton arrived in New York with orders to start negotiations. At once the Board of Loyalists besieged him with pleas to urge Congress to restore the property of the Loyalists who had not borne arms, and to urge Britain to grant land in Nova Scotia or Canada to those who had. William was not sure which way he qualified. He felt lost among the thousands of clamoring Loyalists who jammed the city. He wanted to get out, to get away, to emigrate quickly; yet, if there were a chance he might have his farm restored because he had not borne arms, perhaps he should stay. Elizabeth dissuaded him. Shrewdly she suggested that if the land was going to be reinstated he might find willing buyers in the persons of the husbands of Jane's two sisters still living in New Rochelle. Accordingly they took a day's walk to their old home.

The husbands considered William's offer with typical gravity. Elizabeth made an emotional point; the land should stay with the family and some of it had been Bonnet land. The sisters queried how much money William needed in order to start again. By midnight, as the candles gutted, they came to an agreement. William had met some Loyalists who were praising the advantages of the Island of St. John and proposed to charter a brig to go there to see what it was like. He wanted to join these men and needed passage money as a starter. If he liked what he saw he would take his family there. Sir Guy Carleton was already organizing a great exodus to a wilderness spot in Nova Scotia called Port Roseway. He understood that passage to Port Roseway would be free on government transports, but he also needed money to buy supplies and, if he could find one, a coastal schooner at Port Roseway. He could use the schooner to move his family to the island if he wanted to. The husbands admitted he had a reasonable scheme considering the times, and probably the best of the options available. They went to their coffers, gave him money and received their deeds. Then all said goodbye, knowing in their hearts that they would never meet again. Nor was William ever again to see his cherished Mary. Their parting was being repeated all over the Colonies by families doomed to separation.

In New York William hastened to arrange for his passage to the Island.[8] The passenger list included several families of refugee Loyalists who told him much more about the island than he had known before. He learned that some fifteen years before, England had introduced a form of feudalism there. William thought he would like that, provided he could accumulate enough land to become a feudal lord himself which was his dream. The island, he was told, was now split into sixty-seven lots of about 20,000 acres each. A brilliant surveyor, Captain Samuel Holland, did the job, and, to reward him, England deeded him Lot 28 on the south shore which was where their brig was headed. They would drop anchor at a village called Tryon on the edge of Lot 28.

William's expectations ran high, nor was he disappointed when he saw Tryon — a few boats, a wharf, and a cluster of log huts with small farms stretching back. They spent a few days there with a congenial host named

William Schurman

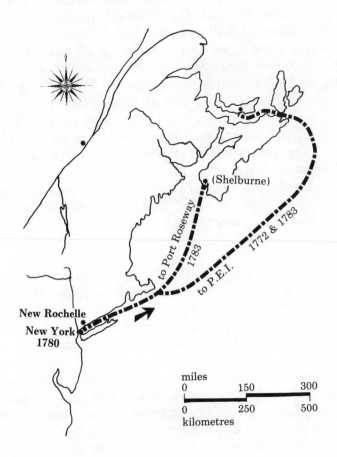

Warren who radiated the optimism he felt for the island's future and urged them to help settle the place. But William kept his plans to himself.

Back in New York he plunged into loyalist activities and made friends with the Port Roseway Associates. The exodus to Nova Scotia would soon begin. Sir Guy Carleton wanted Port Roseway to be 'a great and permanent establishment'. William had a feeling it might not be for him. Yet each day Elizabeth encouraged him. She thought that William, with his usual caution, was actually arranging for two destinies: if all went well, a new life in Port Roseway; if not, the prospects of Tryon. With his Dutch determination and his French *élan* she thought he'd succeed well enough in either place.

April of 1783 proved to be fine and sunny. Three thousand passengers and crew busily prepared for the event. Then, on the 27th, thirteen square-rigged ships and several sloops and schooners, accompanied by two ships of war, sailed out of the harbour.[9]. The Schurman family, with Sook and Bill, found themselves crowded into one of the smaller vessels.

The advance ships entered Roseway Bay on Sunday, 4 May, a week after they had left New York. The rest were safely moored in the bay's northeast harbour by the next evening. From on board, the refugees stared at their future home. Although some groups sent up weak cheers, most were unable to hide their dismay. They knew that Nova Scotia's Governor Parr had made plans in Halifax for the settlement, with streets fifty feet wide, but the plans must still be on paper. What streets? They saw nothing but rocks and acres of forest. On a nearby island were a few tents and log huts, while at the head of the harbour someone had erected a large army marquee. They were told this was the office of the governor's surveyors through whom they would obtain their properties. It appeared that the Surveyors, Messrs. Benjamin Marston and William Morris, had not yet got their bearings; they had arrived only just ahead of the refugees.

Three days went by while the surveyors, the army men, and the representatives of the Associates wrangled over where the town should be located. Following this, a thousand or more men 'began very cheerfully to cut down the trees — a new employment to many of them', so Marston wrote in his journal. William, indeed, cheerfully cut down trees; he was glad of the exercise. While Elizabeth stayed on board, Peter and Bill worked with him. As fast as they cut trees, surveyor Marston came with his compass, his measuring devices, his line poles, and his stakes to determine, so William thought, the dimensions of a man's life — to box him in and confine him to a small town site. William protested inwardly, seeing the streets crossing and re-crossing each other and later the frames of houses going up side by side. But hundreds of others worked in a kind of happy frenzy, exuberant that they were building something for themselves. At one time they may have been soldiers, seamen, farmers, lawyers, merchants, jewellers, potters, barbers, tailors, but now they hacked at trees, limbs, logs, forever cutting, sawing, carrying, heaving, digging. They argued and quarrelled, were impertinent and crude, but more often they sang and joked. This seemed to upset Benjamin Marston, but then Mr. Marston was a tensely worried man. He had never done any surveying before, and also he had the worry of making up tickets with which to draw the land lots.

The day came for the first lottery. William was among the 441 persons selected by the Association to have first chance. The honour brought him luck; he drew a fair-sized strip along the waterside. It was not much to look at, but as soon as he could, he put a tent on it, obtained provisions from the commissary, and moved his family in.[10]

A month after their arrival, the townspeople celebrated the King's birthday. In spite of a perilous fire a few weeks earlier, the celebrants lit a huge *feu de joie* at nightfall, danced and sang around it, let liquor flow, and continued dancing at a 'Ball'. William would not attend the ball, and Elizabeth was furious. She pushed back her hair, pulled out the clay pipe she always used when irritated, puffed at it, and glared at him. He explained that he did not want to stay in Port Roseway. She let down her hair. He had not spoken of this since they had come.

She waited, and intuitively she sensed another turning-point. He said he liked the excitement of building a new town, but he thought the place was already too crowded, with thousands more expected. He said he wanted room for his spirit and his energy. He had no use for a water-side lot, with scarcely enough earth to grow a garden.

Elizabeth said that what she wanted was a happier atmosphere in the town. She recalled how they had gone to the service given by the Methodist preacher, Reverend Black, outside one of the tents. They were shocked when ruffians attacked and blasphemed him.[11] Government support was restricted to the Established Churches of England and Scotland. Did they not know that Methodism had grown out of the Episcopal Church, and that already it was a source of comfort to many New Englanders, especially the Hugenots? She felt ashamed.

But she got to the next 'Ball' as William was unusually happy for that occasion. He had met two agents from the Island of St. John, and one was acquainted with his friend, William Warren, in Tryon. They told him that several of the proprietors of the sixty-seven island lots were now willing to let Loyalists settle one-quarter of their land, about 5,000 acres on each lot. They told William he might get as much as 500 'free' acres. He was elated but at the same time he was practical enough to inquire about the disposition of the other 15,000 acres on each lot. They said they thought some of it could be leased or even purchased, as nearly all the proprietors were living in England and were making little use of their holdings. William took a deep breath, he began to laugh, his eyes sparkled as his enthusiasm mounted. At last, here was his long dreamed chance to get more land, to build enterprises across the face of it to make more money to buy more land, to have acres and acres to leave to his family. He was so fired up he began to splutter in French, then shouted excitedly, 'Tell William Warren I'll be there!' A few nights later he was dancing with Elizabeth at the governor's ball.

On Wednesday evening the town gave a public supper and another ball, 'conducted with the greatest decorum', so it was reported. The supper and ball did not break up until five o'clock the next morning, so the decorum must have disintegrated. Noting this, William and Elizabeth returned to their tent at midnight, but they had had a great time. He had never seen Elizabeth so animated. She was small; he could not say she was *petite*; she was a bundle of strong muscles and vigour, dancing with spirit. In her happy moments her laughter was musical and her smile affectionate. He loved her heart-shaped face, and he thought her brown hair, which she rolled in a bun on top of her head, might grace a princess.

They lifted the tent flap. Elizabeth touched each of the four boys sleeping on their fir boughs, murmured to Sook cradling baby Caleb on a pallet, and turned to William with a grin. She had heard at the ball that the fresh water rationing had ended, so tomorrow she would make her scrub board rattle.

On the day Governor Parr was leaving, three transports arrived from New York with about ninety families.[12] William scowled when he saw them, then his face brightened. He had spotted two small schooners skimming past the larger vessels, and, as he watched them, he knew in his heart that either of these would be what he wanted to move his family to Tryon. The ceremony of the governor's departure seemed unending, but in time William acquainted himself with the two skippers. They were fishermen, natives of Marblehead. To his relief, one of the skippers jumped at the chance to trade his two-master for William's water lot and the hard cash William displayed.

That night at supper William happily announced the news. The boys and Sook wanted to start next day. Bill was not so sure; he had wanted to join the nearby black community of Birchtown, but he would make the trip to help Peter with the sails. Elizabeth cautioned patience; she said arrangements might take longer than they thought. As usual, her advice was wise; it took them a month before they sailed.

After the sharp gale that blew them into the Gut of Canso, the family blessed the little coastal schooner which had safely rocked them to sleep. In the morning they smiled as they looked up along the channel to see the distant gulf, and the blue waters that would carry them to Tryon. The wind favoured the day.

Once in view of Tryon they liked its modest log houses varnished golden by the setting sun. William Warren, on the wharf, caught their hawser and lashed it to a bollard. He had already started a home for them, even provided a thatched roof of seaweed. Compared to their tent in Shelburne, the cabin seemed a luxury. Elizabeth danced a jig, Peter climbed to the chimney, while William stared at the small farm lots running back from the houses. September was too late to farm. His immediate work would be with the schooner and helping Warren build a couple of fish houses he wanted. By spring he would have to move on. The land lots in Tryon were too small for him, and he would have outstayed his welcome.

Until Christmas, William made periodic runs to Charlottetown in his schooner, carrying his neighbours' fish and farm produce and bringing back supplies. In mid-winter he joined the other men in cutting and sawing pine logs into boards; these he hauled on handsleds over the ice along the 48 kilometre shore to the city. He exchanged them for food which was scarce. They were suffering a cold and difficult winter. At one time starvation threatened, and the children grew thin. Then spring came, and the island turned into lovely Abegweit, the Micmac name for a cradle in the waves, with all the warmth and hopes that a cradle means to a family. William dreamed of his land.

Yet no land was being offered free to an individual, as the agents had said it would be.[13] He talked to the government executive council in Charlottetown. They explained that Governor Patterson had in mind an immigration of many families to make up towns and area settlements. They suggested, for a start, that he return to Shelburne and bring back a dozen or so families, and every married man, including William, would receive 500 free acres and every single man 300 on Lot 19 owned by Governor Patterson himself. Unluckily William neglected to inquire if possession of these acres included possession of legal deeds — an oversight that took eighty-three years to rectify.

They continued to explain that the governor sought

prompt action. But this was something William could not offer. Already it was May, he had land to clear, seeds to plant, and a house to build. He had sailed up Bedeque Bay and found the site he wanted. It was at the mouth of the Dunk River, part of Lot 26.[14] The owner of this lot was Chief Justice Peter Stewart;[15] they could put him in touch with Stewart's agent at once. Meanwhile they asked when they could expect his return from Shelburne with the settlers. William answered he would be back by 1 August, and gave his word.

He could never say afterwards that the interview with Stewart's agent was satisfactory; he could not trust the man. But he came away with a signed paper stating that the agent on behalf of the proprietor agreed to sell to William Schurman, for fifty pounds, to be paid within ten years, a stipulated 350 acres on Lot 26 at the mouth of the Dunk River. William was well pleased. He thought this a propitious time to Anglicize his name. When he signed the paper he dropped the 'e' as his family surname had been Schureman.

It took only a day or so for the family to pack up, scrub the cabin, and thank William Warren for the use of it. During their short sail to Bedeque Bay the warm sun glowed over the headlands, and on their arrival they were again greeted with island hospitality, for Thomas Hooper of New Jersey, already settled by the river, came to clasp their hands and wish them well. William showed Hooper his deed and together they staked out a spot for his house. He would build a cabin like the one in Tryon, he and the older boys and Bill would sleep under the stars until the seaweed roof was in place, and meanwhile Elizabeth, Sook, and the two youngsters would share the Hooper home. When the house was finished, William cleared more land and planted what he could so late in the season. By then he had persuaded Thomas Hooper to sail with him on the Shelburne enterprise.

They arrived back in Shelburne early in July, and William found that after less than a year the town now boomed with nearly 10,000 people, over a thousand buildings,[16] and a harbour packed with ships. Yet there must be families who were sick of the crowded conditions. Accommodated at McGragh's tavern, he and Tom

Hooper spent a fortnight searching them out. In all, they persuaded eight families and seven single people to leave. To these they added ten disbanded soldiers, some with families,[17] for the soldiers were dissatisfied and had begun to riot.[18] It was not difficult to charter ships for transportation and William took one family along with him in his schooner. On 29 July, two days before William had promised he would have them there, representatives of the new settlers stood before the executive council in Charlottetown to receive their grants on Governor Patterson's Lot 19. A few of the lucky ones got land adjacent to Malpeque Bay. William had no firm plans for his own reward of 500 acres in Lot 19 other than lumbering; he would reserve them for his sons.

He continued to arrange for settlers arriving from Shelburne,[19] he kept busy using his ship as a trading schooner, he opened a store in his house with Elizabeth's help, he built and equipped a sawmill and a grist mill on the Dunk River, and he took on any job offered by his neighbours. He had a cash box and he wanted to see the money in it grow. In November he helped William Warren shingle his fish store and net shop, carefully recording in his account book that Warren had paid him nine shillings for three days work, one pound seventeen shillings 'to make in two thousand shingles', thirteen shillings 'to fore days work', and six shillings 'to one pair of shues'.[20] Through the year both William and Peter worked at lumbering, coopering, blacksmithing, harvesting, building a bridge — all for a princely three shillings a day for William and less than one shilling for Peter. But the cash box weighed heavier. That summer Elizabeth gave birth to her first daughter who was named Jane.

Much to William's surprise, 150 of his neighbours elected him to the Legislative Assembly in 1785. In politics, however, he found himself up against greed, craftiness, and inflexible controls. The Assembly was 'a mere debating chamber'; the Council, with the sanction of the Crown, had sole power. The Council also opposed the Governor. Patterson was replaced by Fanning, who proved to be worse, dictating in true feudal fashion, as if the island were his own private domain.[21] William was disgusted and he would not run again. The Council, still seeking his support, appointed him road overseer, justice of the peace, and then magistrate in his district. These functions he performed well, but he had no interest in mixing with people who had acquired status and profit by obstructing needed legislation even to the extent of falsifying documents and destroying records.[22]

He had always tried to maintain what he thought was right. Along with this went his sense of guided destiny and the fitness of Christian living. Both he and Elizabeth were Presbyterian but were also interested in Methodism. In 1792 Benjamin Chappell, an impoverished carpenter,[23] helped to promote a great Methodist revival on the island as a memorial to his revered John Wesley who had died the year before. A large group of settlers from Lot 19 and the Bedeque area attended.[24] Nathaniel Wright and his family, whom William had brought from Shelburne, went along with the Schurmans. The Wrights became zealous converts and later built an active Methodist community in the Bedeque area.[25]

While she was at the revival, Elizabeth had left her children to Sook's good care. On her return, she was anxious to see them, but she tarried a moment outside her cabin door to let a rare flood of sentiment take over. She thought: I have been away for the first time; I am back at home now. These are the walls that have enclosed my family for eight years. The bark peels from the logs, the moss from the chinks, the thatch has moulded, but this is our home. I love it, she murmured to herself — the curtains, the mats, the children's beds and bunks, the pots and pans, the water pail, the crane in the fireplace.

The crane in the fireplace reminded her of the wild partridges which the Wrights had given her. She must make a stew of them in the iron pot that hung from the crane. She went inside and added wood to the fire. William, working on his account book, cautioned her. But she wanted a quick fire so she threw on chips and bark as well.

The fireplace flamed, the chimney roared with flame, exploding sparks flamed against her curtains. She screamed to Sook to find the children, and to the boys to save themselves. By now William, with cash box and day book under his arm, had her by the elbow, and together they ran from the inferno. Mutely they all watched as their home collapsed into a mass of fiery embers. One by one they knelt outside and mourned. The cabin had burned in a tragic few moments — such a few short moments.

The cabin could be replaced, but the loss brought further misfortune. William had decided not to rebuild until he had complete ownership of the land which the new house would stand on. Stewart's agent had given him ten years to pay fifty pounds for the 350 acres. The agreement burned in the fire, but William had saved his cash box, and with some confidence he sailed to Charlottetown. The agent received him cordially. He consoled William on the loss of his home. He glazed his eyes when William recounted the loss of the agreement. Coolly he then denied that there had ever been such an agreement. William was astounded. The agent searched his file drawers. He found no copy, he said. Should Mr. Schurman care to pay rent, as did all the other settlers on Lot 26, the agent could quote him eight pence per acre per year. William had no choice. He considered Lot 19 and his 500 acres there, but as yet he had no clear title to these either. He accepted, and continued to pay about ten pounds a year for the rest of his life on land that he could never own. Disillusioned, he commenced work on the new house.

It would be a frame house and larger, with an added ell to accommodate the store. He selected a site nearer to his wharf. He would extend his shipping trade, buy a larger schooner, ship lumber across the gulf to New Brunswick, raise cattle and oxen, buy horses for himself and Elizabeth, but he would no longer cultivate the land.

He became prominent among his neighbours as an imaginative, industrious friend who took on many community responsibilities, yet his great service to all was to open his large store in the ell. At heart a keen merchant, eager to build business, he relished the store and kept a meticulous day book accounting for all his transactions.

The Schurman store, the first in Bedeque, offered hundreds of articles and services the variety of which William proudly recorded in detail, often in his unique spelling! If one walked into the Schurman store, one could find, for example, spices, molasses, rum, applejack, 'hare riben', sail cloth, rope, pitch, potatoes, grain, flax, meat, salt, sugar, tea, tobacco, clay pipes, fine combs, leather soles, tanned hides, pelts, writing paper, ink powder, 'fidel strings', bar iron, nails, tools, lumber, shingles, yard goods, needles, thread, buttons, mittens, 'sope', nutmegs, pails, 'sno shues', moccasins, ladies slippers, clothing, hats, 'gaus for muskeeta net', chinawear, cutlery, wooden noggins, 'blew indigo', powder and shot, chairs, glass, hinges, locks, and the Bible.[26]

Just when he was most needed, old Bill, perhaps resenting having to help build a house at his age, asked to be released, and William took him to Charlottetown to find passage to Shelburne where he wanted to go. The ancient Black man had been part of the family for nearly twenty years; they were sorry to see him leave. But the work got done, the boys were older and the neighbours helped.

Now, at age 50, William moved his family in, relieved to have made a successful start again. Marking the occasion, Elizabeth named her new baby son after him and the next year, William named their next baby, a daughter, after Elizabeth. In 1796 the census listed 12 in the Schurman family, which still included Sook. At that time, now in her early forties, Elizabeth was carrying John, their last child.[27]

Settled comfortably in the new house, William found time for his duties as road overseer, laying out the first road between Bedeque and Charlottetown. And he bought a new vessel, a 23 and 1/2 ton schooner, which he christened *Mary* after his daughter in New Rochelle. The schooner soon began to be profitable. This income was needed, as Peter had married and the ship would have to help support two families.

The *Mary* took a crew of five, one of whom was Benjamin. Now a young man, Benjamin remembered all he had learned about handling ships from brother Peter and old Bill. He was Elizabeth's first child, only 18 when he signed on. He was 19 when the *Mary* sank off New Brunswick in a storm and Benjamin, with all on board, drowned. His body was never recovered. Neither William nor Elizabeth ever got over the solitary death in their family.

William gave up coastal trading and passed the business over to his older boys; he had no heart for it now. He set himself to recover the financial loss of the *Mary* and turned to shipbuilding. The industry was just getting started on the Island, and, when trading goods or selling produce in Charlottetown, from 1800 onwards, he had often chatted with John Cambridge, the Island's most prominent shipbuilder. He learned that many men were entering the business, expanding from the smaller ships they had always built. As a shipbuilder he saw that he could make good use of his own resources: his acres of timber, his sawmills, and nearly everything else he might need was already in his own store. By 1801 his first ship was ready.

All the Schurmans had worked on it, even Elizabeth at times, so the launching became a celebration. Sook and Elizabeth had cooked trenchers of food. The young girls carried these outside to offer to the crowd gathered by the river. Small boys paraded with tankards, mugs, noggins of spruce beer or apple cider. Everybody expressed their admiration for the schooner, *Lively*. The name *Lively* was William's choice. Secretly it did not satisfy him (too common a name, he thought) but the men with the wooden mauls were standing ready. William, on the deck with Peter and Isaac, and with Jacob clinging to the gunnels, gave the order to knock out the wedges. As the keel groaned against the soaped ways, the shouting and whistling commenced, and Sook ran forward just in time to see the prow leave the cradle and skim into the water. She clapped her hands, enchanted by the ship's smooth slide, calling out, repeating a phrase she had heard: 'Oh, how she scoons like a schooner should. She's lovely, Mistah Schurman, lovely!' William's eyes danced. 'The *Lovely* she'll be! Dat's good for you, Sook!' he shouted back. 'You've christened her'. Sook burst into delighted laughter, clasping her old hands to the skies, and the crowd laughed with her as they raised their drinks.

The success of building the *Lovely*, which he sold to a buyer from Newfoundland, excited William enough to build yet a larger vessel and two years later he launched the 168 ton *William*, and three years later the 65 ton *Sally*.

By 1806, he was 63 years old but far from retiring, still his active mind was on land, on getting more land. In 1800 the executive council, 16 years late, had finally granted him full title to his 500 acres in Governor Patterson's Lot 19, the reward for his Shelburne enterprise. But he was not satisfied. Lot 25 stood in his way; it blocked passage between his original rented 350 acres in Lot 26 and his new land in Lot 19. He yearned to own some of this intervening land, and by good luck it became available; one of the owners died and his son was willing to sell. William had profitted well from selling his three ships and he paid £800, a fortune then, for half of Lot 25 — some 6,500 acres. The new property stretched sixteen kilometres around Bedeque Bay, heavy timber land with rich soil, a river, and a perfect valley for his sons to cultivate and to live in. Almost at once he built a dam and a large new sawmill which flourished. William had so much timber it was said that 'when a ship arrived without notice for a load of timber, a crew of men could be assembled to cut down, saw and load it in one day'.[28]

Work at the mill was now his chief interest. He found the long ride from his home both tedious and demanding, so, with his customary verve, he quickly settled the problem. At age 66 he deeded his old homestead in Central Bedeque to Peter and built a new house near the sawmill for Elizabeth, the younger ones, and himself. He lived in the new house until his death ten years later.

The last years were good years. He continued as a respected magistrate and counsellor, 'a man of substance, entrusted to dispense justice in his home and in the court at St. Eleanor's'. He owned well over 7,000 acres of land, two sawmills, his prosperous store, his grist mill, his farm, an interest in his sons' shipping, and a thriving lumber business. All of this he had accomplished after having made a complete new start at the age of 40. His children married and most of them developed the Schurman land. William could sit by his fireside and think leniently about the patroons he had once fancifully admired. The Dutch patroons were proprietors of family tracts of land; they were also magistrates, and protectors. He hoped he had done all this, protecting his family as well, guiding them and starting them on their own. The Wilmot river, the Wilmot valley, the Dunk river, the Bedeque shore, and the Schurman name became inseparable. He was satisfied, now content and happy. He died peacefully at age 76. He was buried 'near the church' as he had requested. Many persons faced with the displacements of William's time needed courage and endurance, but William had imagination, resourcefulness, and strength as well.

The *Prince Edward Island Gazette*, in its 23 September 1819 obituary, noted William Schurman's 'vigorous activity of mind . . . purity of intention . . . and sound judgment', and further commented that his family and numerous 'attached neighbours'must ever retain 'an affectionate and grateful remembrance of the virtues of a good father and a staunch understanding friend'. To his memory 'his wife and sons gave him a marble stone with the most charmingly-worded epitaph in North Bedque cemetery':[29]

> In this place
> Are interred the remains
> of
> WILLIAM SCHURMAN
> Undeviating
> In honesty and sincerity
> Faithful as a Magistrate
> Affectionate as a Husband
> and Father
> Kind as a friend
> Through life
> He exchanged it for Eternity
> on the 15th day of Sept. 1819
> aged 76 years.

In his will, William bequeathed land to each of his children, and one third of his estate to Elizabeth 'as long as she remains my widow'. He provided for 'my Negro Servant, Susannah', and requested that all cattle be sold 'excepting two pair of good oxen for the use of the saw mill and one good horse for the use of my wife'. Peter, Isaac, and William were appointed executors. John his youngest child, now 23 years old, inherited the house. Five years later, when John elected to try his fortune in Nova Scotia, the executors sold the house, the mill, and the Lot 25 property to William Clark of Bedeque. Elizabeth went to live with some of her children — apparently happily, for she lived another 24 years to the good age of 90.

But Peter, the eldest, outlived them all to the age of 98. In 1866, two years before his death, Peter had the ironic satisfaction of receiving full title to William's initial 350 acres on Lot 26. The yearly rental fee ceased at last. He must have chuckled but perhaps without much mirth, for it had taken the government 83 years to recommend 'free grants to those loyalist descendants who can prove that their fathers had been lured to the Island under false promises'.[30]

Some of the Schurman descendants returned to the United States, perhaps the most notable being William's great grandson, Jacob Gould Schurman, President of Cornell University for 28 years, who also headed numerous U.S. government commissions throughout Europe and Asia, including a valued 1899 study of social and political conditions in America's newly acquired Philippines. Many descendants still live today on the old farms in the Bedeque and Wilmot regions. In 1896 Maynard Freeman Schurman and his wife Sarah formed the M.S. Schurman Company. This building firm, today, with head office in Summerside has expanded and serves the people of the three Maritime Provinces.[31]

In 1939 George Artemas Leard, an Island historian researching the Schurman Day Book, wrote the following attractive tribute: For 35 years William Schurman

> had known the clink of Spanish dollars on his counter, the feel of the adze biting into virgin pine, the ring of the hammer on the anvil, the sound of flails on the barn floor, the thump of looms and the hum of spinning wheels in his house, the plodding patience of his oxen ploughing in April, the swish of the scythes on the marsh in August, and the everchanging beauty of na-

ture reflected in the Dunk. But now he was gone from all this, gone from his mill, his forge, his store, his farm, to see the final reckoning of his accounts in a Day-Book kept even more accurately than he had kept his.[32]

1. It is clear from Schurman's Day Book of Accounts that, while he had no desire or perhaps time to learn correct spelling, he seemed to delight in having fun with phonetic spelling. No doubt his lively sense of humor extended as well to his amusement with Dutch-French-English speech mixtures.
2. No document has turned up so far with any description of the voyage from Shelburne to Prince Edward Island, nor of the family other than their names and ages.
3. James Truslow Adams, *The Epic of America*, Boston: Little, Brown, 1931, p. 92.
4. Fort Washington was near what is now New York City's 178th. Street entrance to the George Washington Bridge crossing to Fort Lee and Hackensack.
5. Jared Sparks, *The Life of George Washington*, (Boston: Tappan and Dennet, 1839), p. 199.
6. Jacob ultimately arrived with Loyalists in Saint John, New Brunswick.
7. Again there is a scarcity of documentation on Schurman's life in New Rochelle, his attitudes and business affairs. The harassment of brother Jacob and the pro-revolution attitudes of Jane's sisters through their husbands are recorded by Ross Graves in *William Schurman, Loyalist of Bedeque, Prince Edward Island.* (Summerside, P.E.I. Harold B. Schurman, 1973).
8. It is not known for certain that Schurman made this preliminary trip, but he must have had friends at Tryon who helped him when he and his family arrived there the next year. For Holland's map with the 67 lots delineated see p. 31 of Errol Sharpe, *A People's History of Prince Edward Island,* (Toronto: Steel Rail Publishing, 1976).
9. Mary Archibald, *Gideon White, Loyalist*, (Shelburne, N.S.: Shelburne Historical Society, 1975), p. 8.
10. We have no documented account of Schurman's activities while he was in Shelburne. It is thought that after a few months there he left late in that summer (1783) or early fall.
11. Recounted in a footnote by W.O. Raymond, 'The Founding of Shelburne, Benjamin Marston at Halifax, Shelburne and Miramichi', *Collections of the New Brunswick Historical Society,* (St. John, New Brunswick: 1909), Vol. 8, p. 219.
12. Raymond, p. 225, Marston's entry dated 30 July 1783.
13. Enticements to settle in Price Edward Island were in the form of proclamations from Governor Patterson and his agents, displayed or published. As example, from the *New York Gazette*: 'We, the subscribers (your countrymen and fellow sufferers) . . . think it is our duty to point out to you as the most eligible country for you to repair to of any we know between this and New Jersey. The soil is good, it is well wooded and free from rocks. The climate is so good that fevers and agues are unknown . . . The government is mild. But very few taxes: these are very light and raised solely for the benefit of the Island. There is room for tens of thousands, but the lands in the finest situations, on harbours, navigable rivers and bays to be had exceedingly reasonable'.
In October, 1783, a proclamation in Shelburne read in part: '(Future settlers) shall be put in possession of such lands as they shall be entitled to, free from every expense'.
14. Graves, p. 45.

15. Sharpe, p. 236.

16. Raymond, p. 259 — Marston's reckoning.

17. It is thought that Schurman arranged several trips to find settlers in Shelburne willing to go to Bedeque, the first group arriving 26 July 1784, according to George A. Leard's *Historic Bedeque*, published by Bedeque United Church, 1948, amended 1973.

A list of the first Loyalists who left Shelburne for Bedeque follows: (obtained from the United Empire Loyalists' Association of Canada, 23 Prince Arthur Avenue, Toronto, Ontario M5R 1B2.)

Families
1. William Wright
2. John McDonald
3. Jacob Silliker (& his wife, Mary Strang)
4. Nathaniel Wetherell
5. John Murray
6. David Stags
7. Sarah Palmer
8. William Stairman

Single People
1. Robert Hancock
2. Lawrence Berry
3. John Murray
4. Andrew Eastman
5. James Wharf (Waugh?)
6. Jesse Strang
7. Nathaniel Wright

Disbanded Soldiers
1. George Malby (Mabey?) and wife
2. Richard Moorfield and wife
3. John Shilfox
4. Dudley Wells
5. Thomas Gould
6. John Chambers
7. William Sauchaback (Sencabaugh?)
8. Richard Price
9. Joseph Wood
10. Richard Garrett

Total: 25. Wilbur H. Siebert and Florence E. Gilliam, 'The Loyalists in Prince Edward Island', *Royal Society of Canada Transactions*, 3rd series, IV, section II, (Toronto, 1910) on page 111 gives 27 as the count.

18. See Raymond, p. 265, Marston's entry, 26 July, for the culmination of the riots, leading to Marston's dismissal and the beginning of the tragic remainder of his life.

19. Siebert & Gilliam, p. 111, note that after the July arrivals 26 more men with families came from Shelburne on 13 September and 55 on 19 September and 12 on 25 September. Many of these settled on Lot 19 near Schurman's land.

20. Graves, p. 25, from Schurman's Day Book of Accounts.

21. Sharpe, p. 49-53.

22. Siebert & Gilliam, p. 114.

23. Harry Baglole and Ron Irving, *The Chappell Diary*, a Play, p. 56, denote Chappell as 'the founder of Methodism on the Island'. Chappell had come to the island 18 years before in 1774, indentured to the Quaker visionary Robert Clark whose proposed great city of New London near Malpeque, which he intended as 'a place for recovering sinners' failed. See *The Chappell Diary*, (Belfast, P.E.I., Ragweed Press, 1977).

24. Siebert & Gilliam, p. 117.

25. *Ibid.*, p. 117.

26. The Schurman Day Book of Accounts (in private possession) has been researched by George Artemas Leard and selections with Leard's comments have been published as a series in *The Charlottetown Guardian*, 27 November to 16 December, 1939, under the newspaper's title 'Shop Keeping in Pioneer Days', although Leard preferred his own title, 'Rum and Ribbons' by E.S.D., being the last initials of his real name. (Information from Mrs. Doris Haslam of Springfield, P.E.I.).

27. As recorded by Graves, a list of the eleven Schurman children with dates of birth:
By Jane Bonnet — Peter (1769), Mary (1771), Isaac (1774), Jacob (1777).
By Elizabeth Hyatt — Benjamin (1780), Caleb (1782), Jane (1785), Sarah (1788), William (1793), Elizabeth (1794), John (1796), the last five born in Prince Edward Island.

28. Judy Boss (Boudewyn), *William Schurman*, a monograph in a leaflet series, *United Empire Loyalists*, edited by Mary Archibald, (Toronto: Dundurn Press, 1978).

29. Leard, 'Shop Keeping in Pioneer Days'.

30. Boss, *Schurman*.

31. Graves, p. 39. Schurman today is still pronounced with a 'k'.

32. Leard, 'Shop Keeping in Pioneer Days'.

Sir John Johnson in 1772 at Johnstown

Chapter 8

Sir John Johnson

Knight of the Revolution

by Mary Archibald

Sir John Johnson, son of Sir William Johnson, was in charge of Johnson Hall and responsible for many of the tenants in the Mohawk Valley. Eventually forced to flee, he formed a military company of his Scots tenants and Indian allies, leading raids against the forces of the Continental Congress. He and his 'Royal Yorkers' were some of the earliest settlers of what became Upper Canada (Ontario). Sir John Johnson struggled for years to win the same rights of land holding and government for the Loyalists which they had been accustomed to in the older British colonies. Thus he can be partially credited with the creation of the province of Ontario.

Johnson Hall stood quiet in the October noon-day. The whole Mohawk Valley seemed breathless, as if every living thing in the Valley was being drawn to the edge of a deep chasm by forces they did not understand and could not control.

Lady Johnson (Polly) sat in the parlor of Johnson Hall, watching her husband who stood looking out over the Valley. At his side, he held the letter that had come that morning from the Committee of Safety of Tryon County. Sir John had read her the letter.

The members of the committee wanted to know why Sir John's tenants were not joining the Rebels. They instructed Sir John to turn over to them the Gaol and Courthouse at Johnstown.[1] They demanded that Sir John himself sign the American Association, passed by the First Continental Congress which had met the previous year, 1774, at Philadelphia. The Association bound all who signed not to trade with Great Britain or buy British goods until England had changed her colonial trade and taxation policies.

As Lady Johnson watched, her husband lifted his head, squared his shoulders and turning from the window crossed the room to the table standing against the far wall. He sat down and wrote his answer. After he had closed the letter, he lighted the wax and watched the drops fall on the paper. When he had stamped his seal on the fold, he got up and went to the doorway where the servant stood waiting: 'Take this letter to the Committee of Safety. Tell them that I, Sir John Johnson, sent it'.

He stood in the doorway until Long, the servant, had mounted his horse and rode out of sight. Then he turned to his wife: 'I told them', he said, 'I told them that I had never forbidden my tenants to form companies. I told them that before I would turn over the Gaol and Courthouse, they would have to pay me the 700 pounds the buildings cost my father. And I told them that before I would sign any association or lift my hand against my King, I would rather that my head should be cut off'.[2]

He stood a moment, looking at Lady Johnson almost as if she were the enemy. Then he turned on his heel, walked through the doorway leading to the courtyard, and stood looking out to the forests that banked the view as far as the horizon. As he looked at the surroundings, every tree, every trunk and branch, every red and yellow leaf became etched on his memory.

In his mind's eye, he could see his father standing where he was now standing; he could see his father greeting neighbours from the Province of New York, greeting representatives of the British Government. He could see his father preparing to meet with the Indians and use all his persuasions to hold the Indians firm in their allegiance to the British Empire. Would all of his father's efforts be lost? Would there be a British Empire in America?

William Johnson, Sir John's father, had been a powerful man. He was an Irishman, the nephew of Admiral Peter Warren, one of the most able British sailors of the eighteenth century.[3] Peter Warren was also an astute business man, and by 1738 had accumulated so much property in America that he sent his nephew, William Johnson, to administer his estates in the Province of New York. William took up his headquarters at Amsterdam on the Mohawk River, about forty miles from Albany, the capital. Sir John's mother was Catherine Weissenburg, whose background can best be understood from reading this advertisement which appeared in *Zenger's New York Weekly Journal*, 22 January 1738-39:

> Run away from Capt. Langden of the City of New York a Servant Maid, named Catherine Weissenburg, about 17 years of Age — middle stature — Slender, black ey'd brown complexion speaks good English Altho a Palatine born — had on when she went away a homespun striped waistcoat and Peticoat, blew stockings and New Shoes and with her a Calico Wrapper, and a striped Calamanco Wraper, besides other cloaths whoever takes her up and again shall have Twenty Shillings Reward, and all reasonable Charges; and all Persons are forewarned not to entertain the said Servant at their Peril.

Because Catherine could 'speak good English' she probably had spent some time in England after fleeing religious persecution in the German Palatinate. From the advertisement it is clear that she had found other kinds of persecution across the sea in America. William Johnson found Catherine, gave her shelter and 'entertained her' until her death in 1759. They had three children. Ann, the eldest married Daniel Claus. Then there was John and then Mary, who became the wife of Guy Johnson, William's nephew who became his secretary.

Sir John Johnson was described by Lord Dalhousie, who recorded in his *Journals*[4] that he met him when Sir John was 77 years old, as a 'very tall gaunt looking old man, very lively in countenance and speaks rapidly. Very gentlemanlike manner and with all that a kind of wildness, as if he wished to appear a character tinctured with the intercourse he had had with the Indian tribes'.

All of Sir John's life was intertwined with the Indians. In 1755, when Sir John was only thirteen years old, he and Joseph Brant, who would become a leader of the Six Nation Indians, went along with the other men from the colonies who defeated the French and their Indian allies at Lake George, on 8 September. For his leadership in that campaign William Johnson was created baronet, received £5,000 and the promise that his eldest son would be knighted when he reached the age of 21. In 1760, when he was eighteen years old, son John was commissioned a captain in the Albany County militia, and in 1761 visited Niagara and Detroit with his father. During Pontiac's uprising, John Johnson was in charge of a group of rangers and Indians on an expedition into Indian country.[5]

John Johnson's formal education started in 1757 when he was sent to the Academy at Philadelphia. He stayed for three years, but it was not until 1765, when he was 23, that his father sent him to England. There are two possible reasons for the delay. First, he may not have wanted to go. John Johnson loved the Mohawk Valley and the people who lived there. In December, 1765, after he reached London, he wrote Daniel Claus, his brother-in-law: '. . . you can't imagine the grief I was in at leaving home parting with all I esteemed dear to me in this world . . .'[6] The second reason may have been Sir William's concern for the Indians. From the cessation of hostilities at the end of the French and Indian War — as the Seven Years' War was called in America — until his death in 1774, Sir William spent most of his waking hours trying to pacify the Indians.

After the Peace of Paris of 1763, Sir William and his assistant, George Croghan, tried to tell General Amherst of the importance of following the precedent of the French who had granted hospitality to the Indians at the forts, had given them presents and had seen that the Indians had an adequate supply of ammunition. As soon as possible Sir William favoured reopening the fur trade. However, Amherst and the other British officers followed no such advice and in the fall of 1763 Pontiac, who had become extremely anti-British because of the English and colonial policies, 'provided the force which touched off the violence which spread from Detroit in every direction'.

Whatever the reason for the delay, the 1765 visit of Lord Adam Gordon, the British member of Parliament, and his wife, Lady Gordon and the Scottish actor William O'Brien to Johnson Hall convinced Sir William to send his son John to receive his title at the court of George III of England.

There were three other purposes to John Johnson's mission to England in 1765. He was to press the King to make legal a grant of 80,000 acres along the Mohawk River given Sir William by the Mohawk Indians. He was to ask for a clergyman for Sir William's new church at Johnstown and he was to seek a wife suitable for the station in society his father wanted for his son. Sir William went as far as Albany with the travellers, but was not able to continue to New York City because of the 'possible arrival of Mr. Croghan who will be probably accompanied by Pondiac (sic) and some Western Indians'.[7]

John stayed in England for two years. He received his title, but was unsuccessful in securing the King's approval for his father's 80,000 acre grant, or for a minister for the new church at Johnstown. That he did not bring home a wife from England may well have been due to the advice given by George Croghan who wrote Sir John:

> You will See Some of the finest Women in the World in London you will be held up to them for one of the Greatest fortunes in a Marriage and No Doubt Many young Ladys will Spread their Netts to Catch you My Dear Sir BeWair of their wilds . . . they will make the worst Wife in Ye World for an American Gentleman . . . [8]

Shortly after he returned from England in 1767, Sir John showed he had his own ideas about a suitable wife for an American Gentleman!

In *Clarissa Putman of Tribes Hill*, John J. Vroom tells the romantic story of the love and common-law marriage between Sir John and Clarissa Putman, the lovely blond maiden who lived in the Mohawk Valley about three miles from Fort Johnson. She won Sir John's love, but could not satisfy Sir William's standards as a suitable mother for his grandchildren. Sir John and Clarissa lived at Fort Johnson for several years and had two children, William and Margaret. Although later Sir John did make a marriage that suited his father, and became the father of fourteen 'legitimate' children, he made arrangements through his agent, Daniel Campbell of Schenectady for the support of his 'first' family.[9] He and Clarissa remained in touch with each other till his death in 1830.

In 1771 and 1772 Sir John spent some time in New York City and by 1773 had met Mary Watts, the daughter of the Honourable John Watts, President of the Council of New York. They were married 30 June 1773. Sir John and Lady Johnson, (Polly, as she was known to her friends), moved to Fort Johnson and made their home there until Sir William died 11 July 1774. Sir William's death was a terrible loss to the whole Valley.

As well as being the champion of Indian rights, Sir William had encouraged many Highland Scots to settle on his estates near Johnstown. Some of them had taken part in the 1745 Rebellion but had become reconciled, taken the oath of loyalty, and at the outbreak of the American Revolution were strong supporters of the British Crown. There were also other minorities in the Valley. Huguenots had found refuge along the Hudson River, and in 1710, while visiting England, Saga Yean Qua Prab Ton, the Mohawk Chieftain whose granddaughter, Molly Brant, became Sir John's stepmother, invited refugees from the Palatinate, who were finding a temporary refuge in London, to come to the Mohawk Valley. Over this community of minorities Sir William had presided as if he were a feudal chieftain. After his father's death, Sir John turned down the offer of the position of Superintendent of Indian Affairs and moved to Johnson Hall and assumed the responsibility for his father's tenants.

The next year would prove most unsettling to his peace of mind. With growing anxiety he heard of the troubles in Massachusetts and in the spring of 1775, the Claus and Guy Johnson families, along with John Butler, who later raised a regiment of rangers, and Joseph Brant and a large group of Loyalists left the Mohawk

Valley for Canada. Mary, Sir John's sister, far advanced in her pregnancy, died in childbirth at Oswego.

Sir John was firm in his decision to stay at Johnson Hall as he loved his valley. Polly, his wife since 1773, was pregnant [10] and Sir John keenly felt his responsibility to the settlers of the area who were being coerced into signing the American Association as an expression of their willingness to support the Rebels. In August Sir John assembled 'some 400 armed supporters to protect Sheriff Alexander White from an angry mob of Patriots'. Later, when the sheriff had fled, Sir John met with some of the rebel committee and an uneasy peace was temporarily restored.

The Rebels did not take kindly to the leadership at Johnson Hall. On 27 October 1775, a letter had been sent by the Committee of Safety of Tryon County to the Sachems of Canajoharie Castle (the Mohawk Village near Johnson Hall) telling the leaders that the Indians who had gone to Canada must return.[11] The Committee also wrote Sir John insisting he turn over the Gaol and Courthouse at Johnstown and demanding that Sir John join the American Association. In spite of his desperate attempts to retain command of the situation, Sir John saw that events were moving beyond his control. Some of his tenants wrote him confiding that they had been obliged to 'unite', otherwise they 'could not live there'. The Canajoharie and German Flatts people wrote that 'they had been forced to sign'.

Realizing that people throughout the Valley were being intimidated, in December Sir John sent Allan Macdonnel of Collachie to New York with a letter for Governor Tryon, telling the governor he had resolved to form a battalion and had named all the officers, but could not stir without support and supplies. Evidently Sir John received neither. On 20 January 1776, General Phillip Schuyler marched on Johnson Hall and compelled between 200 and 300 Scottish Highlanders to parade in Johnstown and turn in their arms. Six of them were taken as prisoners to be held as hostages for Sir John's promise that he would not try to escape to Canada.

Strangely enough, it was the threat of a British invasion down the Hudson River that forced Sir John to leave Johnson Hall. After Guy Carleton's forces had held off the rebel attempt to take Quebec City, and British reinforcements had arrived in the St. Lawrence River, the Rebels feared an advance by the British down the Hudson. General Schuyler knew full well that such an advance would be joined by Sir John and his followers and on 14 May 1776, he wrote Colonel Dayton from Saratoga ordering the colonel to proceed to Johnstown with his regiment and remove the Highlanders and arrest Sir John.[12]

Colonel Dayton tried to follow the orders, but Molly Brant, who was living with her family at Fort Johnson, heard of the advance of the Rebels and warned Sir John. He gathered the followers he could, and when he saw Colonel Dayton and his men approaching, started his flight to Canada. His group included 130 Highlanders and 120 others with three Mohawk guides. Colonel Dayton followed them, but a group of Indian warriors carrying arms and wearing war-paint, paraded in front of their tents, 'delaying their pursuit'.[13]

With insufficient food, the plight of Sir John and his followers was desperate. Montreal and the forts along the Richelieu and Lake Champlain were all occupied by remnants of the Revolutionary Army. A large British force under General Carleton was said to be on its way up the St. Lawrence and there was a small British post at Oswegatchie (now Ogdensburg) but weeks of hard travel through an unmapped wilderness lay ahead.

After ten days of pushing through that wilderness, their food ran out and a number of the party gave up and went back to Johnstown. About 7 June, 19 days after they had fled from Johnson Hall, 170 weary refugees reached St. Regis (Cornwall, Ontario).

Sir John and his party were welcomed. In 1760 Sir William had visited the Indian village and had treated the people well. While Sir John and his party were pushing through the Adirondack Mountains from Johnstown, the St. Regis Indians, with Captain Forster and the 8th Regiment, had engaged and defeated the enemy. The victory at the Battle of Cedars, 18 May, had left the Indians in a buoyant mood.[14] Gathering many Indians and Canadians, Sir John obtained a fieldpiece from Oswegatchie and advanced toward Montreal to assist the British.

He was too late for the action. On 15 June, General Benedict Arnold had evacuated the city at night, with 'his reduced garrison . . . when the British were only eleven miles away'. When Sir John reached the city he found it in possession of the 29th Regiment. He crossed to La Prarie hoping to cut off some of the retreating enemy but was met by Carleton who saw the condition of Sir John's followers and ordered him to 'go no further'. Two days later, at Chambly, General Carleton commissioned Sir John as Commandant of the King's Royal Regiment of New York, the second provincial corps raised for the Canadian command, and the first composed entirely of Loyalists.

Back at Johnstown there was chaos. After Sir John's escape, the Rebels had looted Johnson Hall and taken Lady Johnson and her children to Albany under arrest. The Johnson family was permitted to stay with relatives, but held within the city as 'sort of hostages'. All that summer Lady Johnson appealed to General Washington to let her join her husband. In Canada, Sir John, after an expedition with Carleton to Lake Champlain and a trip to New York, took up the active leadership of his regiment and led his men against the rebel forces.

In the fall of 1776 he received leave to go to British held New York City by sea and try to get his wife and children through enemy lines. A letter, written to Daniel Claus tells the story:

20 January 1777

Dear Brother

After Lady Johnson had been at Albany a considerable time, I advised, as I constantly correspond with her by Indians and white men that I sent through the Woods to try to prevail upon Mr. Schuyler or the Committee to let her return home or come down to this Place to her friends they refused saying that while they had her and the children in their possession I would not dare to head the Indians or act against the Congress . . . [15]

205

Even while Sir John was writing the letter, Lady Johnson may have been on her way to meet him.

In December, she had been allowed to go to Fishkill, New York, and then she was allowed to go on to Walkill in Ulster County along with her sister, a nurse, two servants and her children. Sometime between 20 January and 15 February, she and the children, and probably the others, disguised themselves as country people and escaped from their guards. They obtained horses and carriages and, following the inland route down the Hudson to New York, met Sir John who was waiting for them. As soon as they could get passage, the family went by sea to Montreal.

Conditions at Montreal were also in a state of confusion. The British government had been upset with General Sir Guy Carleton's conduct of the army following the rebel attempt to capture Canada. The General had been lenient with the Rebels, allowing them to escape with their guns and ammunition. He had also made it possible for them to take conveyances which could have been used for a British and Loyalist thrust down the Hudson. Carleton was relieved of his command in North America and, a junior officer, subordinate to Howe, General John Burgoyne was appointed Commander-in-chief of the British and Loyalist forces in Canada.

The plan for the attack down the Hudson was master-minded in England where the strategists had little knowledge or conception of the terrain in North America. Two forces were involved in the strategy. One would proceed from Montreal down the St. Lawrence and cross Lake Ontario, land at Oswego, proceed across Lake Oneida and take Fort Stanwix (near Rome, New York), and continue on to Albany. The other would proceed northward from New York. Sir John was appointed second in command of the force under Brigadier Barry St. Leger, an English officer, who would advance to reduce Fort Stanwix.

The force under Barry St. Leger left Oswego 26 July 1777, but was ill-prepared for the mission. Although the British had been told the fort was manned by 60 soldiers, it was garrisoned by some 600 Rebels. The enemy had been warned of their coming and had 'stp up a narrow

River called Wood Creek by cutting of Trees across it for abt 20 Miles' making it necessary for the British and Loyalists to cut a 'Road thro the Woods for 25 Miles to bring up the Artillery'. The force from Oswego did not arrive at Fort Stanwix until the second day of August.[16]

The Indian Loyalists immediately attacked the fort, but for three days the garrison held firm. The third day intelligence was brought by an Indian guide that a large body of Rebels, led by General Nicholas Herkimer from Tryon County, was on its way to relieve the garrison. Taking up a position six miles from the fort, the British and Loyalists ambushed the enemy, killing 'upwards of 500'[17] Rebels and mortally wounding their leader. This was the Battle of Oriskany, the bloodiest battle of the American Revolution.

However, the British and Loyalists failed to capture Fort Stanwix. During the Battle of Oriskany, men from the fort had looted the Indian camp, taking away 'the Indian packs with their cloaths, Wampum & Silverwork . . . .'. When the Indians returned their rage at their losses was intensified by the report that thousands of enemy were converging on Fort Stanwix and that General Burgoyne's army had been cut to pieces. The Indians panicked and many fled, though it was later learned 'that there was not an enemy within forty miles of Fort Stanwix'.[18] St. Leger withdrew and the campaign to capture Fort Stanwix was abandoned. On 17 October 1777, the British and Loyalists were defeated at the Battle of Saratoga, the most decisive defeat of the entire Revolution. Because of this defeat, the French openly entered the conflict and eventually sent thousands of soldiers to America, soldiers that weighed the balance in the outcome of the Revolution.

In the midst of all that tragedy and chaos, Sir John realized the necessity of keeping the Indians as allies. Following the Battle of Oriskany, as Catherine S. Crary records the story, Sir John sent Sarah Cass McGinn 'a Loyalist lady of Tryon County who understood the language of the Six Nations' to the Indians to 'mollify them and assuage the loss of their men and chiefs at Oriskany'. He called on the same lady again after the defeat at Saratoga. General Schuyler had sent a 'Belt of Wampum' to the Six Nations telling them of the defeat of the King's troops and warning them of the consequences if they did not join the Rebels. By intercepting the Belt of Wampum and prevailing upon the Indians to carry an 'Account of a different Nature favourable to Government', she managed to keep the Indians firm in their loyalty. They soon rejoined the white Loyalists in their cooperation with the British in the attempt to halt the rebellion in America.

The British would need all the help they could get from the people of America. After her defeat in the Seven Years' War, France had been building her navy and marshalling her forces to engage England in a global confrontation. By October, 1778, she was ready. Admiral d'Estaing sailed from France bringing 4,000 soldiers across the Atlantic. On his arrival in America he issued his appeal to the French-Canadian: 'Vous êtes nés Français, vous n'avez cessé de l'être',[19] a message that would be very nearly repeated word by word some two hundred years later by another French citizen on his visit to Canada.

Sir John was shattered by the decision of France to enter the war. Perhaps as much as any man who ever lived, Sir John loved the land where he had been born and where he had hoped to raise his family. Every stream, every sunset, every sweep of forest held personal meaning for him. As a child he had been close friends with many Indian children and he and Joseph Brant remained companions during most of their lives. Molly Brant, who became Sir John's stepmother had understood the yearning of this young man for the blond maiden, Clarissa, from Tribes Hill and had remained Sir John's confidant till her death in 1796.

In *An American Knight in Britain; Sir John Johnson's Tour, 1765-1767*, Dr. Milton W. Hamilton wrote that Sir John's career during the American Revolution 'has given Sir John a bad name'. Most of that career was in planning and leading raids by the Loyalists and British into enemy held territory. These raids had two purposes — to destroy supplies which might be used by the Continental Army and to rescue Loyalists who were still in the Valley.

The first of these raids took place October 1778,

when William Byrne and Wm. R. Crawford, two of Sir John's officers led a daring scouting expedition to Johnson Hall and brought back Sir John's papers which he had buried before his flight to Canada in 1776. Unfortunately, these papers were in such bad condition that most of them were illegible. Sir John estimated his loss from their destruction as at least £20,000.

By late summer, 1779, the Indians and other Loyalists still in the Province of New York were asking for help from their friends in Canada. On 30 August Daniel Claus wrote Governor Frederick Haldimand:

> Sir
>
> Sir John and I arrived here last Saturday morning. Soon after My arrival two of the few Mohawks that remain at home came and told me they had received another Message from the Five Nations acquainting them with their present critical Situation with Regard to an Invasion from the Rebels who they heard were 16,000 strong Marching against them . . . I told them in Answer that I apprehended the Five Nations were more alarmed than they had reason to be, but that I would acquaint your Excellency what they had Said . . . [20]

Further cries for help came from the Valley. Captain Angus Macdonell and Lieutenant Archibald Macdonell, taken by the Rebels 7 January 1776, were still held as hostages. Chief David of the Mohawks sent word that his Indians had been driven from their positions at Chemung and that 'they are now almost out of Breath & must yield without you send some strong Body to their Relief'.

It was not until 7 May 1780, that that 'strong Body' in the person of Sir John was sent to the Valley, travelling to Johnson Hall to 'bring off the distressed Loyalist families & destroy supplies' which could be used by the Rebels. According to Sir John's report of 3 June, he 'burned 120 Houses, Barns, Mills, but killed only 11 men and took 27 prisoners'. He wrote, '14 I suffered to Return being either too old or too young to March & was induced by the earnest desire to the Loyal families left to do so'.[21]

During his return journey Sir John escaped scouting parties sent by the Rebels from New York and from New Hampshire. The Oneida Indians, who supported the Rebels, retaliated by burning homes of the Loyalists in the Valley and laying waste their lands. Major Haldimand gave Sir John permission to mount a second battalion. Then in the fall Sir John returned, this time leading 600 men from his own regiment, from Butler's Rangers, from the Six Nation Indians and British Regulars who scourged the Valleys of the Schoharie and Mohawk rivers. In three days his troops burned 13 grist mills, several sawmills and a thousand houses with their barns holding grain and other fodder desperately needed for the rebel armies. The Rebels fought back by plundering even more. Niagara became crowded with Indians and other Loyalists 'half starved and half naked', driven from their homes and desperate for their safety.

By the fall of the next year, the fighting was in its final stages. On 19 October 1781, the British General Cornwallis, blockaded by the French fleet off the Capes of Chesapeake, was defeated by the French and continental armies in Yorktown. Hoping to convince the British to continue the war, Sir John took his family to England in the autumn of 1781. But early in 1782, the British government fell and the new administration wanted peace. Realizing that the war could not continue, Sir John and his family sailed home.

On his return Sir John faced three major crises. The Indian Loyalists were distraught and angry. First they had to be mollified, and then given lands and other considerations to prevent their return to the United States and helping the Rebels mount a possible attack on Canada. As their Indian villages had been destroyed and plundered, they must have new homes in what remained of British North America. As he brought back from England his commission, dated 14 March 1782, as 'Superintendent General and Inspector General of the Six Nations Indians and those in the Province of Quebec', Sir John was now in a position to provide for the Indians.

Also there were the White Loyalists, many of whom had served in Sir John's own regiment, as well as Huguenot and German farmers, minority groups who, after sheltering in England, had settled in separate communities in New York and Pennsylvania where their cultural identity had been respected. During the Revolution they had been harassed by the Committee of Safety who tried to make them conform to the American Association and other dictates of the Rebellion. Now these minorities must be guaranteed cultural freedom and found new homes in Canada.

The Quebec Act, drawn up and passed in 1774 to appease the French-Canadian leaders, created an unpalatable form of government for settlers who had sacrificed everything to support the British Crown and the British concept of government. The Quebec Act would have to be modified for them.

The Indian Loyalists had gone through a terrible nine years, even within their own confederacy. Late in the sixteenth century, the Onondagas, Senecas, Mohawks, Oneidas, Cayugas and Tuscaroras had formed the Six Nation Confederacy, but years later, the American Revolution had been a civil war for them as much as it had been for the white citizens of the Thirteen Colonies. The members of the confederacy had become a divided people. Some had tried to remain neutral or had fought alongside the Rebels, but the majority of the members of the confederacy had supported the King and by 1783 had taken an uneasy stand in what is now Canada.[22]

At first, Governor Frederick Haldimand, who had come to Canada in 1778, planned to settle the Indian Loyalists on the Bay of Quinte and had sent Major Haldimand, the Surveyor-General and a few Mohawks to Cataraqui to survey lands for their villages. He wrote Sir John asking him 'to proceed to Niagara to quiet the apprehension of the Indians by convincing them that it is not the Intention of Government to abandon them to the resentment of the Americans'.[23] But Joseph Brant, the leader of the confederation, was very mindful of the resentment of the Americans, and early the following year asked Haldimand to grant the Six Nations lands on the Grand River where they would be near their friends, the Senecas, vulnerably situated at Niagara.

Although John Deseronto, Joseph Brant's cousin, elected to stay on the Bay of Quinte, by March 1784, Haldimand was convinced of the necessity of heeding Joseph Brant's request and wrote Sir John:

> You will please therefore give Lieutenant [-colonel John] Butler the necessary directions for Purchasing without loss of time the Tract of Country situated between Lakes Ontario, Erie and Huron.[24]

Two months later a tract of land about 9 kilometres on each side of the Grand River was purchased; in 1785 a census recorded 1,843 Six Nation Indians from 19 tribes living on the shore of the Grand River in what is now the Province of Ontario.[25]

But difficulties arose concerning the sale of the Indian lands on the Grand River to white men. It is unclear whether Joseph Brant, who sold large tracts of that land to his white friends, truly felt that they were needed to set an example in farming methods for the Indians, and that the money from the lands sale would be used to provide an assured income for his people, or whether he sold the lands for his own profit. Thomas Douglas, Lord Selkirk, confided in his diary that 'Brant had demanded a 10% commission for his services', and in 1798 the Caugnawaga Indians accused Chief Brant of surreptitiously selling part of their lands in New York State to the American Government.[26] Sir John's role in the land sales is not recorded. Speaking for Governor Carleton (Lord Dorchester) in 1788, Sir John told Aaron and Isaac Hill, two Mohawk chiefs who had left the Grand River for the Bay of Quinte, that the lands on the Grand River 'had been granted to the Six Nations in general and the white People have no right to it & Must Withdraw and if they do not do it of their own accord, measures will be taken to compel them. That all the White people know that they are not to enveigle and work upon the passions of the Indians to obtain Grants of land . . . '[27] Yet, in 1819, John Brant, son of Joseph would claim:

> Sir John Johnson also wished us to Surrender Six Miles on each side of the River at the Mouth, we complied with his request provided it was for our benefit, but that it should be for our benefit.[28]

At a meeting held in 1788, Sir John assured the In-

Sir John Johnson

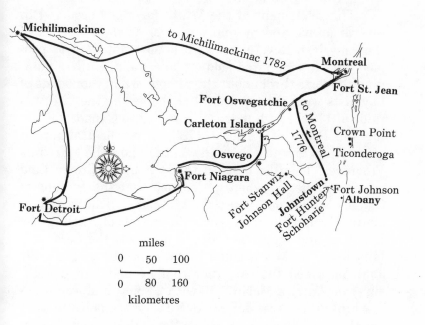

Michilimackinac

to Michilimackinac 1782

Montreal

Fort St. Jean

Fort Oswegatchie

Carleton Island

to Montreal 1776

Crown Point

Ticonderoga

Oswego

Fort Niagara

Fort Stanwix

Johnson Hall

Johnstown

Fort Hunter

Schoharie

Fort Johnson

Albany

Fort Detroit

miles

0   50   100

0   80   160

kilometres

dians that measures would be taken to compel the white man to give up the lands they had purchased from the Indians, but in 1812, when an investigation was carried out, it was too late to set aside the deeds Joseph Brant had given his white friends.[29] Today the Indian reservation on the Grand River in Ontario, still the largest in Canada, takes in only one-twelfth of the original lands given these Loyalists in 1784.

In 1784, Governor Haldimand told Sir John he must be held responsible for the expense if he continued to supply provisions to the Indians who were bringing their children to Montreal for inoculation. Thus Sir John's responsibility to the Indians was much broader than just seeing that they had satisfactory lands in Canada.

The settlement of the White Loyalists occurred in several areas, and by many routes. At the outbreak of the American Revolution what is now Ontario was peopled by a few hundred soldiers and their families manning the forts throughout the region. When thousands of Loyalists were driven from their homes by the Sullivan raids of 1779, and hundreds more fled to Canada following the Peace of Paris of 1783, Governor Haldimand made plans to settle them in what are now the Maritime Provinces. Then he learned that not much Crown land was available, so when he learned that the Indians of Canada would not object to White Loyalists as neighbours, he appointed Sir John in charge of settling the Loyalists and instructed him to purchase the necessary land from the Mississauga Indians. In March 1784, Sir John informed the Governor that he had sent deputy-surveyor Patrick McNiff 'Off with 26 men' and would follow himself in three days.[30] McNiff and Louis Kotté were deputy-surveyors under Major Samuel Holland, Surveyor-General. Major Edward Jessup, and Captain Justus Sherwood aided by Major James Rogers superintended the Loyalists on their journey north.

That spring was a time of challenging activity for Sir John. On 26 April he advised that 'the Highlanders and others, of Roman Catholic and Protestant faiths wished to settle separately for the benefit of religious worship', and by early May the first town plots were laid out 'the big trek up-river, via bateaux, beginning about

24 May'.[31]

Not only were religious differences respected in the granting of land, but also the men of disbanded army units were kept together in the townships. As Gerald M. Craig writes in *Upper Canada, The Formative Years: 1784-1841:*

> The first five of the Royal Townships went to the first battalion of Sir John Johnson's Royal Yorkers, the settlers being divided, at their own request, according to race and religion. Catholic Highlanders, Scottish Presbyterians, German Calvanists, German Lutherans, and Anglicans accordingly occupied these townships in that order. The next three townships were alloted to Major Jessup's corps. No. 1 of the Cataraqui Townships went to Captain Grass's party from New York, No. 2 to remaining members of Johnson's second battalion, to whom were joined men from Major Rogers' Corps and another party from New York City led by Major Van Alstine. The last township in the Cataraqui series, the present Marysburg, was settled by detachments of disbanded regulars, including some Germans.[32]

By 7 July 1784, Sir John reported that 1,568 men, 626 women, 1,492 children and 90 servants had been distributed in these townships.

But even in these successful settlements there were problems. Not only was the Quebec Act of 1774 the law of the land, but also Governor Haldimand had had definite instructions from England that the surveyed lands were to de incorporated into the seignorial system, and that distinct seigneuries or fiefs were to be established and 'lots within them were to be held of the King on the same terms as in the old sections of the province'.[33]

Sir John concentrated his energies on this settlement problem. In April 1785, he and a group of officers petitioned the King on behalf of themselves and their fellow Loyalists who had come to the province. They explained to the British Government that the Loyalists had fought to preserve their British form of government and that the French laws, particularly those pertaining to the holding of land, were quite foreign to them and that these communities would fail if they were compelled to live under a French-oriented system. Sir John proposed that a district within Quebec, separate but subject to the Governor and Council of Quebec, be established which would have British-oriented laws and land tenures without disturbing the French Canadians and their systems and laws in the eastern section of the province. Sir John stressed that the Loyalists who had come to Nova Scotia and to what had become New Brunswick were privileged to live under the British system of government, and if the same privileges were not granted the Loyalists who had come to Canada, those people would not remain. On the positive side, he suggested that if those privileges were granted, more and more dissatisfied citizens of the new United States of America would come north and the region would strengthen and become a vibrant part of the Empire.

Of course, there were objections. The 'French Party' opposed the suggestion, arguing that the Loyalists made up only five percent of the population of the province. Sir John continued his persuasion, emphasizing that he wanted to see a policy adopted 'that would have the effect of assimilating this (the colony of Quebec) into the other of His Majesty's Colonies in America . . . .[34]

Feeling confident that the policy he advocated would be adopted, his world seemed in order. In November 1785, he wrote to his brother-in-law, Robert Watts in New York:

> . . . Neither time, distance, nor the unhappy Revolutions that have taken place can make me forget My friends or lessen in the least the sincere regard I always had for you and your good Lady. Few Men, if any, have greater reason to regret their Separation from friends than myself, particularly as my fate puts an end to the prospect of our ever meeting in the same happy situation we once experienced. However, I have the Satisfaction to assure you that my prospects before me are such as cannot but be Satisfactory to myself and family — having the Appropration of my Sovereign and my Country, at least of that part of it worthy of esteem; for my Conduct with rewards and prospects of future preferment and compensation, the first at least adequate to my Merit, and I hope and have some

reason to Believe, the Latter will he little short of my pretentions. Thus Circumstances in point of honor and Emolument, with a good Stock of Health, a partner I have the Sincerest Affection for, and a fine young family as engaging as they are fine, I think I would be unreasonable, notwithstanding my disappointments and hopes, was not contented and happy.[35]

His life did not work out quite that way. Although he received £38,995 in compensation from the British Government, the second highest sum granted to an individual Loyalist, and saw the creation of the new region he had advocated, the government of the 'new district' was not what he had expected.

When Sir Guy Carleton (Lord Dorchester) returned to Quebec in 1786 as Governor, he consulted Sir John on the proposed councils for the new province and in 1790 strongly recommended Sir John for the post of Lieutenant-governor. But the British parliament turned down Carleton's recommendation and instead appointed John Graves Simcoe, an Englishman who had come to America in 1776 to fight in the Revolution and who had risen to command the Queen's Rangers. The British Government felt Sir John had such large land holdings in the western part of the district that it would be impossible for him to be objective in the administration of the new province. The Canada Act, separating Quebec into Upper and Lower Canada was passed in England and in November, 1791, John Graves Simcoe came to take up his post as Lieutenant-governor of Upper Canada.

By the end of 1791, Sir John was exhausted, as the last two years had drained all his energies. In June, 1790, he had toured the province-to-be, investigating Indian affairs and land irregularities — to purchase Indian lands north of Lake Erie — also to look into complaints of the former Butler's Rangers who had settled under Captain William Caldwell, opposite Detroit in 1784. During July and August he had presided at land boards held in Detroit and Niagara. At the Huron village on 15 and 16 August he held a conference of the principal chiefs of the Huron Confederacy which was also attended by several chiefs of the Mohawks, Shawnee and Delawares. In August 1791, he was present as a member of the Council at Quebec City. In that same month, at the request of the Governor, he attended a meeting of the Governor and Joseph Brant along with twelve other chiefs and warriors of the Mohawk, Cayugas, Tuscaroras and Seneca Nations and deputies of the confederated Western Indians. In December Simcoe visited Montreal to confer with Sir John and to attempt to establish friendly relations with the frustrated Baronet. Simcoe reported 'evidence of good humour'.

In June 1792, it was proposed that Sir John go to the United States to confer with the British representative George Hammond, regarding a new Indian boundary. Sir John refused to go, writing Major-General Alured Clarke:

> The same motives that have ever actuated my conduct, would upon this, as upon every other occasion, influence me to offer services were it not for the very unpleasant predicament I stand in, proscribed by an Act of Attainer, with many other reasons and circumstances that would render it highly improper for me to go into the States at Present.[36]

He was granted permission for a long absence in England and left Montreal with his family during July 1792, and stayed in England until October 1796. During that time he purchased and lived in Twickenham, an estate outside London. Sir John offered his services to the Crown after the Declaration of war by France in 1793 but refused to enter politics. The ladies of the family wanted to stay in England, but by 1796 Sir John had sold his estate at Twickenham and in October landed with his family at Montreal.[37]

In 1796 North America was in a state of great tension. Fearing an attack on the continent by France and Spain, England had agreed to American demands. Jay's Treaty had been signed and on 1 June 1796, the western forts were turned over to the Americans.[38] For other reasons the Indians in Upper Canada were in a state of turmoil. Ever since 1787, Joseph Brant had been agitating for government recognition of the land sales he had made to white men on the Grand River. In 1797, he led 300 Braves in a march on York, the Provincial Capital.

The President of the Legislative Council, the Honourable Peter Russell, fearful of a French invasion, appealed to his council which passed the necessary legislation and the lands on the Grand River became the home of the white man.

All that first year, when Sir John was trying to pull the Indian Department together, Lady Johnson was yearning to return to New York. Even though Sir John had moved his family into a large house on St. Paul's Street, Montreal, she, in 1797 and again in 1798, journeyed to Albany, writing back to Sir John 'in raptures of the United States of America'.[39] In 1801 she went to England.

Sir John's nephew, William Claus, had been confirmed as Deputy-Superintendent General of Indian Affairs in 1800, and in 1801 the Indians sold part of their land to purchase property at Niagara for Anne, William's mother who was Sir John's sister. Anne died early in that same year.[40] Then Sir John suffered another misfortune as he and Joseph Brant had arguments which brought to an end a friendship that had been troubled since the two men had come to Canada.

Now that Anne and Mary his two sisters, were both dead, Sir John knew he would never return to Johnstown in the Mohawk Valley. In 1806 he built 'a small log house on a cone-shaped hill on his seigneury on the Richelieu which he named Mount Johnson' (now Mont St. Grégoire). Here he spent much of his time in his later years and established the family burial vault. Lady Johnson, who had come back to Upper Canada in 1802, returned to England in 1807.

Clarissa Putman came from Schenectady, New York, to be with Sir John in Canada. They had time to share many memories. Perhaps they talked about Peggy, their daughter who had married James Van Horne, the independent young man who had refused Sir John's offer to secure him a position in the Indian trade. Perhaps Clarissa told him how the wardens of the church Sir William Johnson had built in Schenectady had given Peggy permission to use the Johnson pew in the church and how each Sunday, Peggy and her husband dressed in their finest clothes and, with heads held high, went to worship in the church built by her grandfather who had refused his permission for her father and mother to marry.

When Clarissa went back to Schenectady in 1809, Sir John in his continued fondness for her gave her this letter:

Montreal 16th September
1809

Madam

Agreeably to my promise, I hereby bind myself my Heirs, or Executors, to pay to you, Annually, during your life, as heretofore, fifty Pounds New York Currency, or one hundred and twenty Eight Dollars — this, though not a Legal Instrument, I hold as binding on my honor, and on that of My Heirs or would I suppose otherwise of any one of my family, I would not own or Acknowledge them as Such —

The House that was Spoken of, or some other Equally Suitable Shall be procured for you, your Daughter, and her Children — this Arrangement, I hope, will ease your Mind, and Make your latter days more Comfortable, As the Idea of it does Mine. Wishing you health, a Safe Return, and a happy meeting with your Child, And Grandchildren, I remain as ever,

Your faithful, and Affectionate friend

J. Johnson[41]

Mrs. C. Putman.

As he grew older, Sir John became a country gentleman, owning and becoming most interested in seignories on the Ottawa and the Richelieu. He investigated the possibility of bringing out Scottish settlers for his holdings. He planned roads to his eastern settlements and set about bringing pearl-ash, corn and pork to the Montreal markets.

Lady Johnson died in 1815 and the following year his granddaughter came from Schenectady to visit Sir John. When she went home she took this letter to her grandmother:

Montreal 27th August, 1816

My dear Friend

Your Grand Daughter returning to you, I can no longer put off writing to you to assure you that, however my long Silence may appear to you, and the Want of that Aid you Stand in Need of, that it has not been owing to a Want of Gratitude, or regard, but to the heavy losses I have sustained and the very great Expense I have been put to by the Visits my family made to England which involved me in debt, that I am, and have been Selling property to pay off, and hope in a Short time to Accomplish, and have it in my power to give you the Assistance you require I have not had it in my Power to see, or to give your Grand Child the Assistance I otherwise would, for These reasons and the Expense I am now at, in building, having sold my house in Town, and having no other in it, to Dwell. I am now about collecting the Means of Paying off the remainder of the Money due Mr. Robinson for the House, and Will, at the same time remit you as Much as I conveniently can, and hope in the course of Next Summer to clear off all you Claim, at least — but you ought not to charge me with Ingratitude, or want of remembrance of past happy days, nor to let any one Write, or encourage you to unbraid me with what my heart abhors, having every inclination to convince you of that gratitude, and the trust with which I am, and ever will remain

Your Affectionate

and faithful friend
John Johnson

I write this in a great hurry As They are just going off and have much to do —

Adieu[42]

Sir John was seventy-four years old and in debt. He was to live fourteen more years in Canada. He had fourteen 'legitimate' children.[43] Anne (Nancy) born at Fort Johnson in July, 1774, married Major, afterwards Colonel Edward Macdonell, Deputy-Quartermaster General in Canada during the War of 1812. William was born at Johnson Hall in 1775 and married Susan, the daughter of Stephen de Lancey. William was a Lieutenant-colonel of His Majesty's 28th Regt. of Foot and died in Montreal in 1812. John, the child born while Lady Johnson was a prisoner of the Rebels, died in Montreal when he was less than two years old. Warren, born in December 1777, died unmarried in 1801. Catherine was born in 1780 and died in infancy in Montreal. Sir Adam Gordon was born in 1781 and in 1798 he was a prisoner of war in France. In 1814 he commanded a corps of Indians 'destined to take part in the reduction of Plattsburg.' Sir Adam became the third Baronet of the family in 1830 and held this title until his death in 1843. The second John, born in 1782 on the passage to Quebec became Major of the 6th Battalion of the Townships Militia during the War of 1812.

Christopher, born in 1784, lived less than a year. James Stephen, born in 1784, was killed at the siege of Badajos, April, 1812, and is buried in Spain. Catherine, born in 1785 in Montreal, married Colonel Bowes, who was succeeded as commandant of the troops in Upper and Lower Canada in 1806 by Sir Isaac Brock. Colonel Bowes became Major-general and was killed at the storming of the Forts at Salamanca in 1812 and was buried there. A monument in St. Paul's Cathedral, London, commemorates his services to England. Robert was born in 1787 and saw duty with the army in Ireland and Spain but died accidently in Montreal in 1812. Charles became Lieutenant in the army and died in 1854 in England. Marianne, Sir John and Lady Johnson's youngest daughter, was born in 1791 and after her mother's death became Sir John's companion and housekeeper. After her.father's death in 1830, she went to England and died there in 1868.[44]

Sir John's obituary, published by the *Montreal Gazette* of January, 1830, told of his work with the Indians, and of his membership on the Legislative Council of Lower Canada. The *Montreal Gazette* emphasized that most of Sir John's life had been spent in 'the service of his Sovereign', and that at the beginning of the American Revolution Sir John had 'abandoned his very extensive Estates in the Province of New York' to join His Majesty's forces in Canada. The paper wrote of the regiment Sir John had raised and of the fact that he had been appointed 'Colonel and then Brigadier General and continued to serve with distinction until the termination of the conflict'.

The same paper also gave an account of Sir John's funeral. It was a most solemn and impressive occasion. The 24th Regiment 'attended by a fine band led the procession, playing tunes most suited to the solemn occasion'. The hearse was drawn by four black horses; the coffin covered with the 'ensignia of the departed Brigadier General'. Following the hearse were the relations and 'numerous friends of the deceased', then the Provincial Grand Lodge for 'the district and the Officers of the Private Lodges of the city over which Sir John Johnson had long presided as Provincial Grand Master'. Then came about 300 Indians including 100 women from the Missions of Caughawaga, St. Regis and the Lake of Two Mountains.

The service at the Episcopal Church was read by the Chaplain to the forces. Afterwards the cortege proceeded by St. Vincent Street and the New Market Place to the landing on the river where the boat waited to carry the body to the family vault on Mount Johnson. Before the boat started its solemn journey downstream, Lazare Teconwarisan, 'a very old Iroquois Chief from Caughawage' spoke to his people about Sir John, telling of the respect and love the Indians held for 'he who made the house tremble (the title given to the late Baronet by the Indians)'. The troops on the shore 'fired the usual vollies and were answered by a salute of fifteen guns from the batteries on St. Helen's Island'. The boat carrying the remains of Sir John Johnson disappeared into the gathering dusk.

Sir John accomplished much for Canada by holding the Indians loyal to the Crown and in settling them and the White Loyalists on their lands in still British North America. By setting up townships which respected the cultural diversity of the various refugee groups, and by leading the move to establish a separate district in which those groups could live under the laws and systems of land tenure of the British Government, he gave immeasurable service to Canada and helped to create Ontario as a separate province.

1. Johnson Hall was built in 1763 by Sir William Johnson, Sir John's father. After the American Revolution it was expropriated by Congress and eventually sold. It exchanged hands several times before it was purchased in 1808 for $18,000 in gold by Edward Akin, descendant of immigrants who had come to the colonies in 1680. Johnson Hall has been purchased by the State of New York and is now an Historic Site.
Johnstown was established on lands originally granted to Sir William Johnson in recognition of great services to the Crown in the French and Indian Wars, as the Seven Years' War was called in America. By 1770 Johnstown boasted over 500 residents and some one hundred buildings. Brick making and lumbering were vital industries of the time and Johnstown merchants benefitted from Sir William's trade connections in 'New York Town'.
The Court House in Johnstown was the first brick court structure standing between Albany and the Pacific Ocean. In this Court House the first Court of Quarter Sessions was held, September, 1772, thus bringing the old English system of jurisprudence to what was then the western frontier of the colonies. One of the final engagements of the American Revolution was fought at Johnstown. Five days after Cornwallis' defeat at Yorktown, 19 October 1781, a battalion of Sir John's Regiment, the King's Royal Regiment of New York, a body of Butler's Rangers and 200 Indians marched upon Johnstown and battled with Rebel forces in open fields north of Johnson Hall. The Rebels carried the field.
The above information has been taken from 'The Edwards History' and has been made available by Harold Edwards, Jr., Syracuse, New York, who is a descendant of Edward Akin.
2. The Minute Book of the Committee of Safety of Tryon County, p. 84, a copy of which has been made available by Frank B. Risteen, Sr., Belleville, Ontario, who has provided almost all of the research material that has made possible this biography of Sir John Johnson.
3. Admiral Peter Warren was in command of the British Fleet at the capture of Louisbourg in 1748.
4. Marjorie Whitelaw, ed. *The Dalhousie Journals*, (Ottawa: Oberon Press, 1978), p. 147.
5. Frank B. Risteen, Sr., 'Some Highlights in the Life of Cornwall's Founder, Sir John Johnson', a paper presented to the Stormont, Dundas and Glengarry Historical Society, Cornwall, Ontario, 17 March 1976.
6. Public Archives of Canada, Claus Papers, 14: 75-76.
7. Milton W. Hamilton, *An American Knight in Britain, 1765-1767*, New York Historical Society, April, 1961.
8. *Ibid.*
9. Daniel Campbell Letter Books, Schenectady County Historical Society, Schenectady, New York.
10. Frank B. Risteen, Sr., 'Children of Sir John Johnson and Lady Mary (Polly) Johnson, married at New York 30 June, 1773', *Ontario Historical Society*, LXIII, 2, (June, 1971), pp. 93-102.
11. The Minute Book of the Committee of Safety of Tryon County, p. 84.
12. J. Watts DePeyster, Address to the New York Historical Society, 6 January 1880.
13. Peter Force, *American Archives, Series 4, Volume 6*, p. 511.
14. G.F.C. Stanley, *Canada Invaded: 1775-1776*, (Toronto: Hakkert, 1973).
15. Public Archives of Canada, Claus Papers, 1: 230/3.
16. Catherine S. Crary, *The Price of Loyalty: Tory Writings From the Revolutionary Era*, (Toronto: McGraw-Hill Ryerson, 1973), p. 242.
17. *Ibid.* pp. 242-243.
18. *Ibid.* p. 240.

19. Hilda Neatby, *Quebec, The Revolutionary Age: 1760-1791*, (Toronto: McClelland and Stewart, 1977) p. 147.
20. Public Archives of Canada, Haldimand Papers. B. 114, p. 63.
21. E.A. Cruikshank. 'The King's Royal Regiment of New York', *Ontario Historical Society Papers and Records*, XXVII, pp. 233-4
22. Charles Johnston, *The Valley of the Six Nations*, (Toronto: The University of Toronto Press, 1964), p. xxviii.
23. *Ibid.* p. 38.
24. *Ibid.* p. 45.
25. *Ibid.* p. 52.
26. *Ibid.* p. xlviii.
27. *Ibid.*
28. *Ibid.* p. 67. Also see P.A.C. Claus Papers, x1238041, Proceedings of the Indian Council at Hamilton, 4 July 1819.
29. *Ibid.* p. xliv.
30. Frank B. Risteen, Sr., 'Some Highlights in the Life of Cornwall's Founder, Sir John Johnson', p. 8.
31. *Ibid.*
32. Gerald M. Craig, *Upper Canada, the Formative Years: 1784-1841*, (Toronto: McClelland and Stewart, 1963), p. 6.
33. *Ibid.* p. 5.
34. *Ibid.* p. 10-11.
35. Catherine S. Crary, *op. cit.*, p. 421; Robert Watts Papers, Box 11, New York Historical Society.
36. Frank B. Risteen, Sr., 'Notes on Sir John Johnson's Postwar Activity', *The Loyalist Gazette*, Spring, 1976, p. 6-7.
37. *Ibid.*
38. England had refused to hand over the Western Forts until Congress would repay the Loyalists for their losses in the Revolution.
39. Frank B. Risteen, Sr., 'Notes on Sir Johnson's Postwar Activity'.
40. P.A.C. Claus Papers, 16; 34/36.
41. Daniel Campbell Letter Books.
42. *Ibid.*
43. Frank B. Risteen, Sr., 'Children of Sir John Johnson & Lady Mary (Polly) Johnson', *Ontario Historical Society*, LXIII, No. 2, (June 1971), pp. 93-102. Also see, for alternate dates, Mary Beacock Fryer, *King's Men*, (Toronto: Dundurn Press, 1980), p. 348.
44. *Ibid.* p. 93.

Ranna Cossit

Chapter 9

Ranna Cossit

The Loyalist Rector
of St. George's Church
Sydney, Cape Breton Island

by Robert Morgan

Ranna Cossit was an Anglican priest in New Hampshire when his community was struck by revolutionary fever. Like many other clergymen of the Church of England, Cossit was a staunch defender of the British system. Faced with many dangers, he and his family were finally forced to leave and Cossit accepted a Rector's post in Sydney, capital of a newly created colony. Here, he became involved in the affairs of the state as well as the religious life of Cape Breton Island.

The autumn of 1785 was ablaze in Cape Breton Island and in its little capital, Sydney. The town stood among the trees, hardly more than a clearing, on a peninsula jutting out into a magnificent harbour. The settlement had been founded just that spring by a group of Loyalists and British settlers. This was no ordinary settlement, however. Sydney was to be the capital of the new Colony of Cape Breton, which like New Brunswick, had been chosen as a home for the Loyalists forced from the rebellious colonies by the American Revolution.

The island was a wilderness. No appreciable settlement had taken place since the Fortress of Louisbourg had fallen to the British in 1758. After the dispersal of the French from the Fortress, the British had failed to develop the island. Louisbourg lay in ruins and outlying settlements like Spanish Bay, now Sydney, had been abandoned. Then as a result of the American Revolution, thousands of Loyalists began moving northward. First they entered New Brunswick and mainland Nova Scotia, and then the Saint Lawrence River Valley. As these areas filled, one group of New York Loyalists under the leadership of the former Mayor of Albany, New York, Abraham Cuyler, chose to colonize the Island of Cape Breton. Cuyler, who had fought valiantly in the Revolution, had a good deal of influence with the Colonial Office in London. His petitions for the right to settle Cape Breton were answered in the summer of 1784, when word was received that the government had decided to establish the island as a separate government. His little group of Loyalists reached Cape Breton on 28 October 1784. Many of them wintered near the abandoned coal mines on the north side of the harbour.

Cuyler however was not to be the governor of the new colony. This position went to Joseph Frederick Wallet DesBarres, a Frenchman of Swiss ancestry whose family had moved to England when he was a young man. DesBarres was an outstanding engineer, who had just completed a twenty-year survey of the coast of northeastern North America. The results had been published as the *Atlantic Neptune* in 1783. The British Government had not paid him adequately for the labour, and he sought the Lieutenant-governorship of Cape Breton in compensation. Besides, who else knew the coast of Cape Breton and the island's potential as well as DesBarres? In an exhaustive memorandum to the Colonial Office, DesBarres pointed out the great value of the Cape Breton coal fields that were centred on Spanish Bay. He was also familiar with gypsum and other minerals on the island as well as the potential of the fishery which the French at Louisbourg had exploited so successfully. DesBarres claimed that the income from these resources would more than pay for the operation of the new colony's government.

As soon as his appointment was verified, DesBarres loaded a ship, the *Blenheim*, at Portsmouth, England with settlers and supplies, and dispatched it to Cape Breton. He went to Halifax to meet the Lieutenant-governor, John Parr, and arrived to meet his settlers in Spanish Bay in February of 1785. During that winter he had laid out the plans for a new colonial capital and in February held his first Executive Council meeting, thus officially launching the Colony of Cape Breton.

DesBarres and his fellow settlers crossed Spanish Bay in the spring of 1785 and founded Sydney as the Colony's capital. During that summer, troops of the 33rd Regiment were sent from Halifax to garrison and help clear the land. More Loyalists also arrived and an air of optimism prevailed. The governor's house was erected, along with barracks, bake houses and other public buildings.

This was the scene which greated the new prospective minister when he first saw Sydney during the autumn of 1785. Ranna Cossit was greatly impressed with the prospects of the colony as well as its Lieutenant-governor and the settlers. On their part, they seemed pleased with the young 41-year-old cleric with his dark curly hair, deep blue eyes and determined air.

Determination is one thing Ranna Cossit possessed in full measure. For generations his family had sought to lead their chosen way of life free from the tyranny of those who would impose their ideas on them. The name 'Cossit' is of French origin; one René Cossett had emigrated from Paris to Trois Rivières, Quebec as a young man, but around 1712, perhaps unhappy with life there, had migrated to Connecticut where he embraced the Anglican faith. Cossett's son, also René, moved to North Granby, Connecticut and anglicized his first son's name to 'Ranna' and 'Cossett' to 'Cossit'.

The young man was intelligent and persistent so his father sent him off to the newly-formed Rhode Island College where he received his Bachelor of Arts degree in 1771. By that time, Ranna expressed an interest in studying for the priesthood which meant that he had to study in England. After two years of intensive study he was ordained a priest of the Church of England by the Bishop of

229

London on 7 March 1773.

On his return to America, the young man moved westward to the pioneer area of Claremont, New Hampshire, where he served as a missionary for the Society For the Propagation of the Gospel in Foreign Parts (S.P.G.). His charge included an area that extended from Claremont to Haverhill, seventy miles to the north. This meant frequent journeys through semi-wilderness with all the attendant dangers, experiences that would be useful one day in Cape Breton.

But even greater challenges faced Cossit. New Hampshire was rife with dissatisfaction over its links with Great Britain. Cossit had become more and more aware of this, but perhaps because he studied in London, he favoured conciliation and retention of the ancient ties with Britain. The very fact that he returned to the Colonies, and indeed to the backwoods where rebel sentiment was strong, indicated Cossit's fearless sense of determination to support any cause in which he believed. Incapable of doing anything by half-way measures, he stoutly defended the cause of King and Country.

As the clouds of revolution gathered, one bright spot appeared in Cossit's life, for he fell in love with and married eighteen-year-old Thankfull Brooks, one of his parishioners, in June 1774. Thankfull's life was slated to be one of unrelenting hardship.

Far from the centre of law and order, Cossit was open to personal attack from the rebellious backwoodsmen. Six months after his marriage, a mob of 300 men threatened his life. Now he had to think of his wife, who was pregnant and would bear him a son in August. The Claremont rebels organized a Joint Committee of Safety to root out Loyalists who disagreed with their course of action. To Cossit they represented the end of civilized government and he was determined to resist.

Consequently, in the following December he and around twenty other Anglicans were arrested and brought before the Committee of Safety. Upon examination Cossit firmly proclaimed his loyalty and added:

I believe the American Colonies in their dispute with Great Britain . . . are unjust . . . I verily believe the

British troops will overcome by the greatness of their power and the justice of their cause.[1]

Cossit's open defiance, so typical of the man, earned him confinement within the town limits of Claremont, without weapons to defend himself. He continued his clerical duties, openly offering up prayers for the King. This brought further persecution upon him and his fellow Loyalists: they were confined in jails, beaten, and drawn through mud and water. All during the winter and spring of 1776 Cossit was cross-examined for his beliefs, but to no avail, for that May he refused to sign the so-called Declaration of Independence by the People of New Hampshire.

With continued persecution, his fellow Loyalists gradually left the region. 'In sundry places', Cossit wrote, 'where I used to officiate, the Church people are all dwindled away. Some have fled to the King's army for protection, some were banished, and many died'.[2] Many moved northward to Canada but their determined minister stayed, sending information to the British north of the border, and indeed visiting Quebec in November, 1782 to bring information concerning the events in his area. During this time, Abraham Cuyler, the Mayor of Albany, New York, who would one day move to Cape Breton, became familiar with Cossit's work and personality.

In 1783 Britain signed the Treaty of Versailles recognizing the independence of thirteen of her former colonies. Although Loyalist refugees were streaming northward, Cossit still stubbornly remained convinced that at least northern New Hampshire and Vermont might be brought back to British rule. By then as the only Anglican priest in New Hampshire, he had a great many more services to perform. After the Revolution, the S.P.G. was forbidden to employ missionaries in the United States, though former missionaries continued to receive allowances until Michaelmas, 1785. To add to these problems, his family was increasing in size. Between January 1777 and April 1785, Thankfull bore him three more sons and three daughters. One of the boys died, leaving him six children to provide for and a wife. Faced with a dwindling congregation but a growing family, with continued distrust by the surrounding population and fearing the end of his allowance from the S.P.G., even Cossit was forced to give in and seek a new mission.[3]

There was no shortage of positions, since new parishes were springing up in the newly-settled loyal colonies to the north. On 29 April 1785, the Rev. William Morice, Secretary of the S.P.G. wrote offering Cossit a post in Cape Breton which would bring £120 annually. This offer included a house and glebe lands, and even financial help in moving his family and household. To the Cossit family, this seemed like a miracle as Ranna's allowance from the S.P.G. for his work in New Hampshire was due to expire and his young family was facing destitution.

By the fall, Cossit, who had made the long trip to Cape Breton, was standing aboard a ship sailing into Spanish Bay. Within a few hours he was in the forest clearing called Sydney and talking to Lieutenant-governor DesBarres. DesBarres agreed to the terms of Cossit's appointment, and since the minister was also in charge of education in the colony, a temporary schoolhouse-church was promised together with a parsonage. With a promise to return the following spring, Cossit sailed for Boston to gather supplies and make a final plea for his loyal churchmen from New Hampshire among whom he would truly have loved to have settled in the Eastern Townships of Quebec. This would never be, and though Cossit's future seemed assured, the poignant separation from his beloved countrymen was a tragedy faced by all Loyalists. It was a trial he would encounter again one day.

Now, however, Cossit had to start his new life on the northern cape. He decided to leave his wife and children with Thankfull's family and friends, and returned to Sydney in the spring of 1786. Disappointment faced him there. The building intended as a temporary church and school had been blown down in a gale, his rectory had not yet been begun and he was informed that the British government would not supply money for the church until it was completed. It was like starting again at Claremont 13 years earlier.

Ranna Cossit

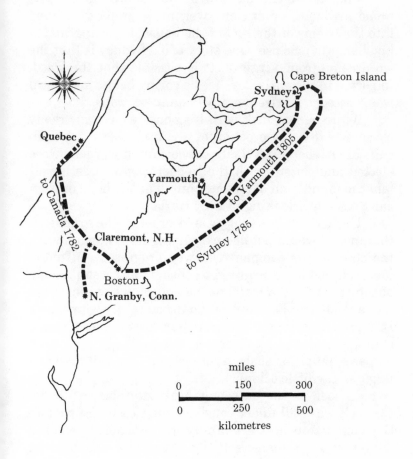

Cape Breton Island

Sydney

Quebec

Yarmouth

to Yarmouth 1805

to Canada 1782

Claremont, N.H.

to Sydney 1785

Boston

N. Granby, Conn.

miles

0   150   300

0   250   500

kilometres

His first duty was to his family and he built a house on Charlotte Street, located midway between the governor's house and the site chosen for the new parish church. The two-storey house with six fireplaces was a fair-sized one for the little colony, but Cossit would need space for his growing family. Since there was no sawmill yet erected, it appears Cossit used lumber previously cut and imported, perhaps first used in the construction of the schoolhouse-church which had blown down. The broad arrow, the mark of government property, carved into the beams of the roof of the house, indicated that it had had previous use. One story of old Sydney is that the wood came from Virginia. It is possible that the wood, imported in the early days of the colony before a sawmill was erected, came from many distant locations.

While he had luck with his house which was ready by early 1787, the erection of a church was more difficult. In October 1786 the first two church wardens were elected and Cossit, with the co-operation of DesBarres, laid the foundation of a stone church at the head of Nepean Street, overlooking Sydney Harbour.

The colony however was poor, and the provision that money would not be forthcoming from London until the church was completed slowed progress even more. Material had to be acquired as cheaply as possible; some of the stone for the walls of the church was taken from the abandoned Fortress of Louisbourg. By Christmas Day 1789, Cossit held the first church service in the new church christened St. George's. Even though there were no pews, pulpit or seats, another step forward had been taken in the little colony.

As soon as the parsonage was habitable, while St. George's was still under construction, Cossit returned to Claremont to collect his family. He probably spent the winter of 1788 there, settling his affairs and bidding farewell to his friends. In the spring he was back in Sydney, which was becoming home.

But Sydney was entering a difficult period.[4] The Colony of Cape Breton had been separated from the jurisdiction of Nova Scotia in 1784, almost as an afterthought, in order to accommodate an expected influx of Loyalists. The division however had been made too late, since Loyalists had already settled in mainland Nova Scotia and New Brunswick in 1783, two years before Sydney was founded. They preferred locating in the more established colony of Nova Scotia or in New Brunswick which was closer to their former homes. Cape Breton was still a wilderness, unattractive to new settlers seeking at least some of the amenities of civilized life. As late as 1790 there was no doctor, no teacher, and before Cossit, no minister in the Colony. When Abraham Cuyler had sought to settle the island, he promised to bring 3,000 Loyalists. Instead, he brought fewer than 150. Although new Loyalists continued to move in until around 1790 from almost all the former colonies, previous settlers emigrated just as quickly. Consequently Sydney grew slowly. In 1795 there were only 121 people living there; 26 of whom were preparing to leave. Houses which had gone up with such promise in 1785 were abandoned; 27 homes lay in ruins.

This problem would be readily understandable if Cape Breton were resourceless. Instead, the island had an abundance of natural resources such as coal, timber, fish and gypsum. But these resources, particularly coal, needed capital for full development. Britain, fearing competition at home from this coal or from industries which might locate near mines, was in no hurry to see the mines flourish and capital was subsequently not forthcoming. The other three resources were still in their infancy and their development did not begin until after the turn of the century.

The management of the mines passed from one lessee to another. In most cases the operators had no mining experience and very little capital. Sydney, which should have been a wealthy industrial centre, languished in its early days.

The main revenue in the tiny capital was money spent by the garrison and officials, largely on rum. If these few officials and merchants could have been taxed, at least their money could have been spent on colonial improvements. Taxation however was forbidden. This may have been the Colonial Office's way of attracting settlers or of insuring that new people would not be exploited, but it meant that the Lieutenant-governor and his council were impotent in trying to build roads or public buildings.

Therefore, the early years of the colony tell a story of frustration. Loyalists like Abraham Cuyler or David Mathews, former mayor of New York City, who had come to Cape Breton hoping to regain some of the losses they had sustained in the Revolution were disappointed in the colony's prospects. They were appointed to high office: Cuyler for example was Secretary and Registrar of the Colony; Mathews was Attorney General; both were on the Executive Council. However, they could hardly use their office to advance their wealth, since the colony was poverty-stricken. This simply angered them, and they blamed lieutenant-governors like DesBarres. DesBarres on the other hand, was a strong-willed man with military training who was opposed to privilege and determined to be sole ruler of the Colony.

The inevitable clashes between the lieutenant-governors and members of the Executive Council may have been settled had a House of Assembly been established. Instead, the Colonial Office had decided that no House of Assembly would be elected until the island's population warranted it. Superficially, this seems reasonable. In reality, it had the effect of keeping settlers away, which in return delayed the granting of an assembly. The meetings of the lieutenant-governor with his executive thus became forums of debate. This delayed decisions and prevented action from being taken to cure the colony's ills. Cuyler and Mathews succeeded in convincing the Colonial Office that DesBarres was a tyrant and unfit to rule. He was recalled and replaced by Lieutenant-governor William Macarmick in 1787.

The struggle to remove DesBarres had not been a complete victory for the powerful Loyalists. Some members of the executive council, and many people, both Loyalists and otherwise, supported DesBarres. A rift developed which led to two factions, which persisted throughout the life of the Colony. The varying success of each side makes up a large part of the political history of Cape Breton until 1820.

Cossit tried to avoid these intrigues. In June 1786 he wrote, 'Seeing I could do no good in these matters, I avoided as much as I conveniently could, hearing or saying anything, as I am determined, as much as in me lieth to live peaceably with all men . . . '.[5] Possibly his mind was on his own responsibilities as another daughter was born in 1789 and another son two years later. With more mouths to feed, finances became more important, particularly when his salary from the S.P.G. was delayed. However, Cossit complained very little about this slowness, but busied himself with his clerical duties. He hired the colony's first teacher, Hiram Payne in 1790 and classes were taught in the parsonage. He managed to obtain £500 from the British government for the completion of St. George's in 1791. Meanwhile his missionary duties continued. They must have reminded him of the early days in Claremont, except that the territory was broader and communications even more primitive. He made trips by horseback to Main à Dieu, Louisbourg and Cow Bay (Port Morien). The dangers of such expeditions are exemplified in this story told by Cossit's great-great-grandson:

> Rev. Ranna, on one occasion was returning from a visit to Cow Bay and nightfall found him at the Inn at Hines Road. He left his horse with a stablehand to be fed and watered and went into the Inn for his supper. During the course of his meal he noticed two very unsavory characters in a corner of the room. They were talking in whispers, glancing in his direction, and soon left the room. Rev. Ranna suspected they were up to no good. When he finished his meal and paid the host, he went outside where he found his horse, fed and saddled. Mounting, he kept a wary eye on the shadows and before long he saw the two outlaws jump from the bushes and seize his bridle. Slipping the sword from its sheath, he caught one of the men across the face and swinging on the other, cut the arm holding the horse. Spurring his mount, he then left the culprits who were howling in pain and rode off. Needless to say, he was not molested after this.[6]

Cossit's reaction offers another insight into the determined spirit of the Cape Breton rector. Such a man would not bow to enemies of what he considered the cause of Cape Breton, and it was not long before Cossit became involved in the Colony's politics. He distrusted Cuyler and Mathews in their opposition to the established authority of the lieutenant-governor. Though he was a democrat, Cossit would not tolerate what he saw as a return to the unruly situation which had led to revolution in New Hampshire.

At first he was too busy organizing his parish and family to participate in politics. He observed however that

> Discontent, Envy and Malice are much more dominant here than true Religion on account of contention of some principal men (having commissions both Civil and Military) with the governor to the great prejudice of the settlement. These contentions, with many false reports against the governor, have kept many industrious farmers and fishermen . . . from becoming settlers on this Island, when they had made all preparations for so doing in order to enjoy the British Constitution which they esteem to be the Wisdom of God and the Glory of the whole Earth.[7]

Cossit firmly believed that the protection of the British Constitution was the duty of the Established Church; it was therefore only a matter of time before he, as that Church's minister, became involved in the political life of the Colony. This was hastened by his appointment to the Executive Council, which brought him in close proximity to Mathews and Cuyler. By the time Cossit became actively involved in politics, Cuyler had left the Colony. Lieutenant-governor Macarmick relaxed for awhile, but asked to be removed in 1795. As senior member of Council, David Mathews was appointed Administrator until a replacement could be found for Macarmick.

Cossit had established himself as the chief enemy of Mathews when the latter tried to form a group to prevent the settlement of Acadians in Cape Breton. Cossit alleged that Mathews' group would 'subvert the good order of Society'.[8] Macarmick agreed and squelched Mathews' alliance, thus allowing the free settlement of Acadians in Isle Madame. After this incident, Macarmick kept a close eye on Mathews, but on Macarmick's departure, Mathews took out his enmity on Cossit and his followers. Cossit's chief ally was James Miller, a mineralogist sent by the Colonial Office to investigate and make recommendations on the operations of the coal mines. Miller condemned the haphazard mining methods followed by the private individuals, Richard Stout and John Tremaine, to whom the mines had been leased. Stout was the Colony's principal merchant and Mathews was in debt to him. Miller's call for public ownership endangered Stout's position and caused Mathews to unleash an unrelenting attack on him.

Cossit and Miller were natural allies, not only in their distrust of Mathews, but also in condemning the overuse of rum in payment to miners. The latter lived gloomy lives punctuated by drunken revelries, during one of which their barracks burned to the ground. Cossit could not countenance this and with Miller argued that the miners should be paid in cash. Mathews not only supported Stout, but also failed to attend church. This alienated Cossit, so when Mathews allowed his name to stand for vestryman, the rector was furious and he and his followers succeeded in preventing the election.

Mathews' revenge came quickly. When in the fall of 1795, Cossit as S.P.G. agent attempted to appoint a new teacher, Mathews and his followers appointed their own, thus diminishing any tuition Cossit's choice might gain. Cossit opened the school at his home, so Mathews had the schoolmaster arrested for debt, but Cossit and Miller gave security for the schoolmaster.

As others became involved in these and other quarrels, the Colonial Office took action to remove Mathews. Two administrators followed: Major General James Ogilvie, the former Commander-in-chief of troops in the Maritime region, and Brigadier-General John Murray. Before Ogilvie arrived, Mathews managed to have Cossit imprisoned for a £25 debt which the latter allegedly owed Mathews' son. Ogilvie released Cossit, blaming Mathews for the factionalism, and Murray, who succeeded Ogilvie after less than a year, agreed. Cossit and his allies accordingly emerged triumphant in 1799.

The victory lasted less than a year, as Murray's successor, General John Despard, arrived to replace him in June 1800. Murray felt he was being unduly replaced and fought to remain in Sydney. While the decision of Whitehall was being awaited, Cossit and his followers rallied behind Murray; Mathews supported Despard. When word arrived that Murray was to be replaced, Mathews emerged triumphant. The gain was also short-lived however since Mathews died before the year was out.

Despard now saw Cossit not only as a political enemy, but also as a clergyman who had become too involved in politics and who had to be removed for the sake of colonial harmony. Despard wrote asking that Bishop Charles Inglis give the rector a new parish.

Cossit who had come to love Cape Breton refused to leave. His oldest boy, also called Ranna, was already in his late twenties and taking a role in colonial politics. Although some of the older children were married, by 1802 Thankfull had given birth to two more children, giving a total family of thirteen, 10 of whom survived. It would normally be difficult to provide for such a large family, but in the poor little Colony it was a trial. At times it was difficult to keep the children in shoes and had the potato patch in the yard of the parsonage not been productive, it would have been difficult to keep all the mouths fed. The demands of birth and inadequate diet led to the greatest tragedy of Cossit's life: the death of Thankfull in childbirth at the age of 46. Her previous child had been delivered 5 years before and the late pregnancy must have come as a surprise to the couple. Their joy ended in tragedy and the grief stricken rector wrote poignantly in the parish register: 'October 20th, 1802. Buried Mrs. Thankfull Cossit aged 46 years the 15th of March last — her whole life was ornamental to Christianity as a Wife, a Parent, a Neighbour ... '.[9]

The burial of his wife in Cape Breton soil, and his children's setting down roots in Sydney were reason enough for Cossit's desire to remain, but the increasing prosperity of the Colony appeared to be a reward for all the hard work of 15 years. In 1802 the first Scots began arriving from Scotland and though poor, they began farming, fishing and shipbuilding which had an immediate positive effect on the economy of the Colonial capital. Moreover, John Despard proved to be an outstanding ad-

The original Cossit house in Sydney, N.S. which is now open to the public

ministrator and soon increased the productivity of the mines and the extent of the colonial revenue.

But Cossit was not to enjoy his family or the brighter economy. Bishop Inglis himself arrived in Sydney in July 1805 and after three days convinced Cossit that his political involvement had caused scandal which could only hurt the Church. The sixty-one year old rector sadly agreed to leave all behind and accept an appointment far from his home in the remote town of Yarmouth.

The responsibilities at Yarmouth were onerous. As new rector, Cossit was charged with organizing the parish and building a church. The first site was abandoned due to wet ground. A second site was selected and the church was erected in July 1807. As in New Hampshire and Cape Breton, the aging man had to minister not only to the centre of population at Yarmouth, but also to Chebogue, Plymouth and Tusket. At first he pleaded to return to Sydney, but soon accepted his charge. He remained out of politics, perhaps because the capital of this Colony lay 300 miles away, and served the growing parish at Yarmouth until his death 13 March 1815.

Ranna Cossit was a man of principle who acted for what he believed. These beliefs were simple: the advancement of the Kingdom of God on earth, and the righteousness of the British constitution as the instrument of that Kingdom. Any person who opposed these causes was his enemy, and he would fight them with all his strength.

Unlike most people, Cossit left behind tangible symbols of these beliefs: churches in Claremont, Sydney and Yarmouth mark his accomplishments. A cairn near Holy Trinity Church in Yarmouth proclaims his work there. His descendants are scattered all over North America in every walk of life.

On any summer day, the traveller to Sydney is able to visit a humble house on Charlotte Street. It is Ranna Cossit's own home, open to the public by the Nova Scotia Museum since 1977. It endures as the oldest standing home in Sydney, as a monument to the lasting qualities of the Loyalist rector and his wife, and as a reminder of the society they and other Loyalists fought to establish in those difficult years after the American Revolution.

1. O.G. Hammond, *Tories of New Hampshire in the War of the Revolution*, (Concord, 1917), p. 26.
2. Mason Wade, *'Odyssey of a Loyalist Rector'*, Vermont History, XLVIII, 2 (Spring, 1980), p. 100.
3. Pearl S. Cossit, *The Cossit Family* (Pasadena, California), *Genealogical and Family History of the State of New Hampshire*, Vol. I, (New York, 1908).
4. Robert J. Morgan, *Orphan Outpost: Cape Breton Colony, 1784-1820*. (Unpublished Ph. D. thesis, University of Ottawa, 1972).
5. 'The Reverend Ranna Cossit' (sic), *The Journal of the Canadian Church Historical Society*, V., 3 (September 1963), n.p.
6. Franklynn MacLean, 'The Reverend Ranna Cossit', in R. Morgan ed. *More Essays in Cape Breton History*, (Windsor, N.S. 1977), pp. 66-67.
7. Ranna Cossit, *Letter Book*, June 1786, Cossit House, Sydney, C.B.; Archdeacon A. Smith, 'The First Seventy Years of St. George's Parish', *The Cape Breton Historical Society* (Sydney, 1932).
8. P.A.C., Cape Breton A Vol. 12, petition enclosed in Macarmick to Dundas, 18 July, 1794.
9. St. George's Anglican Church, Sydney, C.B., Death Records.

The Blue Church built in 1845 is the third church to stand on the town plot which Justus Sherwood surveyed and on which the Sherwood house stood in Augusta Township

Women in authentic costumes carry out household duties at a campsite depicting that era.

Chapter 10

Sarah Sherwood

Wife and Mother
an 'Invisible' Loyalist

by Mary Beacock Fryer

Sarah Sherwood is one of the women who believed in the loyalist ideal and became part of the migrations. Experiencing danger and hardship, she accepted the problems of raising a family virtually alone and shared the agonies of civil war with thousands of other wives and mothers on both sides of the conflict.

Documentation about Loyalist men is often skimpy; on women it is almost non-existent, other than as statistics on numbers migrating or being provisioned. A notable exception is Molly Brant, who, because she was a leader in a matriarchical society, had great influence and her story is well documented. Otherwise, only glimpses of the women are to be found. The moment a door opens on an individual woman, it slams shut almost at once. Many snippets tell of Rebels robbing Loyalists, of families left without shoes or bedding, information insufficient to make a narrative of any length.

One story somewhat stronger in source material is that of Sarah Sherwood. Her husband, Captain Justus Sherwood, held several important appointments under the governor of Canada, General Frederick Haldimand. In Justus' many letters to the governor's secretary, Robert Mathews, Justus often refers to his wife Sarah, probably because the two men were friends. Both Justus and Sarah were natives of Connecticut who after the American Revolution settled in the western wilds, the territory that became Upper Canada.

Sarah was one of five children of Elijah and Dorothy Bothum (later spelled Bottum). She was born in Norwich, Connecticut, in 1754. The other children in the family were her sister Dolly, probably christened Dorothy after their mother, and brothers Elijah Jr., Simon and Lemuel.[1] In 1767, Elijah Sr. took his family to the frontier in quest of cheap land, and settled in Shaftsbury Township, in the New Hampshire Grants which later became the State of Vermont.

This territory, where the first settlers received their land titles from New Hampshire, was disputed territory as it was also claimed by New York. A vigilante group of Connecticut men known as the Green Mountain Boys, led by Ethan Allen, tried to keep New York settlers out of the New Hampshire Grants. Despite the land war that ignited periodically around him, Elijah Bothum carved out a productive farm among the hills and was famous for his fine flock of sheep.

During the winter of 1771-1772, another hopeful from Connecticut entered the New Hampshire Grants and took up land in Sunderland Township, next door to Shaftsbury, land also held under New Hampshire title. He was Justus Sherwood, from Newtown, a twenty-five-year-old surveyor, who was determined to make a success of life at his profession, and in the lumber and potash trade. To protect his property from New York appointed sheriffs and magistrates who might try to evict him and give his land to a New York settler, Justus joined Ethan Allen's Green Mountain Boys. In March he participated in the rescue of one of the ringleaders in Allen's band, Remember Baker.

On 22 March, a local magistrate and posse working for the sheriff of New York's Albany County, had captured Baker and were taking him in a sleigh to Albany gaol. As the sleigh was passing the Bothum farm, Sarah's sister Dolly recognized Remember Baker and the family gave the alarm. Among the thirteen men who rode in pursuit of the posse was Justus Sherwood. The Green Mountain Boys dispersed the magistrate's men and with Baker returned in triumph to Bennington, south of Shaftsbury.[2]

This brought Justus to Sarah's attention; for her he was a man to admire. For Justus, Sarah was equally admirable; she was accustomed to life on the frontier and from her mother she had learned the skills to run a household in a pioneer area. Early in 1774 they were married by a Baptist elder in Shaftsbury, the denomination to which the Bothum family adhered.[3] Soon afterwards Justus put a tenant in his Sunderland farm and purchased a tract in the newly-opened Township of New Haven, ninety miles to the north. With Sarah and his three slaves, the youngest a mere lad named Caesar Congo who was her house servant, Justus set off along a blazed trail through the forest, driving their cattle. They did not have a cabin to shelter them when they arrived, but before long Justus had a decent house for his family. In New Haven their son Samuel was born before the year had ended.

Recognizing his capacity for leadership, the other settlers soon elected Justus as their Proprietors' Clerk, responsible for keeping the records of town meetings.[4] Despite his association with Ethan Allen, Justus' loyalties lay with the King. When in May 1775 the Green Mountain Boys captured Fort Ticonderoga from its British garrison, Justus was in favour, for that act was directed as much against New York as against Britain. However, he soon had second thoughts, and began advocating loyalty to the Crown. If enough people in the New Hampshire Grants remained steadfast, he reasoned, the British government might reward them by granting them a separate province, which would be one way of removing them from domination by New York. Justus made the decision to remain loyal, and he swept Sarah along with him as events unfolded.

In the spring of 1776, while in Bennington, Justus tried to defend his position, but angry Rebels brought him before a judge who sentenced him to a public flogging.[5] In August, when the Rebels suspected that Justus was sending information to the governor of Canada, Sir Guy Carleton, an armed band attacked his house. They smashed furniture, stole clothing and provisions, and searched for incriminating papers, while a terrified Sarah tried to comfort her child throughout the hubbub. They found nothing, for Justus had buried his private papers and the township records in a potash kettle outside his house,[6] but still they arrested him.

He was released on bail and returned to care for Sarah, but that very night the Rebels again attacked his house and took him away. When Sarah learned that he had been escorted all the way to Bennington, she, accompanied by Caesar Congo, her house servant, set out in a chaise with her son Samuel for her parents' farm in Shaftsbury. She was also five months pregnant, but during two terrorist attacks on her home she had not miscarried. Her brother Simon left shortly for New Haven to take charge of the farm and the other two slaves, expecting that Justus would soon be released. Instead he was sentenced to life imprisonment in Simsbury Mines, Connecticut but while being taken there, he broke away from his guards.

The first Sarah knew about that appalling sentence was Justus' sudden appearance at the Bothum farm in Shaftsbury. He stopped just long enough to sign his 50 acre farm in New Haven over to Sarah's father, in the hope that it could not be confiscated, and to bid farewell to his wife and son. He was no longer safe in the New Hampshire Grants and planned to join the British in Canada. When he left the Bothum farm, Sarah's brother, Elijah Jr., went with him.

Sarah remained in Shaftsbury and on 12 December 1776, she gave birth to a daughter, Diana. Once Sarah felt fit again, she was determined to return to her own home in New Haven, where Simon would help her run the place. Before the spring runoff made the trail impassable, she made the journey by sleigh with Samuel, Caesar Congo and the new baby girl. There, in late April 1777, Justus suddenly appeared on a clandestine mission for Governor Carleton, to reconnoitre Fort Ticonderoga, which the Rebels were reinforcing. Carleton needed the information because he intended to launch a massive summer offensive against the Rebels in northern New

York.[7]

When Justus left to continue his investigations, Sarah was in an awkward predicament. She was pregnant again, but she could hardly admit that her husband had been with her. The leaders in the New Hampshire Grants had recently proclaimed themselves the independent Republic of Vermont, but as the British army led by General John Burgoyne began to move southwards from Canada, most were inclined to make common cause with the New York Rebels to defeat the British army. While Justus came with that army, serving as a captain in a provincial corps known as the Queen's Loyal Rangers, he did not manage to see Sarah. He did, however, call at the Bothum farm in Shaftsbury while looking for recruits, and Elijah Sr. told him of Sarah's condition. He was overcome with remorse. Not until the war had ended and he knew he would survive did he want to father another child.

After Burgoyne's successful recapture of Fort Ticonderoga, his campaign was a series of disasters, and he surrendered his army on 17 October. Where, Sarah wondered, was Justus? Had he even survived? Then some Green Mountain Boys who had joined the rebel side reported that they had seen Justus among the prisoners at Saratoga, and a Loyalist who had been spying informed Sarah that he had been wounded. The Loyalists captured with Burgoyne were being sent to the British garrison that Burgoyne had left at Ticonderoga before his army went further south. Sarah immediately made plans to join Justus, but Simon cautioned her against going directly to Ticonderoga. Although the farm was in their father's name, Justus owned nearly 2,000 acres in the Green Mountains. To protect his property from confiscation, she should go to Bennington and ask the authorities for a safe conduct on compassionate grounds.

With Caesar Congo and the children, Sarah again set out for Shaftsbury. Elijah Bothum Sr. agreed with Simon, and arranged for Sarah to see the 'Grand Council of Safety', as the Vermont leaders styled themselves. On 24 October 1776[8] the council granted her safe conduct, and allowed her to take only necessary clothing and one bed. Back in Shaftsbury, Dorothy Bothum helped Sarah pack, concealing many small items in the mattress and adding a supply of provisions. Sarah, the children and Caesar Congo were taken by wagon to Skenesborough; her sides ached with each sway of the vehicle for she was in the seventh month of her pregnancy. At Skenesborough, where a stream led to Lake Champlain, they were put aboard a bateau for the journey to Ticonderoga.

By this time it was early November, and they found Ticonderoga deserted. The garrison had destroyed anything the Rebels could use and withdrawn for the winter to Fort St. Jean (St. Johns), inside Canada on the Richelieu River. Sarah's escort had no choice but to take her towards the nearest British outpost, Pointe au Fer, at the northern end of the lake. About thirty miles from that post, the men in Sarah's escort panicked lest British patrols capture them and left Sarah's little party on the west shore of the lake, to make their way as best they could.

Aided by Caesar Congo, Sarah cached her belongings and marked the spot. Then they started slowly along the trail, Sarah carrying Diana, leading three-year-old Samuel by the hand, and the slave bearing their provisions and blankets. On they trudged, pausing frequently for Sarah to catch her breath. Each night they shivered in their blankets, but they succeeded in gaining the post at Pointe au Fer. There Sarah waited in relative comfort while Caesar Congo went back along the lake with some bateaumen to retrieve the bed and other baggage.[9]

Even the rest of the journey by bateau, past the outpost at Isle aux Noix and down the Richelieu to Fort St. Jean was a trial to a woman in Sarah's condition. Yet Justus' joy at her arrival made the privation worth while. At first Sarah and the children were housed in a barracks with other refugee dependents, accepting government provisions until Justus could find better accommodation and the means to care for them. At first Justus could not draw his captain's pay of ten shillings a day. Like other provincials captured when Burgoyne surrendered, he was a prisoner of war on parole, and not allowed any military duties.[10]

Soon Governor Carleton came to Justus and Sarah's

rescue, by allowing him 30 pounds a year for the support of his family.[11] Using this money, Justus rented a small house in the village of St. Jean, close to the fort, and with Caesar Congo began building furniture.

On 12 December 1777, some three weeks too early, Sarah's labour pains began. Fearful that the journey from Shaftsbury had been too much for his wife, Justus hurried to fetch one of the military physicians. The baby was a boy whom they named Levius Peters Sherwood — the middle name after Justus' commanding officer in the Queen's Loyal Rangers, Lieutenant-colonel John Peters.[12] Despite the furtive circumstances of his conception, the fears that haunted Sarah during Justus' absence, her exhausting journey to Canada and his premature arrival, Levius was a healthy boy who thrived in the humble dwelling at St. Jean. Sarah was happy, but she agreed with Justus that they must not have any more children until they were resettled and knew what the future held.

For Sarah, seven long years of uncertainty began. Her anxieties about the future were heightened early in May 1778, when scouts returning from Vermont brought word that most of Justus' property had been confiscated. All that remained after his years in the Green Mountains were the 50 acre farm in Elijah Bothum's name where Simon had remained, and another 350 acres in New Haven. There the local Rebels still had a healthy respect for their one-time Proprietors' Clerk.[13]

In June, Justus was returned to active duty on full pay. At that time Governor Carleton revoked all the paroles signed by provincial soldiers at Saratoga, when he learned that the Rebels had also broken the terms Burgoyne had signed there.[14] For Sarah, this meant that Justus was often absent for considerable periods of time, during which she had no idea where he was, or whether he would come back safely. In July, he made his first journey into Rebel-held territory on foot, carrying a dispatch for Carleton which he was to leave at a house near Albany. When he returned he brought six women and fifteen children with him, people left destitute when husbands and fathers were imprisoned or had fled to Canada.[15]

Through the years of displacement, Sarah cared for the children, wove yards of linsey-woollsey, made most of the clothing, and provided Justus with a quiet anchorage from the storms of war. Governor Frederick Haldimand replaced Sir Guy Carleton that summer of 1778, and he appointed Justus a Commissioner of Prisoners and of Refugees. He was occupied interrogating prisoners and refugees at the fort, and in going to designated points along Lake Champlain with his flag of truce to exchange prisoners and escort parties of refugees into Canada. The journeys were exhausting, and at the end of each, Sarah was there to lend a sympathetic ear and see that he had a good rest and the right food.

In the autumn of 1779, Anna Sherwood arrived with three children, Reuben, Anna and Adiel, the latter a baby boy born that May. Anna's husband, Thomas Sherwood, was Justus' cousin and serving in the same regiment. Thomas had brought the family from their farm near Fort Edward, New York, and Anna and the children joined Sarah in the house at St. Jean. Most refugee families were sent on to Machiche, on the north side of the St. Lawrence River from Sorel. Thomas, who was employed scouting for intelligence, wanted to have his family close enough to visit from time to time.[16]

The following August, even closer relatives joined what was becoming a Sherwood compound at St. Jean. Justus' brother Samuel, who had moved from Connecticut to Kingsbury Township, not far from Fort Edward, arrived with his wife Eunice and year-old daughter Rachel, accompanied by a slave. Like Thomas, Samuel worked as a scout. That autumn Justus made a journey into Vermont and arranged for the republic to become neutral. Afterwards he went to Quebec by sleigh to report to Haldimand. His return was delayed until after Christmas, and Sarah tried to see that the children's enjoyment of the festival was not marred by Justus' absence.[17] When he returned he went off to Isle aux Noix, for Haldimand had placed him in command of the scouts operating from that base, among them his cousin Thomas and brother Samuel.

By June 1781 Sarah's responsibilities had become too heavy. Being in command of a large household, even with the assistance of Anna and Eunice, had overtaxed her strength and she needed many days of bed rest before she recovered.[18] That month Justus received a promotion that would keep him away from home even more than ever. Haldimand appointed him head of the British Secret Service, Northern Department, and gave him permission to build a blockhouse on North Hero Island in Lake Champlain. He left with a party of men, and for more than a year he was in St. Jean only briefly.[19] As Justus' deputy, Haldimand chose Dr. George Smyth, a physician and long a valuable agent from Albany who had escaped when a warrant was issued for his arrest.

In the summer of 1782, Justus and Sarah discussed the education of the children during one of his visits to St. Jean. Thus far, the Reverend George Gilmore, a chaplain in one of the regular regiments, had been teaching the children around the fort. The parents paid him small fees and Haldimand allowed a subsidy.[20] Justus felt that their elder son Samuel, now nearly eight years old, should attend an academy in Montreal kept by the Reverend John Stuart, the former Anglican missionary to the Mohawks at Fort Hunter, New York.[21] Sarah may have had qualms about sending a young child away from home, but the final decision was Justus'.

In September he took two weeks leave from his headquarters to settle Samuel in school in Montreal. Then, in order to economize as he had to pay both fees and board for Samuel, he decided to give up the house at St. Jean and move Sarah, Diana and Levius to what he called the Loyal Blockhouse, because it was exclusively a loyalist operation. Sarah agreed to live in that primitive place because she disliked being separated from Justus so much of the time. Thomas and Samuel Sherwood preferred to keep their families in St. Jean and they took over the rent for the house. When Justus' leave was over, he and Sarah packed their belongings in a bateau and with nearly six-year-old Diana and five-year-old Levius set out for North Hero Island and the Loyal Blockhouse.[22]

Sarah was the chatelaine of a little community. In addition to her regular housekeeping duties, she tended the sick and brewed spruce beer to ward off scurvy. The garrison consisted of some 50 men, most of them from Justus' company in a new regiment, the Loyal Rangers. Haldimand had amalgamated some older units and the Queen's Loyal Rangers was one of them. In addition to the garrison, Justus had about 50 scouts who came and went in civilian clothing, and several women who lived in cabins with their children and did housekeeping chores for the men. Justus paid a literate soldier to tutor all the children.

In January 1783, Sarah's youngest brother, nineteen-year-old Lemuel Bothum, arrived at the blockhouse to visit her and their brother Elijah, one of the scouts. Lemuel had trekked from Shaftsbury with Judge Luke Knowlton, one of Justus' agents who had left his home at New Fane when he heard that the Rebels were planning to kidnap him. Lemuel had made the journey in cowhide boots, rather than warm fur-lined moccasins, and was suffering from frostbitten feet.[23] Sarah cared for him, and when Lemuel had recovered, Justus gave Elijah a leave of absence and he left the blockhouse with Knowlton and his brother for the comforts of St. Jean.

Late in February, a scout reaching the Loyal Blockhouse reported that 600 Rebels in sleighs had left Albany bound for Saratoga. Justus prepared for seige, and he ordered all the women and children evacuated to St. Jean. In bitterly cold weather he saw Sarah, Diana, Levius and Caesar Congo off in a sleigh bound for the Sherwood house where Anna and Eunice had remained. With them in more sleighs went the other women and their children, as did Justus' private papers which were to be left at Isle aux Noix. The alarm proved to be false, for the rebel expedition turned towards Oswego to attack that post. At the end of March, accompanied by her brother Elijah, Sarah with the two younger children and the slave again took up residence in the Loyal Blockhouse.

On 27 April 1783, the Preliminary Articles of Peace were published in the *Quebec Gazette*. Now that hostilities were ended, Governor Haldimand made plans to resettle the Loyalists who were in Canada or along the frontiers at his outposts. He ordered Justus to select some men skilled in the art of land colonization, pick up a whaleboat at Isle aux Noix, and proceed to Quebec

City. Enclosed with his orders was a passport for Sarah, so that she could visit her family in Vermont. Justus was to explore the east coast in quest of land suitable for the resettlement of the Loyalists.

Sarah, however, had other ideas. Much as she missed her parents, she longed to experience the glittering social life of Quebec which Justus had described on his return from visiting the city. He, too, had no desire to leave his family behind. He was acquainted with Captain Hugh O'Hara, of the Gaspé Bay garrison, and he thought that the O'Hara family would welcome Sarah and the children while he carried out his mission. Among the men Justus chose to accompany him was his cousin Thomas Sherwood. With his party, including Sarah, Diana and Levius, Justus left the Loyal Blockhouse in a bateau for Isle aux Noix, where they transferred to the whaleboat which could shoot the rapids in the Richelieu River at Fort Chambly. At St. Jean, Justus and his family left the men to continue on towards Sorel, where they would catch up with the whaleboat.

The Sherwoods took a stagecoach to the south shore of the St. Lawrence and crossed the river to Montreal in a ferry. Sarah had a dress made so that she would look presentable among the fine ladies of Quebec, and they took Samuel from his school. By May 22 the little expedition had reached Quebec City, and Justus took rooms in a coffee house in the Lower Town. He conferred with the governor on his upcoming journey. In the evenings, usually in company with Robert Mathews and his wife Mary, Justus and Sarah attended dances and theatrical productions staged by officers of the garrison and their wives. Sarah thoroughly enjoyed the social whirl after so many years of temporary living at St. Jean and the Loyal Blockhouse. She had never experienced anything quite as grand as life in a garrison city inhabited by well-to-do British regular officers and their ladies. All too soon the dream had to end. On the 29th the Sherwoods embarked on the Treasury brig *St. Peter* for Gaspé Bay.[24]

They arrived on 7 June, and as Justus hoped, the O'Hara family welcomed them warmly. While Captain O'Hara acted as Justus' guide, Sarah and the children had a glorious holiday and they must rank as the first tourists who visited that magnificent region. The children swam in the sea, fished with the young O'Haras, and feasted on lobsters which they caught by the tails among the shallows. Again, too soon this idyllic interlude ended. On 14 July Justus and his party returned to Gaspé Bay. On the 20th the Sherwoods sailed for Quebec, taking Captain and Mrs. O'Hara's eldest son and daughter, who were to stay with friends in the city. The voyage back to Quebec was tedious, as the brigantine battled both the prevailing wind and the current of the lower St. Lawrence. Whereas the outward voyage had taken only ten days, the return lasted twenty-four, and they did not reach Quebec until 12 August.

Justus expected to see Haldimand, but the governor had gone to his summer château at Sorel. In a whaleboat the Sherwoods and Justus' party rowed upriver, and after a conference with Haldimand and Mathews at Sorel they continued on up the Richelieu to St. Jean. Sarah and the two younger children stayed with Anna and Eunice, and Thomas went to take command of the Loyal Blockhouse from Dr. Smyth, who was complaining that he needed leave. Justus hurried to Montreal with young Samuel and returned the boy to school. Then he prepared to set out with a survey party for the upper St. Lawrence and Lake Ontario. Haldimand wanted him to assist in the exploration and surveying of the upper country because Justus' report on the land available along the east coast was unfavourable. He had found that most of the good land was privately owned and would be difficult to acquire.

When Justus returned to St. Jean, after helping lay out townships and farm lots around Cataraqui, he was suffering from a high fever. On 9 December 1783, Dr. George Smyth reported to Robert Mathews that Captain Sherwood was gravely ill with smallpox.[25] Even before Dr. Smyth had diagnosed Justus' ailment, the house at St. Jean was plunged into a crisis. The moment the doctor became suspicious he ordered the house cleared. Anna and Eunice Sherwood took all the children to the Loyal Blockhouse, and Sarah moved into the barracks to be on hand to receive daily reports. For her own protec-

Sarah Sherwood

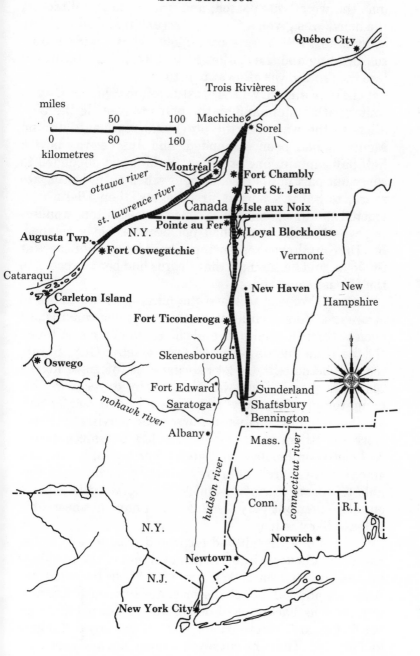

miles

| 0 | 50 | 100 |

| 0 | 80 | 160 |

kilometres

Québec City

Trois Rivières

Machiche

Sorel

ottawa river

st. lawrence river

Montréal

Fort Chambly

Fort St. Jean

Canada

Isle aux Noix

Augusta Twp.

N.Y.

Pointe au Fer

Loyal Blockhouse

Fort Oswegatchie

Vermont

Cataraqui

Carleton Island

New Haven

New Hampshire

Oswego

Fort Ticonderoga

Skenesborough

mohawk river

Fort Edward

Sunderland

Saratoga

Shaftsbury

Bennington

Albany

Mass.

hudson river

connecticut river

Conn.

R.I.

N.Y.

Norwich

Newtown

N.J.

New York City

tion she had to leave the nursing of her husband to people who had had smallpox and were immune. By Christmas the worst was passed, and under Sarah's direction the house was given a thorough scrubbing to rid it of any stray scabs, which were contagious. These, and all Justus' bedding and the clothes he had worn were burnt before the family was allowed to return.

Late in January 1784, Justus left for Quebec City to confer with Haldimand on the plans to resettle the Loyalists to the west. All the provincial regiments around Montreal had been disbanded, and Justus was now a half-pay captain, one on whom Haldimand depended to carry out part of his resettlement scheme. In Justus' absence, to Sarah's horror, first Levius, then Diana contracted smallpox.[26] She was conscience-smitten, wondering whether the house had not been properly cleaned, but Dr. Smyth was reassuring. There were other cases at St. Jean, and he thought that Levius had been exposed to the disease somewhere else.

Sarah refused to leave the nursing of her babes to strangers. Young children tended to suffer convulsions even with mild smallpox, and she could not desert them. By the time Justus returned from Quebec City, Sarah, too, had become ill. On 24 February, he informed Robert Mathews that his son was on the way to recovery, his daughter out of danger, but he was very alarmed for Sarah. Immune himself Justus nursed her, leaving his usual work for others to do, staying by her bedside pressing cool cloths on her face and giving her bits of ice to suck since she was barely able to swallow. By 1 March, he was able to inform Mathews that 'Mrs. Sherwood is, I hope, out of danger but very weak & low. I have not been able to leave her one hour'.

As soon as Sarah had recovered, Justus left for Lachine, to help superintend the movement of the Loyalists up the St. Lawrence. With other officers he doled out supplies, and led one of the brigades himself to Cataraqui, then he backtracked downriver to Township Number 6 (Edwardsburgh) where some of the Loyal Rangers had arrived. There he surveyed a town plot and spent the next two months laying out township boundaries and farm lots. In August he returned to St. Jean and all three

Sherwood families packed their belongings and set out in a bateau for Sorel and on to the new settlements. Sarah found the journey trying, especially while the bateau-men were drawing their craft through the stretches of rapids and the passengers had to walk over rough ground. Neither she nor Justus were feeling fit because her illness was so recent, and he had resumed his duties too soon after his own recovery.

Justus was awarded Lots 8 and 9 in the first concession of Township Number 7 (now Augusta, Grenville County), his brother Samuel Lot 7, Thomas Sherwood Lot 1 in Township Number 8 (now Elizabethtown, Leeds County). Soon Elijah Bothum Jr. arrived from Vermont where he had purchased seed for the settlers, and brought Justus' two slaves from New Haven.[27] Their arrival was timely for Justus and Sarah. Although Elijah had received Lots 26 and 27 in the same township, he wanted to spend the first winter with the family since he would find staying on his own land very lonely. He set to work, aided by the three slaves, Samuel and Levius, building two small cabins on Lot 9. Meanwhile, Sarah and Justus stayed in a tent on the town plot of Township Number 6. Justus was busy handing out lots to other settlers and doing more surveying and had not had time to attend to his own family's needs. In September Sarah was able to leave the tent and live in a primitive but superior cabin. She was undaunted at the prospect for their first cabin in New Haven had been even more rustic. Here the government was allowing each head of family four panes of glass, while in New Haven she had made do with oiled paper at first.

Although their living conditions initially were little different from their neighbours, Sarah enjoyed a position of some prestige. As in New Haven, Justus emerged as a leader in the new settlement, a fact recognized by the government. He was one of the earliest magistrates, and in 1785 he was appointed a member of the Legislative Council.[28] With his half-pay Justus was better able to procure livestock than most of the settlers. He built timber rafts that he floated to Sorel and Quebec City, and made potash, in addition to developing his farm. In 1786, now that they were getting their homestead established,

Sarah became pregnant once more.

In order to provide a better home before the new baby arrived, Justus surveyed a town plot in Augusta and started work on a large, square-timbered house. It was two miles from the farm, where the slaves would remain and he could commute when his other activities allowed him time.[29] There Sarah gave birth to a daughter whom they named Sarah after her. The following year she played host to Robert Mathews, who visited on his way to Detroit to prepare a report on the fort there for Lord Dorchester, the new governor. Dorchester was Guy Carleton with a new title, on a second tour of duty in Canada, and Mathews was his aide-de-camp. Justus was in a back township with a survey party at the time, and he was disappointed when Sarah told him he had missed seeing his old friend.

Schooling, especially for the two boys, was non-existent until the Reverend John Stuart moved to Cataraqui, to the village being called Kingston, sixty miles west of the Sherwood farm. The clergyman reopened his school for a few years, and Justus sent Samuel and Levius to him during the winter months when he could spare them. Diana stayed with Sarah, learning the household skills she would need in order to run a pioneer home properly. In 1788 Sarah gave birth to a third daughter, Harriet.[30]

This child came at a difficult time in the settlements. In the summer of 1787, severe drought struck. This was serious, for the settlers had only coped for two years without government rations. That winter people had been forced to butcher their livestock, and eat the seed they were saving to plant, in order to survive. The government provided some seed, and the harvest along the upper St. Lawrence was better in 1788, but shortages persisted because the quantities of seed each settler received were small. The time from 1787 to 1789 was known as The Hungry Year, depending on where the settlers lived, for the severity of the drought varied.

In 1791, the year Upper Canada was established, Sarah gave birth to their last child, a daughter named Sophia. By that time the Sherwood family had recovered from the losses sustained during the revolutionary war.

Young Samuel Sherwood wanted to study law, and Justus sent him to Montreal to article with Lawyer James Walker.[31] Samuel opened his office in a growing village, now called Prescott, at the east end of the township. There Levius soon joined him to article. Sarah had the care of the younger girls to occupy her while her older children were entering new occupations. In the spring of 1797 Diana, then twenty-one years old, married Samuel Smades, a young farmer with land along the Rideau River. A year later she presented Sarah and Justus with their first grandson, whom she named Elijah Bothum Smades after her favourite uncle.

During the summer of 1798, Justus set off down the St. Lawrence with two timber rafts bound for Quebec City. At Trois Rivières he slipped off one of the rafts and his body was never recovered.[32] For some time Sarah prayed that he would turn up as he had always done during the revolution, but as time passed she came to accept his death. He was only fifty-one, she forty-four when she was widowed so unexpectedly. She still had much to live for — two fine sons, Diana and her growing family, and more important, three little girls to raise. The youngest, Sophia, was only seven years old when her father died.

Sarah managed the farm and the boys took over the lumber trade, as well as operating their law office. In time Sarah's daughter Sarah married Andrew McCollom, a farmer in Augusta, and Harriet chose Dr. Benjamin Trask of Montreal and left the township. In 1810 Samuel moved his law practice to Montreal, and Levius opened his own office in Elizabethtown, the first township to the west. That same year Sophia, aged nineteen, married Jonathan Jones of Augusta, then three years later she died and was buried in the cemetery on Justus' town plot. The province was in the throes of war with the United States at the time, and Levius was the lieutenant-colonel of the first battalion, Leeds Militia. Levius, too, had married, and Sarah was alone on the farm or at the house on the town plot where no town was developing.

Sarah Sherwood sold the farm, gave the house to Levius, and moved to Montreal to enjoy the amenities the city offered and to be close to Samuel and Harriet.

There she died at age sixty-four in 1818. With Justus she had founded a family that would remain prominent in the law and politics of Upper Canada, eventually Ontario, for several generations.

1. Lt.-col. H.M. Jackson, *Justus Sherwood, Soldier, Loyalist and Negotiator.* Published privately, 1953. p. 2.
2. E.B. O'Callahan, ed. *Documentary History of the State of New York.* Albany, 1851, pp. 776-777; Coolidge, A.J. and Mansfield, J.B. *History and Description of New England, General and Social.* Boston, 1859, vol. 1, p. 110.
3. Vermont Public Record Office, Montpelier. Vital Statistics. Marriage and death records indicate that the Bothum family were Baptists.
4. H.C. Mathews, *Frontier Spies.* Fort Myers, Fla., 1971, p. 42.
5. H.P. Smith, *History of Addison County.* Syracuse, N.Y. 1886, p. 526.
6. Abby Maria Hemenway, *The Vermont Historical Gazetteer.* vol. 1, Burlington, Vt., 1867, p. 130.
7. Public Record Office, London. A/O 13-22, p. 351-360. Memorial of Justus Sherwood.
8. E.P. Walton, ed. *Records of the Council of Safety, State of Vermont.* Montpelier, Vt., 1873, vol. 1, p. 192.
9. At that time rebel escorts did not venture close to British posts. Later, handing refugee families over under flags of truce became commonplace.
10. Under Article 8 of the Saratoga Convention, which Burgoyne signed, all captured personnel were to be regarded as British subjects, rather than subjects of the Continental Congress. In this way Burgoyne protected his provincial troops, who otherwise might have been treated as traitors by the Rebels.
11. James M. Hadden, *A Journal kept in Canada upon Burgoyne's campaign in 1776 and 1777.* Albany, 1884, p. 72, footnote.
12. Justus' second son's name is often shown as Livius. His handwriting was responsible. His great, great grandson was named Livius after his mother misread the name in the family Bible.
13. M.G. Nye, *State Papers of Vermont.* No date, vol. 4, p. 17.
14. Public Archives of Canada. Haldimand Transcripts, B 83, p. 97. Order from Headquarters, June 1, 1778.
15. Ibid. B 181, Sherwood to Carleton, July 10, 1778.
16. Thad. Leavitt, *History of Leeds and Grenville.* Brockville, 1879. Memoir of Adiel Sherwood, p. 20.
17. PAC Haldimand Transcripts, B 180, pp. 42-58. Sherwood's journal.
18. Ibid. B 176, p. 123. Sherwood to Mathews, June 2, 1781.
19. Ibid. pp. 142-143. Sherwood to Mathews, July 1, 1781.
20. J.N. McIlwraith, *Sir Frederick Haldimand.* Makers of Canada Series, Toronto, 1926, p. 125-126.
21. Ibid. p. 235.
22. Justus Sherwood's Account Book. Metropolitan Toronto Central Library.
23. PAC Haldimand Transcripts. B 178, p. 22. Knowlton to Haldimand, January 10, 1783.
24. Ibid. B 169, pp. 6-19, Sherwood's journal; PRO A/O 13-22. Memorial of Thomas Sherwood.
25. PAC Haldimand Transcripts. B 178, p. 321, Smyth to Mathews, December 9, 1783.
26. Ibid. B 162, p. 190, Sherwood to Mathews, March 1, 1784.
27. Ibid. B 178, pp. 324-325, Smyth to Mathews, May 20, 1784.
28. PAC *Quebec Gazette*, May 12, 1785.
29. PAC M. G. 23, J. 9. Journal of Major Robert Mathews.
30. Ontario Archives, Biographical Card Catalogue in Alphabetical Order.
31. Leavitt, p. 19.
32. Ontario Archives, Biographical Card Catalogue in Alphabetical Order.

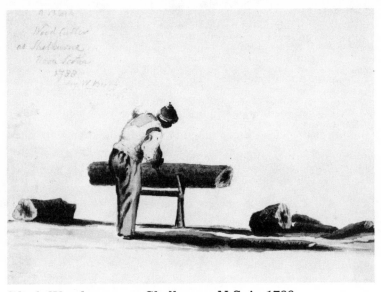

Black Woodcutter at Shelburne, N.S. in 1788

Chapter 11

Boston King

A Black Loyalist

by Phyllis R. Blakeley

Boston King was one of the slaves who seized his opportunity, escaped from his 'master', and after both adventure and misadventure crossed the British lines. From New York, he and hundreds of other former slaves were evacuated to Shelburne where they formed the community called Birchtown. Here, he laboured as a carpenter suffering both the prevelant economic hardships and the additional scourge of racism. After his religious conversion, Boston King became a Methodist preacher and later joined the migration of Black Loyalists to Sierra Leone, Africa.

The civil war between Great Britain and thirteen of her colonies in North America was ending. In Paris commissioners were working out details for Britain to acknowledge the independence of the 'United States' of America and preliminary terms were signed on 30 November 1782. The main headquarters for the British army was in New York City, where thousands of refugees loyal to the Crown had come for protection, many of them former Black slaves who had been promised freedom if they joined the British. One of these was Boston King, who had been a slave in South Carolina, and who wrote in his *Memoirs*:

About which time, (in 1783), the horrors and devastation of war happily terminated, and peace was restored between America and Great Britain, which diffused universal joy among all parties, except us, who had escaped from slavery, and taken refuge in the English army; for a report prevailed at New-York, that all the slaves, in number 2000, were to be delivered up to their masters, altho' some of them had been three or four years among the English. This dreadful rumour filled us all with inexpressible anguish and terror, especially when we saw our old masters coming from Virginia, North-Carolina, and other parts, and seizing upon their slaves in the streets of New-York, or even dragging them out of their beds. Many of the slaves had very cruel masters, so that the thoughts of returning home with them embittered life to us. For some days we lost our appetite for food, and sleep departed from our eyes. The English had compassion upon us in the day of our distress, and issued out a Proclamation, importing, 'That all slaves should be free, who had taken refuge in the British lines, and claimed the sanction and privileges of the Proclamations respecting the security and protection of Negroes'. In consequence of this, each of us received a certificate from the commanding officer at New-York, which dispelled all our fears, and filled us with joy and gratitude. Soon after, ships were fitted out, and furnished with every necessary for conveying us to Nova Scotia.

Boston and Violet King had started on another step on a journey which was eventually to take them to Sierra Leone in Africa. They were part of that more than ten per cent of the 30,000 Loyalists sent to Nova Scotia at the end of the American Revolution who were Black men, women and children.

Boston King's father had been stolen from Africa by the slave traders, but he could read and write and 'was beloved by his master, and had the charge of the Plantation as a driver for many years. In his old age he was employed as a mill-cutter'. He was a Christian and 'lost no opportunity of hearing the Gospel, and never omitted praying with his family every night'. His mother nursed the sick, having learned herbal remedies from the Indians, and was also a seamstress and 'on these accounts was indulged with many privileges which the rest of the slaves were not'. Boston King had been born about 1760 on the plantation of Richard Waring 45 kilometres from Charleston, South Carolina.

Children were put to work at an early age and were trained by the apprenticeship system. Six-year-old Boston was sent to the plantation house to wait upon his master. From nine to sixteen he helped to look after the cattle and horses and had an opportunity to travel with race horses to various parts of America, but one time he lost a boot belonging to the groom who punished him by refusing to let Boston wear any shoes all that winter. The economy of the southern plantations depended on skilled slave labour, as well as field workers, and youths were trained by the apprenticeship system. Plantations had blacksmiths, carpenters, coopers, sawyers, bakers, tailors and weavers. When he was sixteen Boston was apprenticed as a carpenter and after two years had charge of the tools. If any were lost or misplaced his 'master beat me severely, striking me upon the head, or any other part without mercy'. Nails were very valuable, for war had broken out between the American colonies and Great Britain, and nails were expensive because all British manufactured goods were scarce and local blacksmiths could not meet the demand. The workmen had their nails weighed out to them and made the younger apprentices guard the nails at dinner time. Once Boston had to watch the nails until another apprentice returned, when he went to eat. The nails belonging to one of the journeymen disappeared, and Boston was blamed for stealing them. 'For this offence I was beat and tortured most cruelly, and was laid up three weeks before I was able to do any work'. However, Richard Waring who owned Boston, came to town and threatened to take him away, and the master carpenter treated Boston much better and taught him more of carpentry.

While Boston King learned his trade as a carpenter, the political dispute between Britain and her colonies exploded into bitter civil war, offering King and hundreds of other Black slaves an opportunity to strike for freedom. Boston recalled some of these events of the rebel and British forces fighting nearby.

> My master being apprehensive that Charles Town was
> in danger on account of the war, removed into the
> country, about 38 miles off. Here we built a large
> house for Mr. Waters, during which time the English
> took Charles-Town. Having obtained leave one day to
> see my parents, who lived about 12 miles off, and it be-
> ing late before I could go, I was obliged to borrow one
> of Mr. Wats's horses, but a servant of my master's,
> took the horse from me to go a little journey, and
> stayed two or three days longer than he ought. This in-
> volved me in the greatest perplexity, and I expected
> the severest punishment, because the gentleman to
> whom the horse belonged was a very bad man, and
> knew not how to show mercy. To escape his cruelty, I
> determined to go to Charles-Town, and throw myself
> into the hands of the English. They received me readi-
> ly, and I began to feel the happiness of liberty, of
> which I knew nothing before, altho' I was most grieved
> at first, to be obliged to leave my friends, and remain
> among strangers.

Runaway slaves were welcomed by the British who
needed more soldiers, and also needed cooks, orderlies
and waiters, blacksmiths and carpenters, waggoners and
grooms, hostlers, axe-men, guides and pilots, and labourers to work on the fortifications. Also they hoped to crip-
ple the economy of the South by encouraging the slaves
to run away to the British lines. In 1779 the British commander-in-chief, Sir Henry Clinton, issued his Philips-
burg Proclamation in which he promised every Negro
who deserted from an enemy master full security to follow any occupation within the British lines and forbade
any person from selling or claiming any enemy-owned
slave who had taken refuge in the British lines. By seizing slaves the British army increased its resources and
depleted those of the enemy.

Shortly after King joined the British, an epidemic of
smallpox broke out and in an effort to prevent it spreading among the White soldiers, the Blacks were carried 'a
mile' from camp. There were not enough nurses so that
King often lay a whole day without anything to eat or
drink 'but Providence sent a man, who belonged to the

[New] York volunteers whom I was acquainted with, to my relief. He brought me such things as I stood in need of . . . ' The invalids were apprehensive of capture by the American rebel forces but when they realized 'we were ill of the small-pox, they precipitately left us for fear of the infection'. Two days later wagons came to take them to the British army.

When he recovered, King moved with the army to Lord Cornwallis' headquarters at Camden, and since his original regiment was 56 kilometres off, he stayed at headquarters for three weeks. When Cornwallis defeated General Horatio Gates on 16 August 1780, King's friend from the New York Volunteers was wounded. As soon as he heard of this King went to see him and nursed him in the hospital for six weeks. King then became the orderly of a British regular officer, Captain Grey, and went with him to a camp 56 kilometres away, where they stayed for two months. King was off fishing when orders came to break camp in fifteen minutes, and he returned to find all the English were gone and the place occupied by a few Southern Loyalist militiamen. King was alarmed because the militiamen reflected the Southern attitude to slaves. Captain Lewes, who commanded the militia, reassured him.

'You need not be uneasy, for you will see your regiment before 7 o'clock to-night'. This satisfied me for the present, and in two hours we set off. As we were on the march, the Captain asked, 'How will you like me to be your master?' I answered that I was Captain Grey's servant. 'Yes', said he, 'but I expect they are all taken prisoners before now, and I have been long enough in the English service, and am determined to leave them'. These words roused my indignation, and I spoke some sharp things to him. But he calmly replied, 'If you do not behave well, I will put you in irons, and give you a dozen stripes every morning'. I now perceived that my case was desperate, and that I had nothing to trust to, but to wait the first opportunity for making my escape. The next morning, I was sent with a little boy over the river to an island to fetch the Captain's horses. When we came to the Island we found about fifty of the English horses, that Captain Lewes had stolen from them at Different times while they were at Rockmount. Upon our return to the Captain with the horses we were sent for, he immediately set off by himself. I stayed till about 10 o'clock, and then resolved to go to the English army'.

King managed to reach the English headquarters where he informed Captain Grey that Lewes had deserted and the British burned Lewes' house and recaptured forty of the stolen horses. After a year Boston became the servant of the commanding officer at Nelson's Ferry, but this was a dangerous place because they had only 250 soldiers and the American rebels had 1600. The commander decided to send King with a letter to a large English force about 48 kilometres away and promised him great rewards. Boston

set off on foot about 3 o'clock in the afternoon; I expected every moment to fall in with the enemy, whom I well knew would shew me no mercy. I went on without interruption, till I got within six miles of my journey's end, and then was alarmed with a great noise a little before me. But I stepped out of the road, and fell upon my face till they were gone by. I then arose, and praised the Name of the Lord for his great mercy, and again pursued by journey, till I came to Mums-corner [Monk's Corner] tavern. I knocked at the door, but they blew out the candle. I knocked again, and intreated the master to open the door. At last he came with a frightful countenance and said, 'I thought it was the Americans; for they were here about an hour ago, and I thought they were returned again'. I asked, 'How many were there?' He answered, 'about one hundred'. I desired him to saddle his horse for me, which he did, and went with me himself. When we had gone about two miles, we were stopped by the picket-guard, till the Captain came out with 30 men: As soon as he knew that I had brought an express from Nelson's ferry, he received me with great kindness, and expressed his approbation of my courage and conduct in this dangerous business. Next morning, Colonel Small gave me three shillings, and many fine promises, which were all that I ever received for this service from him. However, he sent 600 men to relieve the troops at Nelson's-ferry.[1]

Next King went to Charleston, and after the British

surrendered that city to the Rebels, he was taken to New York on a British warship. When the British finally left Charleston in December 1782 they took 5,327 Blacks — most of whom were sent to Jamaica or East Florida, but a few went to England, New York and Nova Scotia. In New York there were so many refugees that the British authorities encouraged them to support themselves. King expected to follow his trade of carpenter but he did not have any tools and did not have the money to buy any so he had to become a servant. The wages were so low that he could not even buy clothes, and another master who promised more did not even pay him! More than 4,000 Blacks lived in barracks or crowded houses in New York where they worked for the British military departments and drew rations with the King's troops or as labourers, servants, laundresses or tradesmen.[2] King worked at odd jobs around the city until he married Violet, who had belonged to Colonel Young of Wilmington, North Carolina, and who was a dozen years older than King. To earn more money King went to sea in a pilot boat but was captured by an American rebel whale-boat, which carried the crew to New Brunswick in New Jersey. Although his new master treated him well King was unhappy at being a slave again and being separated from his wife and although he admitted that many slaves were well cared for he wanted his freedom.

> . . . indeed the slaves about Baltimore, Philadelphia, and New York have as good victuals as many of the English; for they have meat once a day, and milk for breakfast and supper; and what is better than all, many of the masters send their slaves to school at night, that they may learn to read the Scriptures. This is a privilege indeed. But alas, all these enjoyments could not satisfy me without liberty![3]

Being allowed to walk about when his work was done, King used to go to the ferry and observed that people waded across the river at low tide, but there were guards to prevent the escape of prisoners and slaves. One Sunday morning just after midnight he went down to the river side and found the guards were either asleep or in the tavern and he waded out into the river and reached the shore safely. After hiding all day he crawled through bushes and marshes till he came to the river opposite Staten Island where he found a boat and reached New York safely, and was reunited with Violet.

Boston and Violet King were still in New York when the war ended. The provisional treaty had been signed in Paris by the British and the Americans on 30 November 1782 and was published in the *Royal Gazette* at New York on 26 March 1783. To the consternation of the American Loyalists, it granted independence to the thirteen American colonies and to the horror of the Blacks, Britain agreed in Article 7 to withdraw its land and naval forces 'with all convenient speed, and without causing any destruction, or carrying away any negroes or other property of the American inhabitants'.[4]

The British commander-in-chief in America was Sir Guy Carleton who was also commissioner for restoring peace. Carleton kept Britain's promises to the Blacks and declared that those Blacks who were free behind the British lines before the provisional treaty was signed or had fought for the British King would remain free and would be taken away on British ships with the disbanded soldiers. Most Americans were accustomed to think of slaves as valuable property and field hands would be worth 60 to 75 pounds, domestic servants 50 to 100 pounds and a skilled craftsman like Boston, 150 pounds. Some of the Loyalists had slaves and took them away from New York with their families. Indeed, it is estimated that 1,232 slaves were brought to Nova Scotia.

The American Congress had instructed General George Washington to make arrangements to obtain the delivery of the Blacks and other American property then in the hands of the British. Although Washington had a discussion with Carleton, Sir Guy (whose interpretation of the treaty was later supported by Lord North) insisted that the Blacks who were with the British prior to the signing of the provisional treaty were free, but those acquired after that date were to be given up to their American masters. If it were later proved that Blacks had been wrongly removed, he asserted, the British Government could pay compensation to the American 'masters'. Carleton appointed a board of three persons to compile a

'Book of Negroes' describing all those who sailed away from New York. It listed the names of the Blacks, their ages, their former masters, details of escape or other claim to freedom, military record, names of the vessels and their destination, and general comments such as 'fine boy', 'stout wench', 'blind and lame', and 'nearly worn out'.[5] It included Henry Washington, 43, a former slave of General George Washington, Boston King, 23, who was described as a 'Stout fellow' and Violet King, 35, as a 'Stout wench'.

Before the Blacks could embark on board a vessel which would transport them from New York they had to obtain a certificate from Brigadier General Samuel Birch, the British commander of New York City. The embarkation inspector then marked the magic initials G.B.C., for General Birch's Certificate, beside their names, but turned away everyone without a certificate.[6] Boston and Violet King truly rejoiced that 'each of us received a certificate . . . which dispelled all our fears, and filled us with joy and gratitude'. The Book of Negroes listed 3,000 persons, (1,336 men, 914 women, 750 children), two-thirds of whom came from the south. Most of them sailed from New York from April through November 1783 on the eighty-one vessels which operated on a shuttle service over the 960 kilometres voyage to Nova Scotia.

Among the 409 passengers brought from New York to Port Roseway (now Shelburne) in August 1783 were Boston and Violet King, on board the military transport *L'Abondance*, commanded by Lt. Philips and escorted by the frigate *Cyclops* [7] This ship carried more Blacks than any other making the voyage to Nova Scotia, and they formed the most important Black community in the province at Birchtown, on the north west arm of Port Roseway harbour, opposite the town being settled by the White Associated Loyalists. This was one of the finest harbours in North America, and was surrounded by magnificent forests and offered opportunities for lumbering, shipbuilding, fishing and trade. The White surveyor Benjamin Marston was invited to breakfast on board the *Cyclops* on 27 August 1783 to discuss land for the Blacks 'who by the Governor's orders are to be placed up the

N.W. harbor'.[8] The next day he showed the site to Colonel Stephen Bluck, leader of the Blacks who had been organized into militia companies which were not fighting units. Militia companies were arranged in 1796 from refugees, not belonging to provincial corps.

On the 30th August Marston wrote in his diary that he began the work of 'laying out lands for Colonel Bluck's black gentry' in Birchtown, named for the signer of their freedom certificates, and two assistants continued running lines for a week, perhaps helped by some of the Blacks. The work stopped because another surveyor laid out lots for a group of White Loyalists on part of the land reserved for the Blacks at Birchtown. Marston was angry and intervening for the Blacks, he persuaded the White leaders to 'overhaul that business'. Boston wrote 'we arrived at Birch Town in the month of August, where we all safely landed. Every family had a lot of land, and we exerted all our strength in order to build comfortable huts before the cold weather set in'.

In Birchtown were twenty-one companies commanded by Colonel Stephen Bluck and twenty captains, and they all drew provisions at Birchtown from 3 September 1783 to 24 July 1784.[9] The Kings belonged to Captain Cesar Perth's Company and Boston was listed as the family head, age 24, Violet King, 36, with no children. There were only 25 children in Perth's Company. Ages of the men and their dependents ranged from six months to 63 years. There were 26 men, 32 women, 11 children over 10, and 15 under 10 for a total of 64. Occupations included 4 carpenters, 16 labourers, 1 sawyer, 2 coopers, 1 seaman, and 1 mason. The typical Black household averaged 2.3 persons compared to a White family of 5. All loyalist refugees were entitled to free pork and flour, but if a Black worker left the family he had first registered with, he lost his government rations. Most of the Blacks in Shelburne were registered with White families for whom they were working, and there were many cases where the Blacks left or were dismissed and their White employers kept their free rations.[10] In January 1784 a total of 6845 persons were victualled at Shelburne, of whom 5969 were listed as Loyalists, 1191 as Disbanded soldiers, and 1485 as Free Blacks. It was 5

Boston King

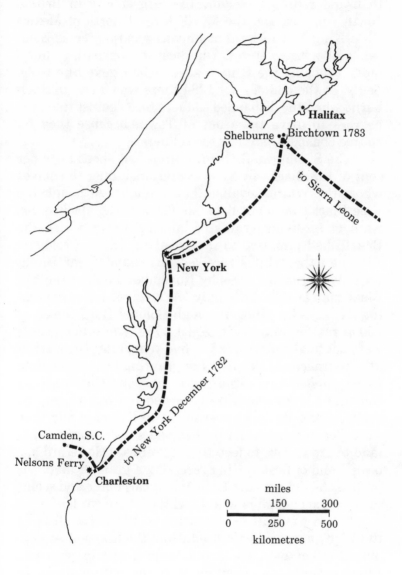

Halifax

Shelburne • Birchtown 1783

to Sierra Leone

New York

to New York December 1782

Camden, S.C.

Nelsons Ferry

Charleston

miles
0   150   300

0   250   500
kilometres

kilometres along a rough trail through the woods from Birchtown to Shelburne.[11]

Port Roseway had been renamed Shelburne by Governor John Parr, and soon, with a population of over ten thousand refugees, became the largest city in British North America and the fourth largest north of Mexico City. King was lucky that he was a carpenter as thousands of houses, stores, wharves and barns had to be built. Probably the British government gave him tools. Sadly, at the end of July 1784 there was a riot in Shelburne when the disbanded soldiers rose against the 'Free negroes to drive them out of Town, because they laboured cheaper than they the soldiers'.[12]

The Shelburne-Birchtown area had about forty per cent of the Blacks in Nova Scotia, including the slaves whom the White Loyalists had brought. Although the Free Blacks were not listed as farmers they looked forward to receiving grants of land for farms which the British had promised to the Loyalists and the soldiers. Although the Whites received farm lands near Birchtown averaging 74 acres by November 1786, of the 649 Black men at Birchtown only 184 received farms averaging 34 acres by 1788. Although Colonel Bluck received 200 acres for himself in April 1786, the other grants were not finalized till 1788 — five years after their arrival. The tragedy of this delay in granting land to the Free Blacks as one man explained to Lt. John Clarkson was that the Blacks desperately needed the free provisions given by the British Government to live on while they were clearing trees and bushes and stones from enough land to grow crops to feed their families.[13] No record has been found of Boston King receiving a grant of land, but perhaps he did not care as he was a carpenter and seems to have had enough land at Birchtown for a garden.

There were also settlements of Black Loyalists in the Digby area and at Tracadie and the towns of Annapolis, Guysborough, Halifax, Liverpool and Preston had Black communities near by or living within them. In New Brunswick the Free Blacks were given land along the Nerepis River and the Saint John River as well as in the town of Quaca (St. Martins), Saint John, Otnabog (near Gagetown), Fredericton and Maugerville.[14]

King did not worry about land grants or the problems of day to day living, but he was concerned about his religious experiences. He wrote that during the first winter in Nova Scotia:

> The work of religion began to revive among us, and many were convinced of the sinfulness of sin, and turned from the error of their ways. It pleased the Lord to awaken my wife under the preaching of Mr. (Moses) Wilkinson . . . she was struck to the ground, and cried out for mercy: she continued in great distress near two hours, when they sent for me . . . . The trouble of her soul brought affliction upon her body, which confined her to bed a year and a half . . . many were convinced by her testimony, and sincerely sought the Lord. As she was the first person at Burch Town that experienced deliverance from evil tempers, and exhorted and urged others to seek and enjoy the same blessing, she was not a little opposed by some of Our Black brethren. But these trials she endured with the meekness and patience becoming a Christian: and when Mr. FREEBORN GARRETSON came to Burch Town to regulate the society and form them into classes, he encouraged her to hold fast her confidence, and cleave to the Lord with her whole heart.

King himself attended Methodist class-meetings and prayer meetings but did not feel that his soul was saved, 'I thought I was not worthy to be among the people of GOD, nor even to dwell in my own houses, but was fit only to reside among the beasts of the forest. This drove me out into the woods, when the snow lay upon the ground three or four feet deep, with a blanket, and a firebrand in my hand. I cut the boughs of the spruce tree and kindled a fire. In this lonely situation I frequently entreated the Lord for mercy — but in vain'.

King was one of sixteen persons working for Mrs. Robinson and these men held a prayer meeting morning and night and read some portion of Scripture. The first Sunday in March as King 'was going to the preaching, and was engaged in prayer and meditation, I thought I heard a voice saying to me, 'Peace be unto thee!' . . . . All my doubts and fears vanished away: I saw, by faith, heaven opened to my view, and Christ and his holy angels rejoicing over me'. Sermons of the Rev. Freeborn Garretson, an enthusiastic young American preacher who had freed his slaves, and was on a preaching mission for the Methodists in Nova Scotia, confirmed his faith. 'Soon after, I found a great concern for the salvation of others, and was constrained to visit my poor ungodly neighbours, and exhort them to fear the Lord, and seek him while he might be found . . . . In the year 1785, I began to exhort both in families and prayer-meetings, and the Lord graciously afforded me his assisting presence'.

John Wesley sent books from England for the use of the Methodist classes, and wrote on 3 July 1784: 'The little town they have built is, I suppose, the only town of negroes . . . in America — nay, perhaps in any part of the world, except only in Africa'. King wrote:

> In the year 1787, I found my mind drawn out to commiserate my poor brethren in Africa, and especially when I considered that we have the happiness of being brought up in a christian land . . . . As I had not the least prospect at that time of ever seeing Africa, I contented myself with pitying and praying for the poor benighted inhabitants of that country which gave birth to my forefathers. I laboured in Burchtown and Shelwin [Shelburne] two years, and the word was blessed to the conversation of many . . . .'

Others, too, noted the misery of the Blacks in Nova Scotia. When Captain William Dyott visited Shelburne in 1788 on a naval cruise with Prince William Henry (later King William IV) he walked from the barracks through the woods to the 'negro town called Birch Town' where 'their huts miserable to guard against the inclemency of a Nova Scotia winter, and their existence almost depending on what they could lay up in summer. I think I never saw such wretchedness and poverty . . . '[15]

The free rations which the British government provided for the Loyalist refugees while they were getting settled in their new homes came to an end in 1786 and few people had cleared enough land to raise sufficient food for the winter. Although the land along the Atlantic coast of Nova Scotia is poor and rocky, the Blacks at

278

Shelburne had been given such barren land that they were forced to work the land of white men 'for which they were entitled to half its produce. It has reduced them to such a state of indigence' wrote John Clarkson in his journal in 1791; 'that in order to satisfy their landlord and maintain themselves they have been obliged to sell [all] their property, their clothing and even their very beds'. Boston King observed:

> About this time the country was visited with a dreadful famine, which not only prevailed at Burchtown, but likewise at Chebucto, Annapolis, Digby, and other places. Many of the poor people were compelled to sell their best gowns for five pounds of flour, in order to support life. When they had parted with all their clothes, even to their blankets, several of them fell down dead in the streets, thro' hunger. Some killed and eat their dogs and cats, and poverty and distress prevailed on every side, so that to my great grief I was obliged to leave Burchtown, because I could get no employment. I travelled from place to place, to procure the necessaries of life, but in vain. At last, I came to Shelwin [Shelburne] on the 20th of January. After walking from one street to the other, I met with Capt. Selex, and he engaged me to make him a chest. I rejoiced at the offer, and returning home, set about it immediately. I worked all night, and by eight o'clock next morning finished a chest, which I carried to the Captain's house, thro' the snow which was three feet deep. But to my great disappointment he rejected it. However, he gave me directions to make another. On my way home, being pinched with hunger and cold, I fell down several times, thro' weakness and expected to die upon the spot. But even in this situation, I found my mind resigned to the divine will, and rejoiced in the midst of tribulation, for the Lord delivered me from all murmurings and discontent, altho' I had but one pint of Indian meal left for the support of myself and my wife. Having finished another chest, I took it to my employers the next day, but being afraid he would serve me as he had done before, I took a saw along with me in order to sell it. On the way, I prayed that the Lord would give a prosperous journey, and was answered to the joy of my heart, for Capt. Selex paid me for the chest in Indian-corn, and the other chest I sold for 2 s

6d and the saw for 3 s 9d altho' it cost me a guinea, yet I was exceedingly thankful to procure a reprieve from the dreadful anguish of perishing from famine . . . .

While I was admiring the goodnes of GOD, and praising him for the help he afforded me in the day of trouble, a gentleman sent for me, and engaged me to make three flat-bottomed boats for the salmon-fishery, at £1 each. The gentleman advanced two baskets of Indian-corn, and found nails and tar for the boats. I was enabled to finish the work by the time appointed, and he paid me honestly. Thus did the kind hand of Providence interpose in my preservation, which appeared still greater, upon viewing the wretched circumstances of many of my black brethren at that time, who were obliged to sell themselves to the merchants, some for two or three years, and others for five or six years. The circumstances of the white inhabitants were likewise very distressing, owing to their great imprudence in building large houses, and striving to excel one another in this place of vanity. When their money was almost expended, they began to build small fishing vessels, but alas, it was too late to repair their error. Had they been wise enough at first to have turned their attention to the fishery, instead of fine houses, the place would soon have been in a flourishing condition, whereas it was reduced in a short time to a heap of ruins, and its inhabitants were compelled to flee to other parts of the continent for sustenance.

The next winter the same gentleman hired King to build more boats, and then asked him to go to Chedabucto (Guysborough) to build a house because he planned to move there with his family. He offered to pay King two pounds a month in cash, and give him a barrel of mackerel and another of herring for his next winter's provision. But when they arrived the employer did not have enough men to go on a fishing voyage to the Bay of Chaleur for the salmon fishery, and persuaded King to accompany him. King found the captain a fine man to work for, except that he cursed and swore continually. In August they returned to unload the vessels, and then set herring nets at Pope's Harbour.

On October 24, we left Pope's harbour, and came to

Halifax, where we were paid off, each man receiving £15 for his wages, and my master gave me two barrels of fish agreeable to his promise. When I returned home, I was enabled to clothe my wife and myself, and my Winter's store consisted of one barrel of flour, three bushels of corn, nine gallons of treacle, 20 bushels of potatoes which my wife had set in my absence, and the two barrels of fish, so that this was the best Winter I ever saw in Burchtown.

In 1791 Boston King moved to Preston, near Dartmouth across the harbour from Halifax where 'Bishop' William Black had appointed him to care for the Wesleyan Society of about thirty-four. There a few Whites also attended his preaching. Boston supported himself by working for a gentleman in Dartmouth who paid him two shillings a day plus food and lodging.

While King was preaching at Preston, Lieutenant John Clarkson, brother of Thomas Clarkson, the famous anti-slavery agitator, arrived at Halifax as the agent for the Sierra Leone Company.[16] This company had been incorporated in Great Britain to trade in Africa and to re-establish former slaves on the African continent to show that the Negroes could support and govern themselves in their homeland. The British Government had agreed to pay all the expenses of those Free Blacks in Nova Scotia and New Brunswick who wished to migrate to Sierra Leone and ordered the Governor of Nova Scotia to help Clarkson. Five days after he arrived in Halifax, Clarkson went to Dartmouth and four miles further to Preston where he 'called at the huts of several of the inhabitants and stated to them the offers of the Sierra Leone Company. Their situation seemed extremely bad from the poorness of the soil and from their having nothing to subsist upon but the produce of it'.

On 14 October Lieutenant Clarkson received a letter from Colonel Stephen Bluck from Birchtown asking for more details and he decided to visit various parts of Nova Scotia to arrange to transport the Free Blacks to Halifax and then to Sierra Leone because he ran into some opposition from Whites who did not want to lose a source of cheap labour and from others who claimed that the Blacks owed them money and could not leave until their debts were paid. On 25 October Clarkson was met at Shelburne 'by a black man of the name of David George, one of the principal Baptist Ministers among the blacks in this district' who arranged a visit to Birchtown where 400 Blacks came through the rain to the church.

Clarkson explained that His Majesty had ordered the Governor and Council of Nova Scotia to give them their promised land grants immediately if they wished to stay in Nova Scotia or they could enlist in a regiment in the West Indies or they could go to Sierra Leone where the company would give each man twenty acres of land for himself, ten for his wife and five for every child 'upon such terms and subject to such charges and obligations . . . as shall hereafter be settled by the Company'. He assured them these quit rents would be small taxes for education and charity and that Blacks and Whites would be treated equally. He also reminded them of the hot climate of Africa.

Most of those who decided to go said it was 'for the sake of their children . . . ' and explained that if they received their land grants in Nova Scotia they had nothing to live on while they cleared away the trees. There was also the desire to return to their homeland and one said: 'Massa, if me die, had rather die in me own country than this cold place . . . ' Others were convinced that back in Africa they would be the magistrates and be able to rule — not the Whites. By 28 November 560 persons at Birchtown and Shelburne had decided to go to Sierra Leone and they asked Clarkson to settle them in Sierra Leone 'as near as possible to the inhabitants of Preston, as they and us are intimately acquainted'.

Practically all the Blacks — about 200 — decided to leave Preston to move to Sierra Leone. The Baptist congregation as well as several Methodist congregations moved as a body. The Preston spokesmen volunteered to support the unmarried women and widows among them until they could support themselves in Africa. Clarkson promised to buy the poultry and garden produce for the voyage from them and after he arranged for them to sail on the *Eleanor* he wrote: 'This vessel will contain the flower of the Black people'.

Boston King left Nova Scotia because of his dream

to preach Christianity to 'my poor brethren in Africa'. He approved of the Sierra Leone Company's intention 'as far as possible in their power, to put a stop to the abominable slave-trade' and told Clarkson that 'it was not for the sake of the advantages I hope to reap in Africa, which induced me to undertake the voyage, but from a desire that had long possessed my mind, of contributing to the best of my poor ability, in spreading the knowledge of Christianity in that country'.

On 15 January 1792, the Sierra Leone fleet of fifteen ships sailed from Halifax with 1190 Free Blacks and by early March they were all anchored at the mouth of the Sierra Leone River. King said that the storms were the worst the sailors remembered. Violet was so ill that her husband expected her to die but the Lord answered their prayers and 'restored her to perfect health'.

Joyfully the men cleared a roadway through the jungle at Freetown for their landing and put up canvas tents for the women and children. Then they all disembarked and marched towards the thick forest with the Holy Bible and their preachers before them singing hymns. Africans brought the newcomers presents of cassava and groundnuts but the Nova Scotians did not know how to cook them or how to speak Temme.[17]

Clarkson had been ill for most of the voyage and looked forward to turning over his responsibilities to the Company's Governor, Superintendent and Council. He found however that there was no Governor, and that the Council of White men appointed by the English Company had failed to prepare for their new settlers and the land had not been cleared or surveyed as they had promised. Reluctantly Clarkson carried on. In spite of temperatures which reached 45 degrees Celsius the Black Captains organized their companies and began clearing eighty acres for town lots for four hundred families and began building huts of grass and clay. Soon the four month rainy season arrived which ruined food supplies, rotted cloth, rusted tools, brought plagues of insects and 'putrid fever' [malaria] to which Violet King succumbed in April. Over 112 had died by 11 April, and in July 800 were sick at once. In June King himself became ill with malaria but recovered although the people were dying so fast it was difficult to bury them. The first year in Sierra Leone was one of the worst seasons of rain the West African coast had known. There was plenty of fish and tropical fruit but it was not the expected 'land flowing with milk and honey.'

Because of his good opinion of the natives of Sierra Leone and 'knowing that there could not be any people in existence, in every point of view, better calculated for forming a new settlement, than those I brought with me from America . . . ' Clarkson decided 'to remain with the poor Nova Scotians till the Colony is established or lost'. Clarkson tried to prevent the Whites showing racial prejudice 'for the people are taught to believe from me that they are to become men and that no distinction is to be made, between them & the Whites.'

It took a year before the town lots were surveyed and occupied, and instead of the promised twenty acres, farms were only five acres. Like most of the Nova Scotian settlers, King was employed by the Sierra Leone Company. His work as a carpenter earned him three shillings a day and he paid four shillings a week towards his food ration. He took his turn preaching with the other Methodist preachers and when the rains were over they erected a small chapel, but he wished to preach the Word of God to the Africans. He went to the Governor and asked for employment on the Company's plantation on the Bullom Shore

> in order that I might have frequent opportunities of conversing with the Africans. He kindly approved of my intention, and sent me to the Plantation to get ship-timber in company with several others. The gentleman who superintended the Plantation [James Watt], treated me with the utmost kindness, and allowed six men to help me to build a house for myself, which we finished in 12 days. When a sufficient quantity of timber was procured, and other business for the Company in this place compleated, I was sent to the African town to teach the children to read, but found it difficult to procure scholars, as the parents shewed no great inclination to send their children . . . . The poor Africans appeared attentive to the exhortation, altho' I laboured under the disadvantage of using an interpret-

er. My scholars soon increased from four to twenty, fifteen of whom continued with me five months. I taught them the Alphabet, and to spell words of two syllables; and likewise the Lord's Prayer. And I found them as apt to learn as any children I have known . . .

Governor Richard Dawes on 3 August 1793 appointed King a missionary and schoolteacher at 60 pounds a year. King married again but he was anxious to obtain more education, and Dawes promised to send him to England for study for two or three years. On 26 March 1794 he embarked for England and arrived at Plymouth, after a pleasant voyage, on the 16th of May. 'On the 1st of June we got into the Thames, and soon after, Mrs. Paul, whom I was acquainted with in America, came to Wapping, and invited me to the New Chapel in the City-Road, where I was kindly received'. One example of jealousies among Sierra Leone officials was that King had been promised free passage to and from England if he would support himself there, but the promise was broken because he went down the Thames to visit Clarkson and his wife at Purfleet. Henry Thornton, chairman of the company, ordered the captain to charge King fifteen guineas.

At first King was shy about preaching to White people, but he was coaxed to preach at Snowfields Chapel

and I found a more cordial love to the White People than I had ever experienced before. In the former part of my life I had suffered greatly from the cruelty and injustice of the Whites, which induced me to look upon them, in general, as our enemies: And even after the Lord had manifested his forgiving mercy to me, I still felt at times an uneasy distrust and shyness toward them: but on that day the Lord removed all my prejudices: for which I bless his holy Name.

In the month of August 1794 King went to Bristol and then Dr. Thomas Coke, John Wesley's right hand man, took him to Kingswood School where he studied until the summer of 1796. His Memoirs are dated Kingswood-School, 4 June 1796 and had a note added: 'About the latter end of September, 1976, Boston King embarked for Sierra Leone, where he arrived safe, and resumed the employment of a school-master in that Colony, and in 1798 had about forty scholars and we hope to hear that they will not only learn the English Language, but also attain some knowledge of the way of salvation thro' faith in the Lord Jesus Christ'.

King was away in England during the trouble about quit-rents when the Nova Scotians were rebellious because of delays in receiving their land grants and because the Company was going to charge them a yearly tax called quit-rent. The Company said Clarkson did not have the authority to make promises about quit-rents when he was in Nova Scotia. In Africa the Nova Scotians had expected to take part in the government as equal British subjects and instead they were ruled by White officials sent from England. The Nova Scotians did however annually elect tithingmen and hundredors who enforced minor laws, were consulted by the Council about laws and passed along the wishes of the people to the Governor and Council.

On the death of James Jones, King became the Granville Town teacher, where he earned Governor Zachary Macaulay's praise for being 'humble & teachable & willing to adopt any plan I suggest'. When the school enrolment dropped to twelve, King was transferred to a Freetown school. He died about 1802 in the Sherbo, but it is not known whether he was a teacher or a trader there.[18]

Of the thousands of Loyalists who fled the Revolution, a relatively small number left sufficient records to recount their story. Very few of these were Black. Boston King, a Black slave, whose hunger for freedom led him into the great loyalist adventure, left an account of his story and of the quest of those Blacks who accompanied him to Africa and of those who remained in Canada to contribute to their chosen land.

1. This article is based on Phyllis R. Blakeley, 'Boston King: A Negro Loyalist Who Sought Refuge in Nova Scotia', *Dalhousie Review*, 48, 1968, pp. 347-356; and Boston King, 'Memoirs of the Life of Boston King, a Black Preacher, Written by Himself, During his Residence at Kingswood-School', *Arminian* [or *Methodist*] *Magazine*, XXI, March, April, May, June 1798, 105-11, 157-61, 209-13, 261-5.

2. Benjamin Quarles, *The Negro in the American Revolution*. (Chapel Hill, N.C.: University of North Carolina Press, 1961), pp. 113-114.

3. Quarles pp. 167-181; Ellen Gibson Wilson, *The Loyal Blacks*, (Toronto: Longman Green Ltd & New York: G.P. Putnam, 1976), Chapters 3 and 4; James W. St. C. Walker, *The Black Loyalists*, (Halifax: Dalhousie University Press, 1976), Chapter 1.

4. Wilson points out on pages 45 to 50 that this clause was added by the suggestion of Henry Laurens, who had built his fortune on slavery and who was bitter because his son Col. John Laurens had been killed by the British at Charleston. The chief British negotiator at Paris was Richard Oswald, a 'particular friend' of Laurens and a wealthy merchant and army contractor who owned the British slave post on Bance Island on the Sierra Leone River. Oswald's cargoes of slaves had been handled at Charleston for a ten per cent commission by Laurens.

5. Book of Negroes, Carleton Papers, PRO 30/55/100; Transcript in PANS RG1 Vol. 423.

6. PANS RG1 Vol. 170 doc. 344 for an example of such a certificate.

7. For more information about the Blacks in Shelburne see Chapter 5 of Ellen Wilson's *The Loyal Blacks*; and Chapter 2, 3 and 4 of James Walker's *The Black Loyalists*; and Chapter 2 of Walker's *A History of Blacks in Canada*, (Ottawa, 1980); Robin W. Winks, *The Blacks in Canada: A History*, (New Haven and Montreal, 1971).

8. Marston's Diary, *Collections of New Brunswick Historical Society*, 8, pp. 227-8.

9. PANS MG100 Vol. 220 No. 4, Muster Book of the free blacks of Birch Town, Port Roseway from original at PAC MG9 B6(1)

10. Wilson p. 87 and comments written in the Muster Book of Free Blacks.

11. The breakdown of the Free Blacks was 630 men, 485 women, 133 children above 10 and 247 children under 10. PANS MG100 Vol. 220 No. 4, p. 102.

12. Marston's Diary, *Collections of New Brunswick Historical Society*, 8, p. 265.

13. Charles Bruce Fergusson, ed. *Clarkson's Mission to America 1791-1792*, (Halifax, N.S.: Public Archives of Nova Scotia Publication No. 11, 1971), pp. 58-59.

14. James Walker in *A History of the Blacks in Canada* p. 30 says that in Upper Canada Governor John Simcoe interpreted the land policy as meaning that only those Blacks who had actually served in the army were eligible for free land grants and provisions so that a few Blacks obtained farms east of Cornwall, in the Niagara district and near the Detroit River.

15. Dyott's Diary 1781-1845, I, p. 57 (Toronto: Champlain Society), I, p. 57.

16. Information about Clarkson's activities are taken from Charles Bruce Fergusson ed. *Clarkson's Mission to America 1791-92*, (Halifax, N.S.: Public Archives of Nova Scotia Publication No. 11, 1971).

17. For additional information on Sierra Leone see Chapters 5, 6, 7 and 8 in James Walker, *The Black Loyalists* and Chapters 8, 9, 10 and 11 in Ellen Wilson *The Loyal Blacks*.

18. Wilson, p. 339.

William Jarvis and his son, Samuel Peters, in the uniform of the Queen's Rangers. William Jarvis' colonel uniform is on display at Fort York, Toronto

Chapter 12

Mr. Secretary Jarvis

William Jarvis of Connecticut and York

by Robert S. Allen

William Jarvis an active member of the Queen's Rangers, fought in many battles against the Rebels in the Revolutionary war. For a few years after the war, he was an exile in England. Then in 1791, he was appointed Secretary and Clerk of the Executive Council of the newly created colony of Upper Canada (Ontario). Soon Jarvis was helping shape the new life of this province, first from Niagara and then from York (Toronto).

'Canada is one of the finest countries that I ever saw', wrote a seemingly enchanted William Jarvis from Kingston on the banks of Lake Ontario in early July 1792, 'the improvements of the Loyalists are beyond anything one could imagine'.[1] Jarvis and his family had been in the country for barely a month, yet their journey along the upper St. Lawrence had afforded them the opportunity to view firsthand the remarkable achievements of the Loyalist pioneers in the newly created province of Upper Canada. The Loyalists were political refugees, victims of a bitter civil war and rebellion in colonial America and during that conflict they had supported the royal cause. Many had fought to preserve the unity of the empire, hence their initials 'UE'. Although these men and women represented a variety of cultural and ethnic minorities, they believed as a group in the sovereignty of the King and Parliament. Perhaps above all else, although a liberal democratic element was present, they espoused conservative principles, and desired peace, order and good government. For their leaders this presupposed a society based on British political institutions, an established church and a graded social order. Within this evolving political and social milieu the newcomer Jarvis, a Loyalist himself, and soon to be formally appointed 'Secretary and Registrar of the Records of the Province of Upper Canada', was determined to rebuild a life, after spending nearly nine years as an exile in England following the war. Indeed, he had every confidence that his American Loyalist background, political appointment and personal character would combine to assure him a prominent role in the emerging colonial autocracy of the new province. For William Jarvis, and the majority of the Loyalists, the prospects of sharing a peaceful and prosperous future in a British North America appeared bright.

William Jarvis was born 11 September 1756 at Stamford, Connecticut, the fifth son of the respected and influential Samuel Jarvis, the town clerk, and Martha Seymour Jarvis.[2] They were a close-knit and loving family, adherents of the Church of England and equally proud of their American colonial and British roots. For them loyalty to the King and the British parliament was sacred. Young William received educational instruction in Connecticut and England. Although his schooling was of a general nature, he was well-read, demonstrated a fair ability for business, and as well, proved to be eminently suited for military life. As an adult, Jarvis was physically impressive, being over six feet tall, well proportioned and robust.[3] A later oil portrait shows a fine head and expressive face, yet suggests that he had become rather stout.

Before he reached the age of nineteen, the serene and happy life of William Jarvis, like that of thousands of other colonial Americans, was shattered by the shots 'heard round the world' at Lexington and Concord. The outbreak of the bitter civil war and rebellion in colonial America was the result in large measure of the long-standing British colonial policy of 'salutary neglect'. Apart from the imposition of some administrative regulations and trade restrictions which emanated from London, the character and direction of the individual colonies had evolved through internal initiative and energy. Following the last great war for empire between France and England in North America which ended in 1763, the colonial spirit of independence developed with the removal of the French threat from the north. The conflict which had been fought to preserve and defend the British colonies in North America, had left Britain staggering under the weight of a huge war debt.

British ministers therefore reasoned that in order to reduce expenditures, the American colonies should at least be willing to help defray the costs of colonial administration and frontier defence. Without consulting the American colonial assemblies, import duties were placed on specific items like glass, paint and tea entering colonial ports. This decision to raise revenue ignited the already smouldering ideological passions of some of the colonial leaders who argued forcefully against 'taxation without representation'. The political-constitutional debate was further inflamed when the British countered by insisting that the colonies were duty-bound to honour the sovereignty of the King and the supremacy of parliament. Although often motivated by personal gain and economic profit, the eloquent and clever rhetoric of the militant colonial leaders, nonetheless convinced significant and volatile elements of the colonial population to grasp the cause of American liberty and independence. The final and tragic result was the outbreak of overt hostilities between British regulars and American colonials in April 1775. Although the causes of the rebellion were complex and pluralistic, British intransigence on parliamentary supremacy formed the keystone of the ideological and constitutional conflict, and the inability of the British ministers to resolve the problem of reconciling the aspirations of colonial autonomy with imperial authority and unity, demonstrated in the last analysis, a failure of British statesmanship.[4]

Colonial Connecticut was torn apart by the savagery of the civil war and rebellion. Among those colonial Americans steadfast in their loyalty to the King and the royal cause, was the Jarvis family. In particular, William Jarvis had been taught to 'Fear God and Honour the King'. Also, he believed in the wisdom of preserving the unity of an Anglo-American empire which could be a future source of strength and power in the world. Jarvis abhored violence, and was disgusted with the antics of the democratic mob which heaped verbal abuse, physically harassed, or tarred and feathered those who opposed their concept of liberty.

As the opinions of the Jarvis family were wellknown, at the commencement of the conflict the colonial rebels siezed William and his brothers, Munson and John. In August 1775, however, 'on a clear night', the brothers escaped, and were transported in an open boat across the Sound to Long Island. Here they found sanctuary in the home of a sympathizer.[5] There were about 2000 loyal Americans from Connecticut. They came from all areas of the province — places like Stamford, Fairfield, Newtown, Norwalk, Stratford, New Haven, Waterburg, New London and Reading. Many of them took passage to New York where they responded to the 'beating orders' and enlisted in one of the newly formed Loyalist provincial corps. In particular, a significant percentage of the officers and men of the Prince of Wales American Regiment, the King's American Regiment and the Queen's Rangers were loyal Americans from Connecticut.[6] William Jarvis, for example, enlisted in the Queen's Rangers sometime before the spring of 1777.[7]

The military exploits and achievements of the Queen's Rangers throughout the civil war and rebellion in colonial America were outstanding. Raised in August 1776 by the controversial Lieutenant-colonel Robert Rogers, the officers and men of the Queen's Rangers were drawn chiefly from the Queen's Own Loyal Virginia Regiment, and from Connecticut and New York. Subsequently, independent companies, Europeans and deserters from the army of George Washington augmented the strength of the corps.[8]

The first major military engagement of the Queen's Rangers was somewhat of a frenzied affair, as the corps was surprised, and mauled in a rebel night attack at Heathcote's Hill, near the village of Mamaroneck, New York on 22 October 1776.[9] Nonetheless, under the experienced supervision of Rogers and his successors, Lieutenant-colonel Christopher French and Major James Wemyss, the Queen's Rangers were molded into a disciplined and efficient unit of light infantry. In June 1777, they engaged the enemy at Brunswick, New Jersey. Later in the year, during the Philadelphia campaign, the Queen's Rangers were praised 'for their spirited and gallant conduct' at the battle of Brandywine Creek on 11 September 1777. Here the corps suffered the loss of 72 officers and men killed and wounded, their highest single casualty toll throughout the war. At the battle of Germantown on 4 October 1777, the Rangers were posted on the British right flank, and participated in this second successive victory of the royal forces within a month.[10]

In mid-October 1777, Major, later Lieutenant-colonel John Graves Simcoe, future Lieutenant-governor of Upper Canada and founder of York (Toronto), was appointed to command the Queen's Rangers. Simcoe not only rigorously trained the corps, especially in the use of the bayonet, but also re-organized the Rangers into a mixed force of infantry and cavalry. As well, a battery of two small guns — an amuzette and a 3-pounder, was attached for a time to the unit. By the end of the war, the Queen's Rangers consisted of eight battalion companies: one light infantry company, one grenadier company, one company of highlanders, three troops of Queen's Rangers Huzzars and two troops of dragoons. The basic uniform of the corps was green.[11]

For four hectic years this daring and innovative British officer directed the operations of this partisan corps which raided and skirmished with the enemy almost constantly. Some highlights of the military activities of the Queen's Rangers for the year 1778 alone, included two raids and actions at Quintain's Bridge on 18 March 1778 and Hancock's Bridge on 21 March 1778 in New Jersey; participation at the battle of Monmouth Court House on 28 June 1778, before and after which the corps covered the withdrawal of the royal forces from Philadelphia to New York City; and a sharp fight at Kingsbridge on 31 August 1778 where a combined force of Indians and Rebels was put to flight. Following this series of unbroken successful efforts, the Queen's Rangers went into winter quarters at Oyster Bay, Long Island.[12]

The faithful and zealous service provided by the Queen's Rangers was rewarded in the spring of 1779 when the corps was designated and numbered by His Majesty as the First American Regiment on 2 May 1779.[13] This Royal favour put the Queen's Rangers, and other Loyalist provincial corps so honoured, on a more equal level with British regular regiments. Throughout the year the Rangers continually raided and harassed rebel positions in New York and New Jersey. The raid of 25 — 26 October was particularly dramatic, as Ranger cavalry and infantry marched through enemy held territory in the Brunswick South Amboy area for a day and a night, and either eluded or defeated each rebel attempt to capture them, before returning safely to Richmond, Staten Island. The next year, the Queen's Rangers formed a part of the expedition to South Carolina, where they took part in the seige and capture of Charleston on 12 May 1780.[14]

From mid-December 1780 until the surrender of Lord Charles Cornwallis and the royal forces at Yorktown on 19 October 1781, the Queen's Rangers campaigned in Virginia. Initially under the general command of Loyalist Benedict Arnold, the Rangers took part in the capture and partial burning of Richmond from 5 to 7 January 1781, in the dispersal of the rebels at Charles City Court House on 8 January 1781 and in the capture of Petersburg on 25 April 1781.[15] As well, the Rangers, who were considered by their enemies as 'formidable and well mounted', raided along the James River, as at Point of Fork on 5 June 1781, where they skirmished with the Rebels and destroyed supplies.[16] Along the Chickahominy River, as Cornwallis was moving towards Yorktown, the Queen's Rangers clashed with the advance of the rebel army, and fought a smart engagement at Spencer's Ordinary on 26 June 1781, near Williamsburg.[17] During the succeeding French and rebel siege of the royal forces at Yorktown, the Rangers were based across the York River at Gloucester Point. When Cornwallis capitulated, the Queen's Rangers also surrendered but did not relinquish their regimental colours, which were hidden and secretly removed. These colours subsequently remained in England for many years, and finally, were sent to Toronto. With the war virtually over, the Queen's Rangers, First American Regiment, became part of the British military system as a regular unit, the officers being given permanent rank by 25 December 1782.[18] The corps was disbanded in October 1783. Throughout the war, the Queen's Rangers had been skilful and enterprising, and time and again those loyal Americans in the corps, both officers and soldiers, had shown themselves to be 'disciplined enthusiasts in the cause of their country'.[19]

Although there is little personal information for William Jarvis, the military records available suggest that he was an active participant throughout the war in the campaigns of the Rangers. As noted previously, he enlisted sometime between the late summer of 1776 and the spring of 1777. His change of officer classification indicated that he served at various times in both the infantry and cavalry of the corps. During the Virginia campaign, he was wounded at Spencer's Ordinary while 'acting with the grenadiers'.[20] His rank then was given as ensign, yet in December 1782, he was formally commissioned as cornet.[21] The young officer was not listed on the regimental nominal roll at the Yorktown surrender of 19 October 1781. Undoubtedly, Jarvis was given sea passage to New York with the other wounded and sick prior to the capitulation. He remained in that city, a British and Loyalist bastion, until at least the late summer of 1783.

Towards the end of his last stay in New York, Jarvis foolishly decided to cross the Sound in a whaleboat with a picnic party which included his sister and two other young ladies, and visit family and friends in Stamford. The neighbouring towns of New London and Groton had been sacked in September 1781 by royal forces, and following the capture of Fort Griswold, a part of the rebel garrison had been massacred by members of Arnold's

Loyal American Legion. Not surprisingly, the rebel population of Connecticut, still seething over these and other atrocities, took every opportunity to wreak havoc and revenge against any British and Loyalist intruders. Although the Jarvis group succeeded in spending the night at Stamford, 'distributed among several Houses in the Town', their crew and whaleboat were discovered the next morning at daylight by a rebel coastal patrol. Immediately, the Rebels attacked the crew and 'beat them most unmercifully'. Jarvis and the other gentlemen, 'carrying the Ladies a great part of the way, up to our knees in water', scrambled in hasty retreat, pursued by a mob. At last, they regained the whaleboat and rowed all night until they reached New York at 'Sunrise next morning', in a state of total physical exhaustion.[22] The prankish incident nonetheless convinced Jarvis, and many other loyal Americans like him, that after the rebellion, there would be no hope of returning to their former homes.

Following the achievement of separation, and the creation of the new republic of the United States, the Queen's Rangers, along with a multitude of other Loyalist refugees, joined the diaspora and found sanctuary in a British province. The Rangers and their families, totalling 361,[23] settled along the upper St. John Valley in what became the new 'Loyalist Province' of New Brunswick, where they contributed significantly in the evolution of British North America and Canada.

William Jarvis did not accompany his brother officers and men to the St. John Valley. Rather, he sailed for England. As a half-pay officer, he possessed modest, but adequate means. In England, his firm intention was to gain social and business contacts, Loyalist compensation and political appointments. Socially, he was happily successful. After a courtship of unknown intensity and duration, he married Miss Hannah Owen Peters (1762-1845), daughter of the Reverend Dr. Samuel Peters of Hebron, Connecticut, at St. George's in Hanover Square, London, on 12 December 1785.[24] The Peters family were staunch Loyalists. Just prior to the outbreak of rebellion, Dr. Peters was a wealthy landowner and Church of England missionary. His elevated position and church affiliation aroused the envy and suspicion of the rebel mob.

As well, Dr. Peters' manner was considered offensive, since he 'aped the style of an English nobleman, built his house in a forest, kept his coach and looked with some degree of scorn upon republicans'. These characteristics apparently provided sufficient reason for those 'Sons of Liberty' to smash his house and furniture, wound his eleven-year-old daughter Hannah with a sword, drag him 3 kilometres to their Liberty Pole, and after beating him about the head, condemn him as a traitor to the rights and liberties of America. Dr. Peters was literally chased to the sea, where he was rescued by a vessel of the Royal Navy and removed to England. In 1776 his daughter Hannah was smuggled from Hebron to Boston, and subsequently joined her father in London.[25]

For the newly married Mr. and Mrs. Jarvis, 'Americans transplanted to London', life was more than tolerable, as they amused themselves with the pleasures of the theatre, zoos and public gardens.[26] While in England, three children were born` Samuel Peters in 1787, who died very young; Maria-Lavinia in 1788; and Augusta in 1790.[27] In 1787, the couple were gravely disappointed with the decision of 'The report of the Commissioners on American (Loyalist) Claims'. Incredibly, none of the Jarvis family was granted compensation by the British government for their losses suffered on behalf of His Majesty's Government during the late rebellion. In a letter from Pimlico to his brother Munson, a merchant in Saint John, a shocked William Jarvis noted that the dividends paid to individual Loyalist claimants were so small that 'some have run mad with despair and disappointment'. He further commented on the suspicions of the claims commissioners noting that 'the report is here that all you that are Refugees in Nova Scotia and New Brunswick are only waiting to get your dividends and then away back to the Rebel States again, and that many have already gone back into Egypt'.[28]

Following this setback William Jarvis became most active as a purchasing agent and shipper to his brother Munson. One 'Invoice of Goods Shipped on the Sloop *Ann* . . .', listed a wide variety of items for domestic and foreign sale, and included 'Iron Bars, Iron Pots and Kettles, Knitting Pins, Steel Compasses, brass Curtain rings, fire shovels and tongs, Pewter ware, tea pots, Paint, Rope and Twine, Nails, Playing Cards, Lead shot, Casks and Chamber Pots'.[29] Protected and favoured by the Navigation Acts which now barred American goods from British ports, New Brunswick and Nova Scotia expected to replace the former American colonies in the reciprocal and traditional trade with the British West Indies. Thus, the Jarvis brothers fully recognized the potential of these new commercial routes as they had plans of developing a general trade with New England, Great Britain and throughout the Second British Empire. William Jarvis wrote enthusiastically that 'there certainly must be a very great profit made upon this circuitous trade', for he rightly deduced, 'while the Navigation Act is in force the American trade is so cramped that they are starving almost which will render our plan three times as profitable sas it would otherwise be'.[30] Indeed, the monopoly of the carrying trade provided the impetus for the burgeoning ship-building industry of New Brunswick, as well as markets for the natural resources of the province.

Throughout these years in England, William Jarvis also remained active in military life. In 1787 he was commissioned as Lieutenant in the Western Regiment of Militia in Middlesex, and in 1791 he was promoted to Captain. His social and military contacts, and especially his continued association with John Graves Simcoe, first Lieutenant-governor of the newly created province of Upper Canada, finally resulted in Jarvis obtaining a lucrative political appointment. In August 1791, Simcoe recommended 'Mr. William Jarvis' for the offices of 'Secretary and Clerk of the (Executive) Council' of the new province 'as held by Mr. (Jonathan) Odell in New Brunswick'. This reward was altered to the more important and prestigous civil post of provincial secretary and registrar. Service in the Queen's Rangers made Jarvis a clear favourite, as Simcoe wrote that 'this Gentleman' had demonstrated a 'firm and faithful attachment which at a very early period of his Life led him and his family to take up Arms for its protection'.[31]

Before he left for Upper Canada, which had been formally created by a Royal Proclamation following the passing of the Constitutional (Canada) Act of June 1791,

William Jarvis astutely entrenched his position by becoming a member of the Grand Lodge of Ancient Free and Accepted Masons. Many influential Loyalists in the new province and elsewhere were Masons, and membership could be helpful. For example, Jarvis' own father-in-law was a prominent Mason. Within a month of his joining, Jarvis was appointed on 7 March 1792 as 'Substitute Grand Master of Masons for the Province of Upper Canada'.[32] These three quick and successive appointments thrilled Jarvis who found great difficulty in suppressing his joy in family letters. In April 1792, Jarvis and his family departed 'the Downs with a fair Wind' aboard *HMS Henneken,* and sailed for British North America. In many ways they were not only beginning a new life, they were returning home.

The voyage was rough. The journal of William Jarvis notes that on 22 May, they spent an 'awful Night' in a storm. Mrs. Jarvis, he explained, 'supported these calamities with uncommon Fortitude' and 'in the midst of our Horror . . . she boldly said — do not attempt the Boat but stay with me and the children and let us live or die together. I saw her lips tremble with her voice.'[33] Despite these literary dramatics, purportedly demonstrating the courage and spirit of the Jarvis family, the *Henneken* managed to persevere and survive the storm. The winds had abated by 30 May and on 5 June, the ship entered the Gulf of St. Lawrence which was covered with a thick fog. By 11 June it had arrived off Québec. Jarvis was becoming somewhat vain, and wrote that 'many Gentlemen at Québec gave a great deal of Attention to me'. The family soon reached Montréal, and in late June embarked at Lachine for Kingston with Jarvis reporting that 'my baggage fills three Batteaux.'[34]

As they travelled along the upper St. Lawrence, Jarvis marvelled at the impact of the arrival and settlement of the loyalist pioneers. Although these settlers had only been in the country since 1784, Jarvis observed many farms 'with the ninth Crop of wheat on them upon the same Field without manure and the wheat up to a mans shoulder . . . and not a Plough ever put into the Ground — an Harrow is the only implement of husbandry used'.[35] The vast majority of the refugees were soldiers and farmers, tough and resilient individuals who had lived in frontier regions, and mainly in 'the back parts of New York Province'.[36] Upon their arrival, they received land grants, and during the early difficult years, His Majesty's Government alleviated the plight of the families by providing them with a Royal Bounty of provisions, clothing and tools. In addition, grist-mills and saw-mills — the King's Mills — were built to lessen further the economic hardships of frontier life. Housing initially consisted of tents and log huts, but a pleasing 'progress of industry' was noted, as a 'neat house' was usually built after two or three years.[37] The educated and officer class especially fared well. Their larger land grants and political appointments ensured an elevated economic and social status in the communities. One observer remarked that most of the officers had built good houses, and 'with the assistance of their half-pay; live very comfortably and increase and multiply at a great rate'.[38] These inequalities produced 'a very dangerous Jealousy and want of Confidence . . . between the Majority of the settlers, and their late Officers . . . ', which became a source of future controversies in the province.[39]

Most significantly, the Loyalists who settled in the western part of the province of Québec soon created a formalized duality in British North America. Rooted in British political and legal traditions, they naturally disliked the feudal concepts of the 'système seigneurial' which was practiced in the province of Québec. They therefore petitioned for a redress of conditions. Next to assuring the economic welfare and security of their families, these Loyalists wanted freehold land tenure and 'the Government and Laws of England' restored to them. These considerations, they pointed out, had already been granted 'to their Fellow Sufferers in Nova Scotia'.[40] Their several petitions were received sympathetically by British ministers, and as a result, the Constitutional (Canada) Act was devised which produced the division of the 'old' province of Québec into Lower Canada and Upper Canada. Thus, within a decade of the Loyalist arrival, 'central Canada' in contemporary terms was split into two solitudes — one French-speaking and homogeneous, with the notable exceptions of the British merchants at

300

William Jarvis

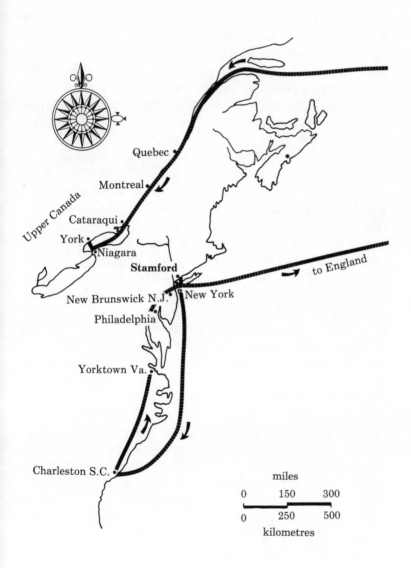

Quebec

Montreal

Upper Canada

Cataraqui

York

Niagara

Stamford

New Brunswick N.J.

New York

to England

Philadelphia

Yorktown Va.

Charleston S.C.

miles

0   150   300

0   250   500

kilometres

Montréal and the Loyalist settlements of Missisquoi Bay; the other a hybrid. In the new province of Upper Canada, the Loyalists were composed of several ethnic, religious and linguistic groups, but they formed in time, and with some exceptions, an English-speaking province.

At Kingston, Lieutenant-governor John Graves Simcoe formally took the oaths of office on 8 July 1792. The following day, William Jarvis was officially appointed 'Secretary and Registrar of the Records of the Province of Upper Canada'.[41] The entourage then sailed for Niagara (Newark) where the first provincial legislature met at Navy Hall on 17 September. Here the formal parliamentary history of the province began. During his administration, Simcoe did his utmost to inculcate 'British Customs, Manners, and Principles' upon the province. He also firmly believed in an established church which would superintend the creation of schools and control education. Finally, the Lieutenant-governor possessed a violent antipathy against American republicanism, and wished to be instrumental in the 'Reunion of the Empire'. For him, Upper Canada would be a show place to demonstrate the superiority of life under British institutions. Although Simcoe's 'enthusiasms' were not universally shared by the settlers, his vision for the province generally correlated with the ideals of articulate Loyalists.[42] Unquestionably, the early character and direction of the evolving province was in large measure molded by Simcoe and a coterie of influential Loyalists.

At Newark, William Jarvis, who hoped that one day he would be an integral part of the élite of the province, initiated his duties as provincial secretary. Much to his chagrin, he soon discovered that his salary of £300 per annum provided insufficient financial security. He was responsible for the full expense of processing the granting of land patents. But changing land regulations sometimes invalidated his work, and as well he was often inefficient and careless in his operations. As a result, he was actually losing money on each land grant processed. To supplement his income Jarvis charged a small fee for his services. He finally petitioned for relief, but received no compensation until after the War of 1812.[43]

In contrast his family life was happier. In July 1792, Jarvis informed his brother Munson that a fourth child was expected. He wrote that he didn't know 'what gender my Canadian will be but I hope of the masculine',[44] and William Jarvis was not disappointed. In November a son, Samuel Peters was born; another son, William Munson followed in 1793; and a daughter, Hannah-Owen in 1797.[45] Life for the family was hectic and exciting, and Hannah Jarvis wrote long, loving and detailed letters to her 'Honoured and Dear Father', detailing incidents of their daily lives. For example, at the celebration of St. John's Day on 27 December 1792 in the Free Mason's Hall in Newark, William Jarvis was formally 'received and honoured as the Provincial Grand Master of Upper Canada'. Fellow Loyalist Lieutenant-colonel John Butler of Butler's Rangers fame was Senior Grand Warden, and merchant Robert Hamilton was Provincial Deputy Grand Master. Unfortunately, the harried, sometimes arrogant and increasingly headstrong William Jarvis soon caused both embarrassment and dissension among the Masons by his frequent absenteeism and irregular conduct in exceeding his power. The resulting internal friction, retarded the progress of the Craft in Upper Canada.[46]

For William Jarvis and the Loyalists, however, the dominant concern during these years at Newark was the threat of a renewal of war with the United States in the summer of 1794. Since the Anglo-American peace of 1783, 'His Majesty's Indian Allies' south of the new international boundary had continued their struggle to preserve and defend traditional lands and culture. Initially, the tribes were 'thunderstruck' by the 1783 treaty which appeared to suggest that the British were going to abandon them to the mercy of American expansion. Fearful of the possible ravages of Indian retaliation, the British quickly revised their frontier policy for North America, and decided that the retention of the western posts, such as Fort Niagara, contrary to the terms of the treaty, was nonetheless both prudent and necessary.

The British then promoted the idea of establishing a national home for the Indians in the Ohio Valley. This suspicious philanthropic undertaking would provide, of course, a convenient native barrier state between the fledgling Loyalist settlements in Upper Canada and the expansive ambitions west and north of the aggressive American republic. To bolster tribal resistance, the British military, and Loyalist officers in the British Indian Department covertly issued them with provisions and war supplies. Encouraged and confident, the Indians won two decisive and successive victories in 1790 and 1791 against American invasion armies under Josiah Harmar and Arthur St. Clair. As a result, American peace commissioners were despatched in the spring of 1793 to attempt a compromise truce. They spent about six weeks at Newark, closely scrutinized by William Jarvis and other Loyalists, awaiting the response of the Indians who were assembled at Sandusky.

The tribal gathering at Sandusky soon degenerated into internal bickering among the native leaders, and this factionalism destroyed the spirit of unity and purpose among them. Peace negotiations with the United States were thus terminated. In August of the next year, a third American invasion army, spearheaded by the Legion infantry of 'Mad' Anthony Wayne, dislodged the Indians from their defensive position at Fallen Timbers, and the British who had earlier built the small post of Fort Miami nearby, refused to assist the fleeing warriors. Thus the existence of an Indian state became the merest of fictions, and the tribes lost the Ohio Valley to the Americans.[47]

The threatened war with the United States in the summer of 1794 threw Upper Canada into speedy military preparations 'for the reception of our neighbours'. William Jarvis was appointed a deputy county lieutenant, and as such took command of the militia of the county of York, with the rank of full Colonel. In a letter to his father-in-law, he commented on the continued determination of the Loyalists, noting that the militia was embodied at Newark 'and a fine body of men they are, almost to a man soldiers that served in the last war'.[48] Other Loyalists actually fought at the battle of Fallen Timbers. Jarvis sadly recounted that a member of his staff, Charles Smith, an adopted chief among the Shawnee and dressed in Indian garb, was killed fighting as a warrior. He 'received shot through the knees', stated Jarvis, 'and was then quartered alive, tho' shocking to relate, nevertheless true'.[49] The alarm and danger of the summer soon subsided, and following the signing of the Jay Treaty later in the year, whereby the British agreed to evacuate the western posts by June 1796, peace returned to the frontier. But, the British retention of the western posts from 1783 to 1796, coupled with the Indian resistance wars, had bought thirteen years of valuable time for the entrenchment of Loyalist settlements and British political institutions. These twin factors in stalling American expansion helped ensure the survival of Upper Canada.

The Jarvis family remained at Newark until 1798. Secretary Jarvis continued to perform his duties, but his inability to improve his financial position made him increasingly cantankerous. During these years, he challenged four individuals to duels, and actually met with one, before his horrified administrative superiors ordered him to desist and keep the peace. Jarvis was also irritated by the haughty arrogance of recently arrived British appointees to the province who possessed undue influence in the Executive and Legislative Councils, and who apparently had a low opinion of colonials. They 'think an American knows not how to speak', fumed Mrs. Jarvis.[50] The social and class tensions, and perhaps a growing lack of confidence, were sufficient reasons to discourage Jarvis from seeking the desired membership in the prestigous Executive Council. I 'am too proud to ask them (the councillors) to recommend me . . .', he confessed to his father-in-law.[51] Hannah Jarvis was more direct in assessing the reasons for her good husband's career difficulties at this time by explaining that Simcoe was surrounded by 'a lot of Pimps, Scycophants and Lyars'.[52] With mounting frustration, mixed with resignation, the Jarvis family which had lingered at Newark contrary to orders, finally vacated their quarters and moved across the lake to the new provincial capital of 'muddy' York.

The town of York was founded in 1793 by Lieutenant-governor Simcoe. The site possessed a fine natural harbour, and was initially designated solely as the military and naval arsenal of the province. But York, situated on the north side of Lake Ontario, was also less exposed to a possible American attack, unlike Newark and Kingston, and thus officially became as well the seat of the provincial government three years later. The choice was not popular with government officials, like William Jarvis. He had with difficulty established his family at Newark, and was not keen on relocating to a tiny, isolated, new capital surrounded by dense forests. In addition, noxious odours arising from the Don marshes apparently caused fevers and agues. Notwithstanding these vexatious concerns, and after several months of defiance and delay, William Jarvis shifted the duties of his office to York.

As early as 1793, in expectation of an official move to York, government officials had been granted town lots at the site. William Jarvis, for example, was granted 'A Front Town Lot and No. 2 first Concession (100 acres)'.[53] He was subsequently granted, as well, considerable 'wild lands' to the north of York. In 1794 Jarvis entered an agreement with a contractor 'to build a Log House of Square pine Timber at or near the Town of York on Lake Ontario', at the reasonable cost of £256.8.0.[54] The house took four years to complete owing to 'want of materials', structural alterations and a manpower shortage. Constructed on the outskirts of town, at what became the corner of Duke and Caroline (Sherbourne), the two and one-half storey building was finely finished of hewn logs, clapboarded on the outside, and painted white. A spacious room in one corner of the ground floor served as the office of the provincial secretary. The living rooms of the family were located at the rear and upstairs. On the second floor above the office, and reached by a handsome winding staircase from the main hall, was a large drawing-room where parties and balls were frequently held. Outbuildings consisted of barns, sheds and a root house. Fruit trees, especially pear, a favourite with the settlers, were planted, and a large garden established. Horses, cows, sheep and pigs were kept on the property which was surrounded by a solid fence with a high peaked gate marking the entrance. As well, Jarvis used in his employ, six Black slaves.[55] The estate reflected an affluent, even ostentatious lifestyle, and the house was one of the two or three largest and finest buildings in early York.

Living beyond his means, William Jarvis was comfortable and enjoyed the powers of his official position in the snarly, status-conscious and increasingly clique-riddled provincial capital. Headstrong, often haughty and somewhat of a prig who for a time showed pretentions of being a member of the York élite, Jarvis became generally dubbed in mocking terms as 'Mr. Secretary Jarvis'. An incident in early 1800, however, deflated his personal sense of importance. Jarvis had shown a personal partisanship in granting land patents, and eventually a Quaker delegation complained to Lieutenant-governor Peter Hunter of the difficulties and delays that they were experiencing in obtaining properly processed grants for their lands north of York. Hunter was furious and sought an explanation. Jarvis could merely reply that his exhaustive duties were so great that he had been unable to prepare these particular patents. The explanation was insufficient for the Lieutenant-governor and provoked an humiliating reprimand — 'Sir — if they are not forthcoming, every one of them, and placed in the hands of these gentlemen here, at noon on Thursday next (it was now Tuesday), by George, I'll un-Jarvis you!'[56] The patents were duly prepared. But unquestionably, the character or temperament of William Jarvis, his lack of popularity, and occasional lapses of administrative efficiency, retarded his career at York.

Yet in civic matters, Jarvis became generally concerned for the welfare of the town. In 1800 he was appointed a magistrate in the Home District (York etc.), and between 1801 and 1806 he served as chairman of the General Quarter Sessions of the Peace, where the district magistrates met. The magistrates were responsible for law enforcement and therefore held the real power in local government. They issued various regulations concerning the safety, respectability and sanitation of the town, and annual tavern licences. As well, the magistrates were expected to pay various expenses and the salaries of the Sheriff, High Constable, Clerk of the Peace, jailer, Court-keeper, coroner and the members of Parliament of the two York ridings. Since expenditures were much greater than the income derived from the Home District, the magistrates faced a hopeless task in attempting to control and manage the steady growth of the town of York. Nonetheless, the magistrates, including William Jarvis, were a dedicated, hard-working and respectable body who, in spite of severe financial difficulties, gave good government to York and the Home District.[57]

For William Jarvis in particular, the development and prosperity of York became a priority, in spite of his initial reluctance to settle there. He enthusiastically assisted in subscribing to a town fire hall; sat on a committee to improve and open Yonge Street further north in order to facilitate farmers in bringing their provisions to market; and encouraged the trade in that one-time delicacy 'York salmon'. He was instrumental in contracting the first schoolmaster, and insisted in sending his children to the District School at York, rather than to the prestigious and well established Cornwall Grammar School of the future Bishop John Strachan. He also, of course, believed firmly in the established Church of England, and fully supported the building of St. James, where he was one of the earliest pew-holders.[58]

Throughout these years at York, the family and social life of William Jarvis, apart from some bickering and jealous rivalries between families, was reasonably pleasant and active. In 1801 a final child, Ann-Elizabeth was born.[59] The Jarvis family participated in caroling, sleighing, boating and country excursions. They attended plays, theatrical performances and delighted in puppet shows. Books were exchanged, and reading novels aloud was a favourite evening pastime. Dinner parties and balls were always popular. For Jarvis personally, shooting wild pigeons, riding, and fox hunting which he introduced and organized, were especially exhilarating diversions.[60]

William Jarvis was less interested in politics. He was an unsuccessful candidate in the first provincial election at York, held in July 1800. His attitude toward 'vulgar democracy' was best illustrated by his one election address in which he emphasized to the crowd that he had 'not solicited the suffrages of my fellow subjects from door to door, such conduct, I am confident, you would think ill became a man who, ardently wishes, shortly to be in the character of your Representative'.[61] The common features of disruption and violence at the polls disgusted Jarvis. He was so incensed at a mob in a York by-election in September 1805 that he actually attempted to intervene and halt their antics. The results of his boldness was reported in a letter by his wife Hannah who wrote that . . . 'Mr. Jarvis is sick, having gone out to suppress a Mob, four men fell upon him and cut his head very bad — and bruised him so much that he is not able to lift his hand to his head or open his left eye — it happened at midnight — he took his Broad sword with him which saved his life — he cut one mans hand off a little below the Fingers, saving the fore Finger and thumb, disarmed another, the others ran away — but have since been taken and thrown into Gaol one who endeavoured to escape is shackled with 50 lb. of Iron . . . '.[62] The fiery and impetuous conduct of William Jarvis on this occasion was clearly understandable. The violence of the mob surely reminded him of the thugs in Connecticut, and the horrors they perpetrated in the name of liberty and freedom prior to the civil war and rebellion in colonial America. He could not bear the thought of such a repetition in Upper Canada. For Jarvis, and many others like him, no sacrifice was too great to crush the threat or even suggestion of American mobocracy and republicanism in order to preserve the peace, order and stability of the British and Loyalist province.

The ruffled nature of Jarvis was also in part explained by his frustrating and plaguing financial problems. His salary could not support his lavish life-style, and a major business venture in land speculation proved embarrassing and unprofitable. Just before Jarvis left Newark, he had bought Block 5, about 30,800 acres, of the Grand River lands for £5675, but put down only £600. The Grand River lands, north of Lake Erie, which totalled approximately 570,000 acres, were supposedly a 'fertile and happy retreat' granted by the King to the Mohawk and other loyalist Iroquois of the Six Nations Confederacy as a partial substitute for their land losses on behalf of His Majesty during the rebellion. Yet their leader Thayendanegea (Joseph Brant), a Mohawk Loyalist, warrior and statesman who had fought valiantly for the British during the war, saw his dream of forming a United Indian nation vanish at the Sandusky Conference of 1793.[63]

From that tragic moment, Brant turned from high idealism and general confederacies to practical self-interest and regional concerns. Three years after Sandusky, Brant acquired in council the power of attorney to sell portions of the Grand River lands. After considerable haranging, bitter debate and threats, Brant forced the British provincial authorities to accept a formal transfer of the Grand River lands to the crown, following which, designated portions, nearly 342,000 acres, were then sold on behalf of Brant and the Iroquois to the various white purchasers with whom Brant was negotiating. Although Brant was allegedly selling these lands to improve the economic welfare of his people, his personal wealth was considerably augmented, and the Native people of the Grand River did not prosper. In fact, a later report noted that these people were unable to provide even 'supplies of flour from the annuities arising oue of the late sale of their lands'.[64]

Block 5 yielded no dividends for William Jarvis. He could not meet his payments, and after five years the Executive Council suggested that he relinquish his pretence or claim to that particular tract. Brant pointed out that Jarvis 'has in no one instance complied with his contract'. By November 1806 the situation was ludicrous and humiliating, particularly when the chiefs in council publicly announced that 'the Secretary of the Province [Jarvis], and some others have received grants for certain parcels of this our land, without either making payment or giving the proper securities'. In the spring of the following year, Jarvis formally surrendered Block 5, and received his original £600, although he argued in vain that he should have been compensated with more financial consideration. The whole land gamble had been a disaster for him.[65]

Frustrated, disappointed and angry because of his dormant career and lack of funds, William Jarvis, for one brief period in 1806, actually supported an anti-government element led by the recently arrived Judge Robert Thorpe. This newcomer contended that the Loyalists were being neglected by the government, and that excessive British appointments had 'stunted the prosperity of the Province and goaded the people until they have turned from the greatest loyalty to the utmost disaffection'.[66] Jarvis agreed with this interpretation. He first arrived in Upper Canada bursting with confidence and pride that his American Loyalist background, political appointment and personal character would assure him a prominent place in the emerging provincial autocracy. But this had not happened. Seeking scapegoats, Jarvis and others of similar persuasion, jealously resented the British and American intrusion into the Loyalist province, and often blamed these people for their personal failures, and for the real or imagined woes of the province. Although Thorpe handily won a seat in the Legislative Assembly, he was soon suspended, and left the province in 1807. The disquiet that he engineered quickly subsided. The flirtation with disloyalty ended, as well, for Jarvis, and for the next five years, he remained engrossed in his professional and family life at York. Yet this tranquility was suddenly destroyed in June 1812 when the United States, prompted by national honour and frontier imperialism, declared war on Great Britain, and then promptly proceeded to invade Upper Canada.

The War of 1812 was the critical test for the survival of British values and Loyalist ideals in the province. For two and one-half years, British regulars, His Majesty's Indian allies and the militia of Upper Canada fought with dogged determination in opposing the American invasion forces. Certain of the old Loyalists and their sons and daughters fervently participated in the defence of their settlements and beliefs against the hereditary American republican foe. The two sons of William Jarvis, for example, campaigned with the British forces. Samuel Peters Jarvis was attached to the 49th Foot, the regiment of Major General Isaac Brock, and was present at the battle of Queenston Heights on 13 October 1812 where the Americans were driven 'off the Mountain', but not before 'Poor General Brock' was killed. William Munson Jarvis was wounded and captured at the battle of York on 27 April 1813, and lost the sight of one eye during the ferocity of Lundy's Lane on 25 July 1814 at Niagara Falls. Both sons, according to one British officer, always showed a 'willing disposition to render themselves useful'. For his part, William Jarvis who remained at York throughout the war, corresponded extensively with his sons and various British officers, encouraging them to their duty. As well, through his influence and patriotism, he frequently assisted young gentlemen officers in particular, by providing them with comforts or favours.[67]

His age and duties did not allow the provincial secretary the opportunity to experience field service in the War of 1812. Yet the violence of the conflict reached him directly in late April 1813 when an American fleet 'hove in sight' and attacked York. The enemy force was overwhelming, and after a stout and bloody resistance, especially by the British regulars and some local Mississauga and Ojibwa Indians, the British retreated, but not before, according to one American participant, they 'devised the inhuman project of blowing up their Magazine (containing 300 Bbls. powder), the explosion of which, shocking to mention, had almost totally destroyed our Army. About 300 were wounded, and about 60 killed dead on the spot by stones of all dimensions falling like a shower of hail in the midst of our ranks'.[68] Angry and partly in retaliation, the Americans proceeded to plunder private homes and public property, destroyed a number of buildings which included burning 'the Houses of Legislature, Courts, and Public Records', and even managed to steal the Speaker's wig which they insisted was a scalp. After an occupation of several days, the Americans left. They returned a second time in late July, and committed similar depredations. In both these attacks, the whereabouts of William Jarvis remains a mystery. He probably removed his family north along Yonge Street in advance of the enemy, and found sanctuary in the woods. During the second capture of York, it was reported that 'the principal Gentlemen had retired from an apprehension of being treated with . . . severity' by the enemy. York was not threatened for the remainder of the war.[69]

The War of 1812, and particularly the capture and

occupation of York on two occasions, was immensely stressful for William Jarvis. Two months after the first attack, a prominent citizen of the town wrote that the 'Secretary of the province is a distressed Man who has no duties to perform which call for Energy'.[70] Indeed, the expenses of the provincial secretary had been unpaid for months. Jarvis pleaded for funds in order to continue his duties, but the war made it difficult to routinely prepare warrants for the payment of his office. Finally, he did receive an insufficient credit for £50. Happily the war ended in December 1814 on the basis of 'status quo ante bellum' and Upper Canada and British North America were preserved. But Jarvis never really recovered from the strain of the war years and the depressed state of his official position. He resumed his duties after the war, but without his normal zeal. In the spring of 1817, his wife Hannah wrote despairingly to her father that 'Mr. Jarvis has been very ill this Winter'.[71] Four months later her worst fears were realized, and in the quiet of his home at York on 13 August 1817, William Jarvis died.[72] The provincial secretary was buried with full Masonic honours in the churchyard of St. James.

William Jarvis did not fulfill his ambitions, and did not become a prominent member of the York-based provincial autocracy. His prickly personality and American Loyalist background were not assets. York, riddled with patronage and self-interest, was not a Loyalist town. Rather, the town was the seat of government, and was mostly inhabited by political appointees, officials and immigrants who arrived after the loyal refugees of 1784. The original Loyalists had settled principally along the upper St. Lawrence, the Bay of Quinte, and at Newark and along the Detroit River area, notably at Amherstburg and Sandwich (Windsor).

As provincial secretary and magistrate, however, Jarvis did have some prestige as a ranking member of the small provincial bureaucracy. In addition, he was moderately successful in advancing the careers of his sons. Samuel Peters Jarvis became Chief Superintendent of Indian Affairs, and Jarvis Street in Toronto was named after him. William Munson became Sheriff of Gore District. William Jarvis was not rich. His extravagant lifestyle and the financial burdens of his office, had resulted in a debt of £1830 at the time of his death. Only later did the Jarvis family become wealthy, largely through the sale of the 'wild lands' granted to William Jarvis, and which became worth a fortune in real estate value with the growth, expansion and prosperity of the city of Toronto.

William Jarvis was determined to create something better out of the catastrophe, humiliation and defeat of the civil war and rebellion in colonial America. The Loyalist diaspora in 1783 had resulted in the establishment of new settlements in British North America extolling British values and Loyalist ideals. More specifically, in Upper Canada the military thrashing of the Americans during the War of 1812 symbolized for these political refugees, like William Jarvis, not only vindication, but Loyalist redemption. The prosperous evolution of the province and the dominion, along with an emerging and distinctive Canadian character separate and different from that of both the United States and Great Britain, was affected in large measure by the United Empire Loyalists who helped weave the basic political and cultural fabric of the nation. William Jarvis stands as a representative example of these proud and resolute people who shall always remain an integral part of our national heritage.

1. The Jarvis Papers, Ross-Ross Collection, New Brunswick Museum (Saint John), William Jarvis to his brother, Munson Jarvis, 3 July 1792.
2. The Jarvis-Powell Papers, Ontario Archives (Toronto); and John Ross Robertson, *The History of Free Masonry in Canada* (2 vols., Toronto, 1899), Vol. 1, p. 466.
3. John Ross Robertson, *Masonary*, Vol. 1, p. 461.
4. The background and causes of the colonial rebellion can be gleaned from: L.H. Gipson, *The British Empire before the American Revolution* (14 vols., New York, 1936-1971); J.M. Bumsted, 'The American Revolution: Some Thoughts on Recent Bicentennial Scholarship', *Acadiensis*, Vol. 6 (1977), pp. 3-22; Jack P. Greene, ed., *The Ambiguity of the American Revolution* (New York, 1968); Bernard Bailyn, *The Ideological Origins of the American Revolution* (Cambridge, Mass., 1967); and Ian R. Christie, *Crisis of Empire: Great Britain and the American Colonies, 1754-1783* (London, 1966) and 'The Imperial Dimension: British Ministerial Perspectives During the American Revolutionary Crisis, 1763-1776', in Esmond Wright; ed., *Red, White and True Blue: The Loyalists in the American Revolution* (New York, 1976).
5. John Ross Robertson, *Masonry*, Vol. 1, p. 461.
6. Epaphroditus Peck, *The Loyalists of Connecticut* (New Haven, 1934); and John W. Tyler, *Connecticut Loyalists* (New Orleans, N.D.).

7. The 'Narrative of Colonel Stephen Jarvis', in James J. Talman, ed., *Loyalist Narratives from Upper Canada* (Toronto, 1946), pp. 158-9.
8. Lieutenant Colonel John Graves Simcoe, *Simcoe's Military Journal* (London, 1784, reprinted Toronto, 1962), p. 2; John R. Cuneo, 'The Early Days of the Queen's Rangers, August 1776 — February 1777', *Military Affairs*, Vol. 22 (1958), pp. 66-67; Burt Garfield Loescher, *Rogers Rangers: The First Green Berets* (San Mateo, California, 1969), pp. 170-72; and W.O. Raymond, 'Loyalists in Arms', *New Brunswick Historical Society. Collections*, No. 5 (1904), pp. 202-3.
9. B.G. Loescher, *Rangers*, pp. 172-76; and Mark M. Boatner, ed., *Encyclopedia of the American Revolution* (New York, 1966), p. 671.
10. H.M. Jackson, 'The Queen's Rangers, 1st American Regiment', *Journal of the Society for Army Historical Research*, Vol. 14 (1935), pp. 147-81.
11. J.G. Simcoe, *Military Journal*, p. 1; Capt. W.H. Wilkin, *Some British Soldiers in America* (London, 1914), pp. 90-117; and W.Y. Carman, 'The Uniforms of the Queen's Rangers', *Journal of the Society for Arm Historical Research*, Vol. 57 (1979), pp. 63-70.
12. J.G. Simcoe, *Military Journal*, p. 45 ff.
13. *Ibid.*, p. 53; and D.B. Read, *The Life and Times of General John Graves Simcoe* (Toronto, 1890), pp. 38-9.
14. J.G. Simcoe, *Military Journal* pp. 58-63, and pp. 75-7.
15. *Ibid.*, p. 88 ff.
16. Richard K. MacMaster, ed., 'News of the Yorktown Campaigns: The Journal of Dr. Robert Honyman, April 17 — November 25, 1781', *The Virginia Magazine of History and Biography*, Vol. 79 (1971), p. 395.
17. J.G. Simcoe, *Military Journal*, pp. 130-5.
18. *Ibid.*, p. 150.
19. *Ibid.*, p. 133.
20. *Ibid.*, p. 135.
21. PAC, MG 23, H1 3, William Jarvis: Correspondence and Papers, 1782-1813, Vol. 1, 25 December 1782.
22. Stephen Jarvis, 'Narrative', pp. 222-3.
23. W.O. Raymond, ed., *The Winslow Papers, A.D. 1776-1826* (Saint John, 1901), p. 244.
24. The Jarvis-Powell Papers, Ontario Archives (Toronto).
25. North Callahan, *Royal Raiders: The Tories of the American Revolution* (New York, 1963), pp. 130-2, taken from the supposed works of Dr. Samuel Peters, *A General History of Connecticut . . . from a Gentlemen of the Province* (London, 1781).
26. For the Loyalists in England, see: Wallace Brown, 'American Loyalists in Britain', *History Today* (October, 1969), pp. 672-8; and Mary Beth Norton, *The British-Americans, The Loyalist Exiles in England, 1774-1789* (Boston and London, 1972).
27. The Jarvis-Powell Papers, Ontario Archives (Toronto).
28. The Jarvis Papers, New Brunswick Museum (Saint John), letter dated 9 July 1787.
29. The William Jarvis Papers, Metropolitan Toronto Library, Baldwin Room, 'Invoice', dated London, 20 May 1788.
30. The Jarvis Papers, New Brunswick Museum (Saint John), William Jarvis to Munson Jarvis, Pimlico, 20 August 1787.
31. E.A. Cruikshank, ed., *The Simcoe Papers* (5 vols., Toronto, 1923-31), Vol. 1, p. 47, Simcoe to Henry Dundas, Secretary of State at the Home Department, London, 12 August 1791.
32. John Ross Robertson, *Masonary*, Vol. 1, p. 339.
33. PAC, MG 23, H1 3, Vol. 2, the 'Journal of William Jarvis to Canada'.
34. *Ibid.*
35. The Jarvis Papers, New Brunswick Museum (Saint John), William Jarvis to Munson Jarvis, Kingston on the Banks of Lake Ontario, 3 July 1792.
36. Richard A. Preston, ed., *Kingston Before the War of 1812: A Collection of Documents* (Toronto, 1959), p. 112, comments of the Reverend John Stuart, Cataraqui, 2 November 1785.

37. Mrs. John Graves Simcoe, *The Diary of Mrs. John Graves Simcoe* (Toronto, 1911), with notes by John Ross Robertson, p. 119, entry of 14 July 1792.

38. Anne Powell, The Anne Powell Diary, 1789, Ontario Archives (Toronto), p. 3.

39. Richard A. Preston, ed., *Kingston*, p. 122, 'Loyalist Grievances', Kingston, 18 August 1787; and also, The William Dummer Powell Papers, Metropolitan Toronto Library, Baldwin Room, B77 'Papers relating to . . . complaints by (Loyalist) settlers' . . . , 1787'.

40. A. Shortt and A.G. Doughty, eds., *Documents Relating to the Constitutional History of Canada, 1759-1791* (2 vols., Ottawa, 1907), Vol. 2, pp. 775; and for general details of Loyalist settlement and ideals in Upper Canada, Robert S. Allen, Loyalist Commemoration in Canada: A Resource Study, unpublished manuscript, Parks Canada, Ottawa (Autumn 1980), esp. pp. 112-19.

41. PAC, MG 23, H1 3, Vol. 1, Kingston, 9 July 1792.

42. E.A. Cruikshank, ed., *Simcoe*, Vol. 1, p. 27 and scattered comments throughout; and S.R. Mealing, 'The Enthusiasms of John Graves Simcoe', *Canadian Historical Association Report for 1958*, pp. 50-62.

43. PAC, MG 23, H1 3, Vol. 1, William Jarvis, Memorial, Newark, 10 November 1795; and for general details, Gilbert C. Paterson, 'Land Settlement in Upper Canada, 1783-1840', *Sixteenth Report of the Department of Archives for the Province of Ontario*, 1920 (Toronto, 1921); and Lillian Gates, 'The Loyalists and the Crown Lands', *Land Policies of Upper Canada* (Toronto, 1968).

44. The Jarvis Papers, New Brunswick Museum (Saint John), letter of 3 July 1792.

45. The Jarvis-Powell Papers, Ontario Archives (Toronto).

46. John Ross Robertson, *Masonry*, pp. 358; and 367-8.

47. For details, Robert S. Allen, 'The British Indian Department and the Frontier in North America, 1755-1830', *Canadian Historic Sites: Occasional Papers in Archaeology and History* (Ottawa, 1975), No. 14, esp. pp. 26-58.

48. E.A. Cruikshank, ed., *Simcoe*, Vol. 3, pp. 29-30, William Jarvis to the Reverend Dr. Samuel Peters, Niagara, 3 September 1794.

49. *Ibid.*

50. PAC, MG 23, H 3, The Jarvis-Peters Papers, Hannah Jarvis to her father, Niagara, 26 July 1796.

51. *Ibid.*, letter of 1 July 1797.

52. *Ibid.*, Hannah Jarvis to her father, letter of 26 July 1792; and for other opinions and general comments, 'Letters from William Jarvis . . . and Mrs. Jarvis to the Reverend Samuel Peters', *Women's Canadian Historical Society of Toronto, Transactions*, No. 23 (1922-23), pp. 11-61.

53. Edith G. Firth, ed., *The Town of York, 1793-1815* (Toronto, 1962), p. 15.

54. The William Jarvis Papers, Metropolitan Toronto Library, Baldwin Room, dated Newark, 26 August 1794.

55. *Ibid.*, John Ross Robertson, *Masonry*, p. 464-5; and Edith G. Firth, ed., *York*, lxxvi, lxxviii and pp. 224-5.

56. John Ross Robertson, *Masonry*, p. 465.

57. Edith G. Firth, ed., *York*, xlix-li and pp. 97, 99, 100 and 235.

58. *Ibid.*; liii and pp. 101, 150, 198-200 and 203.

59. The Jarvis-Powell Papers, Ontario Archives (Ontario).

60. Edith G. Firth.ed., *York*, lxxxiii and pp. 274-5; and for fox hunting, p. 241.

61. *Ibid.*, p. 162; and pp. 162-4.

62. *Ibid.*, p. 256.

63. C.M. Johnston, 'Joseph Brant, the Grand River Lands and the Northwest Crisis', *Ontario History*, Vol. 55 (1963), pp. 267-82.

64. Charles M. Johnston, ed., *The Valley of the Six Nations* (Toronto, 1964); and for specifics, Robert S. Allen, 'Indian Department', esp. pp. 63-64.

65. *Ibid.*, pp. 133-9.

66. Edith G. Firth, ed., *York*, lxvii and p. 174; and for details on the political temperament and personalities of York throughout this period, Robert J.

Burns, 'God's Chosen People: The Origins of Toronto Society, 1793-1818', *Canadian Historical Association Report for 1973* (Ottawa).

67. PAC, MG 23, H1 3, Vol. 1, scattered letters.

68. Edith G. Firth, ed., *York*, p. 307; and Charles W. Humphries, 'The Capture of York', *Ontario History*, Vol. 51 (1959).

69. *Ibid.*, p. 317; and for general details for York and the War of 1812, pp. 279-338.

70. *Ibid.*, p. 315.

71. PAC, MG23, H1 3, Vol. 2, dated York, 11 April 1817.

72. The Jarvis-Powell Papers, Ontario Archives (Ontario).

Appendix A

Chronology of Major Events
1763 to 1791.

1763   1st Treaty of Paris
- France concedes North America possessions to
Britain. Britain, dominant on continent, ends years
"salutory neglect" and embarks on a new Imperial
policy.

1763   Proclamation of 1763
- Established to prevent further encroachment into
Indian lands and thus help prevent Indian Wars
and regulate settlement.

1764   Revenue (Sugar) Act
- 1st law ever passed by Parliament for the specific
purpose of raising money for crown in colonies.

1764   Colonial Currency Act
- Limited right of colonial governments to print
paper money.

1765   Stamp Act
- 1st direct tax levied by Parliament on American
colonies; aroused great opposition in colonies.

1765   Stamp Act Congress
- Meeting of colonial representatives to discuss opposition to Stamp Act.

1765   Sons of Liberty organized
- Secret organization formed to protest Stamp Act
by violent methods.

1766   Repeal of Stamp Act
- British Parliament retreats on issue thus setting
precedence and building colonial confidence.

1766   Declaratory Act
- British Parliament re-asserts right to tax colonies.

1767   Townshend Act
- New taxes disguised as duties; new opposition in
colonies.

1770 Repeal of Townshend Act
- All taxes removed except that on tea.

1770 Boston Massacre
- British soldiers fire on mob Act

1772 Tea Act
- British Parliament gives East India Company preference in colonial markets.

1773 Boston Tea Party
- Sons of Liberty disguised as Indians destroy cargo of East India Co. Tea.

1774 Coercive or Intolerable Acts
- British Parliament decides to punish colony of Massachusetts.
(a) Boston Port Bill - closed the port of Boston
(b) Administration of Justice Act - trials could be transferred to England
(c) Massachusetts Government Act - virtually annulled the charter of Massachusetts
(d) Quartering Act - legalized quartering of troops in private homes.

1774 Quebec Act
- Provided for Government of Quebec and gave the colony new enlarged borders.

1774 1st Continental Congress
- Representatives of most colonies meet to discuss problems.

1775 Battles of Lexington and Concord
- 1st military skirmish of revolutionary war; "shot heard around the world".

1775 2nd Continental Congress
- Again colonial representatives meet; decide to raise army and name George Washington as Commander in-chief.

1776 Evacuation of Boston
- British troops and Loyalists sail for Halifax.

1776 Eddy and Allen Rebellion in Nova Scotia when Fort Cumberland was attacked, but the Rebels were defeated. Washington refuses to send assistance.

1776 Declaration of Independence
- Congress declares colonies independent of Britain; many individuals forced to now declare for Congress or King.

1778 Franco-American Alliance
- After some time of secret support, France openly declares support for the colonies.

1779 Spain enters War in Support of Congress
- By 1780, Russia, Denmark, Sweden, The Netherlands, Prussia, Portugal, Austria, Kingdom of the Two Sicilies opposing Britain; colonial rebellion becomes a world war.

1781 Battle of Yorktown
- British surrender; last major battle of the war.
1783 2nd Treaty of Paris
- Britain recognizes independence of 13 of her colonies.

1783 Major immigrations of Loyalists to British North America.

1784 Creation of Cape Breton Island and New Brunswick
- Nova Scotia split in three parts. Prince Edward Island had previously (1769) been made a separate colony.

1791 Establishment of Upper Canada (now Ontario) as separate political unit.
- Quebec split to form Upper (Ontario) and Lower (Quebec) Canada.

J.N.G.

Appendix B

A Diary of the Military
Events of the American
Revolution 1775-1784

Background Note

To conduct operations against the Rebels in her colonies, Britain organized four military departments. These were the Northern Department, with headquarters in Quebec City, the Eastern (or Northeastern) centred on Halifax, the Southern based on St. Augustine, Florida, and the Central at New York City. In addition to the troops who were campaigning against the rebel armies, these departments had garrisons and Provincial Corps of the British Army were attached to each military department — regiments established for loyal colonials in or from all the American colonies.

New York City, close to the more populous middle colonies, with year-round port, was the main base of operation, and to it were attached the largest number of provincial corps. At New York City, too, most of the civilian Loyalists took refuge as the war went on. This Central Department, closest to the action, with local resources at hand and a wealthy class, and good access for British naval and supply vessels, was the most important base. While there were shortages of fuel and food at times, and the city was badly damaged by two serious fires, none of the other military departments could have coped with like numbers of displaced persons. Many of the provincial corps that fought in the southern campaign belonged to the Central Department. Halifax was more remote, and neither Canada nor the Floridas could provide facilities for the Loyalists that were comparable to those available at New York City.

While many Loyalists at New York City joined provincial corps such as Delancey's Brigade, Skinner's New Jersey Volunteers, Simcoe's Queen's Rangers or other regiments, a far larger proportion were able to exist as civilians. Men of military age served in the militia. One group formed what was known as the Loyal American Association, and asked for permission to harry the Rebels along the coast. The King approved and allowed commissions, but "without Pay or Rank in the Army or Command over other Corps". Other Loyalists formed associations towards the close of the war, to expedite resettlement. Sir Guy Carleton, the Commander-in-chief at that time, organized his civilian Loyalists into militia companies for administrative purposes, before they sailed from New York City in 1783 with their dependents.

1775

Apr. 19	Battles of Lexington and Concord, retreat of British to Boston.
May 5	Capture of forts at Ticonderoga and Crown Point by Allen and Arnold.
June 17	Battle of Breed's/Bunker Hill, costly victory for British.
July 3	George Washington takes command of Rebels' Continental Army.
Sept. 4-Nov. 3	Seige of Fort St. Johns by Rebels.
Oct. 10	Sir Wm. Howe succeeds Gage as Commander-in-chief; Carleton given command in Canada.
Oct. 17	Fall of Fort Chambly to Rebels.
Nov. 13	Rebels under Montgomery occupy Montreal.
Dec. 4	Rebels under Arnold besiege Quebec.
Dec. 9	Battle of Great Bridge, Virginia, British defeated.
Dec. 31	Battle for Quebec, Montgomery, Arnold routed by Carleton.

1776

Feb. 27	Moore's Creek Bridge, North Carolina, Loyalists defeated.
Mar. 17	British evacuate Boston, withdraw to Halifax.
May 5	Relief of Quebec by Burgoyne, von Riedesel, reinforcements.
May 16	Battle of the Cedars, Forster defeats American Rebels.

June - Oct	Carleton and Burgoyne drive Rebels out of Canada, fail to retake Ticonderoga.
June 4	British open campaign in South Carolina.
July 21	British fail to capture Charleston.
Aug. - Dec.	British campaign in New York, New Jersey.
Aug. 27	British victory on Long Island.
Sept. 15	Battle of Harlem Heights, Howe occupies New York.
Oct. 11	Battle of Valcour Island, Lake Champlain, Carleton's fleet defeats Arnold's.
Oct. 18	Delaying action by Rebels at Pell's Point, New York.
Oct. 28	Battle of White Plains, New York, indecisive.
Nov. 16	British capture Fort Washington, New York.
Dec. 25-6	Washington defeats Germans at Trenton, New Jersey, a turning point for the Rebels in the middle colonies.

1777

Jan. 3	Rebels take Princeton, New Jersey.
Feb. 1-May 9	Minor campaigning in New Jersey.
June - Oct.	Burgoyne's campaign in northern New York.
July 5	Rebel army escapes from Ticonderoga
July 7	Battle of Hubbardtown, Fraser, von Riedesel, Peters rout rebel rearguard.
Aug. 3-23	Siege of Fort Stanwix, Mohawk Valley by St. Leger.
Aug. 6	Battle of Oriskany, Johnson, Butler, Brant defeat Herkimer's militia.
Aug. 16	Battle of Bennington, Germans, Loyalists defeated.
Sept. 11	Battle of Brandywine, Howe defeats Washington.

Sept. 19	Battle of Freeman's Farm, costly victory for Burgoyne.
Sept. 20	Rebels attacked at Paoli.
Sept. 26	Howe occupies Philadelphia.
Oct. 7	Battle of Bemis Heights (or 2nd Battle of Freeman's Farm), Burgoyne routed by Gates, Arnold.
Oct. 17	Burgoyne surrenders at Saratoga.
Oct. 22	British fail to take Fort Mercer.
Nov. 15	British take Fort Mifflin.
Dec. 18	Washington's army winters at Valley Forge.

1778

Feb. 6	France forms a military alliance with the Continental Congress.
May 24	Clinton replaces Howe as Commander-in-chief.
June 27	Haldimand replaces Carleton as Commander-in-chief in Canada.
June 28	Battle of Monmouth, indecisive.
July 4	Butler's Rangers, Indians, raid Wyoming, Pennsylvania.
Aug. 29	French, Rebels fail to take Rhode Island.
Nov. 11	Raid on Cherry Valley, Walter Butler, Brant.
Dec. 29	British take Savannah, Georgia.

1779

Jan.	British capture Sunbury and Augusta.
Feb. 23	Capture of Fort Sackville and Vincennes by Rebels under George Rogers Clark.
May - June	Bitter civil war in the South.
May 8	Spain declares war on Britain.
July 15	Wayne takes Stony Point from British.
Aug. - Sept.	Sullivan's expedition against the Six Nations (Iroquois).

Aug. 13	Massachusetts attacks Penobscot Bay, repulsed.
Aug. 13	Battle of Chemung, New York, Butler's Rangers, Indians pushed back by Sullivan.
Aug. 29	Battle of Newtown, New York, Butler's Rangers, Indians repelled by Sullivan.
Oct. 9	French, Rebels fail to retake Savannah.
Dec. 26	British fleet sails to attack Charleston.

1780

Mar. 14	Spaniards capture Mobile.
May - June	Raid on Mohawk Valley, Johnson and his Royal Yorkers.
May 12	British capture Charleston.
July 11	French troops reach Newport, Rhode Island.
Aug. - Sept.	Raid on Mohawk Valley by Johnson, Royal Yorkers, Butler's Rangers, regulars, Indians.
Aug. 16	Battle of Camden, Rebels defeated.
Sept. 25	Benedict Arnold defects to the British.
Oct. 2	Hanging of Major John André.
Oct. 7	British, Loyalists defeated at King's Mountain.
Oct. 29	Sherwood negotiates a truce with the Republic of Vermont.

1781

Jan. 17	British, Loyalists defeated at Cowpens.
Mar. 15	Greene, Cornwallis fight indecisive battle at Guildford Court House.
Apr. 25	Battle of Hobkirk's Hill, costly British victory for Rawdon.
June 30	British hold on Carolinas broken.
Sept. 8	Battle of Eutaw Springs, British retreat to Charleston.

Sept. 28	Washington and Rochambeau march towards Yorktown, Virginia.
Oct.	Ross expedition to the Mohawk Valley, with regulars, Royal Yorkers, Butler's Rangers, Indians.
Oct. 6	British besieged at Yorktown.
Oct. 19	Cornwallis surrenders at Yorktown.
Oct. 25-30	Battles of Johnstown and West Canada Creek as Ross expedition withdraws.

1782

Feb. 23	Carleton replaces Clinton as Commander-in-chief.
Mar. - Aug.	Bitter frontier warfare continues.
Mar. 20	North ministry resigns, Rockingham forms a government.
Apr. 12	Rodney defeats French fleet in the West Indies.
June	Haldimand ordered to cease all offensive operations.
July 11	British evacuate Savannah.
Aug. 18	Battle of Blue Licks, Kentucky Valley, Butler's Rangers, Indians defeat Daniel Boone.
Nov. 30	Preliminary peace treaty signed in Paris.
Dec. 14	British evacuate Charleston.

1783

Feb.	Rebels under Willett fail to capture Oswego.
Apr. 19	Congress proclaims end of hostilities.
Apr. 26	"Spring Fleet" sails from New York for Nova Scotia with Loyalists needing resettlement.
June 15	Second fleet sails from New York for Nova Scotia.
Aug. 26	Third fleet leaves for Nova Scotia.
Sept. - Nov.	Evacuation of remaining Loyalists, regulars from New York.

Sept. 8	Final peace treaty signed.
Oct. 6	The last of the provincial (Loyalist) troops leave New York.
Nov. 25	Evacuation of New York completed.

M.B.F.

Bibliography

Archibald, Mary. *Gideon White, Loyalist*. Shelburne: Shelburne Historical Society, 1975.

Barkley, Murray. 'The Loyalist Tradition in New Brunswick: The Growth and Evolution of an Historical Myth, 1825-1913', *Acadiensis*, 4, 2 (Spring, 1975), pp. 3-45.

Berger, Carl. 'The Loyalist Tradition', *The Sense of Power: Studies in the Ideas of Canadian Imperialism, 1867-1914*. Toronto: University of Toronto Press, 1970, pp. 78-108.

Brown, Wallace. *The Good Americans: The Loyalists in the American Revolution*. New York: Morrow, 1969. *The King's Friends: The Composition and Motives of the American Loyalist Claimants*. Providence, R. I.: Brown University Press, 1965.

Crary, Catherine S., ed. *The Price of Loyalism: Tory Writings from the Revolutionary Era*. New York: McGraw-Hill, 1973.

Cruikshank, E.A., ed. *The Settlement of the United Empire Loyalists on the Upper St. Lawrence and the Bay of Quinte in 1784: A Documentary Record*. Toronto: Ontario Historical Society, 1934.

Evans, G.N.D., ed. *Allegiance in America: The Case of the Loyalists*. Reading, Mass: Addison-Wesley, 1969.

Fraser, Alexander, ed. *Second Report of the Bureau of Archives for the Province of Ontario for 1904*. Toronto: The King's Printer, 1905. 2 vols.

Fryer, Mary Beacock. *Buckskin Pimpernel, the Exploits of Justus Sherwood, Loyalist Spy*. Toronto and Charlottetown: Dundurn Press, 1981. *King's Men, the Soldier Founders of Ontario*. Toronto and Charlottetown: Dundurn Press, 1980. And Lieutenant-colonel William A. Smy. *Rolls of the Provincial (Loyalist) Corps, Canadian Command American Revolutionary Period*. Toronto and Charlottetown: Dundurn Press, 1981.

Gilroy, Marion, comp. *Loyalists and Land Settlement in Nova Scotia*. Halifax: Public Archives of Nova Scotia, 1937. Reprinted by the Royal Nova Scotia Historical Society, 1980.

Graves, Ross. *William Schurman, Loyalist of Bedeque, Prince Edward Island*. Summerside, P.E.I.: Harold B. Schurman, 1973.

Gundy, H. Pearson. 'Molly Brant, Loyalist', *Ontario Historical Society Papers and Records*, XLV, 1 (Winter 1953), pp. 97-108.

Hoerder, Dirk. *Crowd Action in Revolutionary Massachusetts 1765-1780*. New York: Academic Press, 1977.

Jarvis, Stephen. 'The Narrative of Colonel Stephen Jarvis', *Loyalist Narratives from Upper Canada*, James J. Talman, ed., Toronto: The Champlain Society, 1946.

Johnson, Charles M. *The Valley of the Six Nations: A Collection of Documents on the Indian Lands of the Grand River*. Toronto: The Champlain Society, 1964.

Johnston, Jean. 'Molly Brant, Mohawk Matron', *Ontario History*,

LVI, 2 (June, 1964), pp. 105-124.

Jones, E. Alfred. *The Loyalists of Massachusetts: Their Memorials, Petitions, Claims, Etc. From English Records*. London: The Saint Catherine Press, 1930. Reprinted by Genealogical Company of Baltimore, 1969.

MacKinnon, Neil. 'The Changing Attitudes of the Nova Scotian Loyalists towards the United States, 1783-1791', *Acadiensis*, 2, 2 (Spring, 1973), pp. 43-54. 'The Loyalists, A Different People', *The Ethnics of Nova Scotia*. Port Credit, Ontario: The Scribblers Press, 1978.

MacLean, Franklynn. 'The Reverend Ranna Cossit', in R. Morgan, ed., *More Essays in Cape Breton History*. Windsor, N.S.: Lancelot Press, 1977, pp. 66-67.

MacNutt, W.S. *The Atlantic Provinces: The Emergence of Colonial Society 1712-1857*. Toronto: McClelland and Stewart, 1965. *New Brunswick, A History: 1784-1867*. Toronto: Macmillan, 1963. 'The Loyalists: A Sympathetic View', *Acadiensis*, 6 No. 1 (Autumn, 1976), pp. 3-20.

Morgan, Robert. 'The Loyalists of Cape Breton', *Dalhousie Review*, 55, 1 (Spring, 1975), pp. 5-22.

Raymond, W.O. 'The Founding of Shelburne, Benjamin Marston at Halifax, Shelburne and Miramichi', *New Brunswick Historical Society Collections*, 8, Saint John, N.B.: 1909, pp. 204-277. ed. *Winslow Papers 1776-1826*. St. John, N.B.: 1901.

Reid, William D., comp. *The Loyalists in Ontario: The Sons and Daughters of the American Loyalists of Upper Canada*. Lambertville, N.B.: Hunterdon House, 1973.

Risteen, Frank B., Sr. 'Children of Sir John Johnson and Lady Mary (Polly) Johnson, married at New York 30 June, 1773', *Ontario Historical Society*, LXIII, 2 (June, 1971), pp. 93-102.

Robinson, Helen Caister. *Mistress Molly, The Brown Lady: Portrait of Molly Brant*. Toronto: Dundurn Press, 1980.

Ryerson, Egerton. *The Loyalists of America and Their Times*. Toronto: N. Morang, 1880. 2 vols.

Siebert, Wilbur H. 'The American Loyalists in the Eastern Seignories and Townships of the Province of Quebec', *Proceedings and Transactions of the Royal Society of Canada*, VII (1913), pp. 3-41.

Stark, James H. *The Loyalists of Massachusetts and the Other Side of the American Revolution*. Boston: Clarke, 1907.

Talman, James J., ed. *Loyalist Narratives from Upper Canada*. Toronto: The Champlain Society, 1946.

Upton, Leslie F.S., ed. *The United Empire Loyalists: Men and Myths*. Toronto: Copp Clark, 1967.

Walker, James W. St. C. *The Black Loyalists*. Halifax: Dalhousie University Press, 1976.

Wilson, Bruce. *As She Began: An illustrated introduction to Loyalist Ontario*. Toronto and Charlottetown: Dundurn Press, 1981.

Wilson, Ellen Gibson. *The Loyal Blacks*. Toronto: Longman Green, 1976.

Wright, Esmond, ed. *Red, White and True Blue: The Loyalists in the American Revolution*. New York: AMS Press, 1976.

Wright, Esther Clark. *The Loyalists of New Brunswick*. Fredericton, N.B., 1955.

Illustration and Map Credits

With one exception, all maps have been prepared by Mary and Geoffrey Fryer.

Chapter 1
Artist unknown, "The Landing at Newport, Rhode Island." No. 2891, National Maritime Museum, London, United Kingdom.
Dr. Robert Morgan, photograph of St. George's Anglican Church.

Chapter 2
Artist unknown, "John Howe, Sr." New Brunswick Museum, St. John.

Chapter 3
E. Hicks, "South Aspect of Halifax, Nova Scotia, in 1780." Aquatint, hand coloured. No. C 11214. Public Archives of Canada.

Chapter 4
W. Booth, "Part of the Town of Shelburne in Nova Scotia, with the Barracks Opposite in 1789." Wash Drawing. No. C 10548. Public Archives of Canada.

Chapter 5
J.R. Simms, "Fort Johnson." Engraving. *Frontiersmen of New York,* Vol. I, in the collection of the History Department, Metropolitan Toronto Reference Library.

Chapter 6
Artist Unknown, "Ward Chipman, Sr." New Brunswick Museum, St. John.

Chapter 7
Captain Samuel Holland, "A Plan of the Island of St. John." Printed at London, 1775. NMC-1850. National Map Collection, Public Archives of Canada.

Chapter 8
John Mare, "Sir John Johnson." Painted in 1772 at Johnstown. Johnson Hall State Historic Site, Saratoga Capital Park Region, New York State Office of Parks and Recreation Division for Historic Preservation Bureau of Historic Sites.

Chapter 9
Artist unknown, "Ranna Cossit." Beaton Institute, Sydney, Nova Scotia. Photograph of Cossit's House. Both courtesy of Dr. Robert Morgan.

Chapter 10
Photographs courtesy of the author, Mary Beacock Fryer.

Chapter 11
William Booth, "A Black Woodcutter at Shelburne, Nova Scotia, 1788." Water Colour. No. C 40162, Public Archives of Canada.

Chapter 12
Matthew William Peters, "William Jarvis and his son, Samuel Peters." Oil painting. Royal Ontario Museum, Toronto, Ontario.

Contributors

Robert Allen, a resident of Ottawa, is Deputy Chief of the Treaties and Historical Research Centre for the Department of Indian and Northern Affairs. He researches and writes on various topics and has just completed an annotated bibliography of Loyalist literature.

Mary Archibald is a resident of Shelburne, Nova Scotia. A retired school teacher she is an active member of the local historical society. The author of *Gideon White Loyalist* and editor of *United Empire Loyalists: Loyalists of the American Revolution,* she is currently working on other Loyalist projects.

Dr. Phyllis Blakeley of Halifax is the Provincial Archivist of the Public Archives of Nova Scotia. A descendant of Carolina Loyalists she has researched and written extensively on Nova Scotian history. A member of the Order of Canada, Dr. Blakeley has received numerous awards for her contribution to our knowledge of Canada's past.

Darrel Butler is Head of Research and Interpretation for King's Landing Historical Settlement at Prince William, New Brunswick. His work and his residence in Fredericton, N.B., have given him the opportunity to know well the history and traditions of the Loyalist pioneers of that area.

Mary Beacock Fryer, a descendant of a loyalist family, is from Brockville, Ontario, but now lives in Toronto. Among her many books are *Loyalist Spy, Escape, King's Men,* and *Buckskin Pimpernel, the Exploits of Justus Sherwood.*

John N. Grant is a research Associate at the Atlantic Institute of Education. He is a former public school history teacher and has published in various journals of history and education. Raised in Guysborough and now living in Enfield, N.S., he wrote *Black Nova Scotians.*

Dr. Robert Morgan is the Director of the Beaton Institute at the College of Cape Breton in Sydney, Nova Scotia. Formerly an historian at the Fortress of Louisbourg Historic Site, his doctoral work was on the history of Cape

Breton Island. Dr. Morgan has researched and written on various aspects of Cape Breton history.

Helen Robinson's strong interest in Canadian history has resulted in three books: *Joseph Brant, A Man for his People; Mistress Molly, The Brown Lady: A Portrait of Molly Brant;* and *Laura, A Portrait of Laura Secord.* A member of the Big Sister Association, she resides in Toronto.

Donald Wetmore of Tantallon, N.S., formerly served as Arts Supervisor of the Adult Education Divison of the Nova Scotia Department of Education. A recipient of the Order of Canada and a past president of the Canadian Authors Association, he is actively writing plays on historical themes including one on the landing of the Loyalists at Shelburne, Nova Scotia.

Index